Lord James:

The Biography of
James William Bayless

By

Sarah Zale

ISBN: 1-4107-2579-0 (e-book)
ISBN: 1-4107-2578-2 (Paperback)
ISBN: 1-4107-2577-4 (Dust Jacket)

This book is printed on acid free paper.

1stBooks - rev. 09/10/03

I asked Jim about a dedication for his book.
He said there would not be one, so I will contribute mine.

To our family, without whom I cannot imagine.
Jim, our life together has been highs, lows, and in-betweens—
a long, well-traveled path—never dull.
I am glad I was there for the trip. Thank you, Jim—and God.
Jim says, "In that order."

> *Lovingly,*
> *Jean Bayless*

Acknowledgements

The book *Mountains to Climb: A Biography of Inez Yeager Bayless Blanchard* by Grace Thrasher Blanchard (self-published, 1986) provided invaluable information about the early years of James Bayless' life. With the publication of *Lord James,* James William Bayless honors *Mountains to Climb* as the beginning of a tradition.

My thanks to Jim's children: Craig Bayless, Christie Gorsline, and Joanie Madden.

My appreciation to Jim's sister, Martha May Davis, for her tour of Grants Pass' past and present, and to his brother, Roy Junior Bayless. Additional thanks to other family members: Bill Wilkinson, Lisa Kelley Parmentier, Amy Jean Kelley Goodwin, and Rick Gorsline. Taylor Bayless' essay on Molokai provided a rich addition.

Many others offered their time and resources: Cathy Gach, principal of Warrenton High School; Reverend Douglas D. Rich of Pioneer Presbyterian Church; Pastor Wallie Nichols of Freedom Baptist Church; Tim Welch, 1999 recipient of the Bayless Scholarship; Mary Ellen Callahan; Gene Sauce; Sue Thuemmel Helzer; Nancy Smith; and Alan J. Zell. Thanks as well to individuals James worked with: Ron Kutella, Bill Burch, and Jim Hefty.

Deep gratitude for the enthusiasm of Larry Epperson, great-grandson of Ary Bayless and webmaster of www.54in.com, and the work with his mother, Dolores Bayless Epperson, on the map of Browns Valley. The Indiana Gen Web Project provided an extensive listing of the Bayless Genealogy.

Warm appreciation for those who offered feedback and caring support: Michael Hindes, Dan Statz, Roger Aplon, Jeanne Peterson, Suzanna Neal, and Patrick McMahon.

Prologue

James William Bayless has achieved the American dream. He believes it and says so in a manner that every American would love to: matter-of-factly—as if his hard work and unflinching belief in himself made it his right. His life, which spanned most of the 20th century, embodies the world's sense of America itself during that period: Not always right, but never in doubt. It is the phrase Jim Bayless claims best describes him.

He told his story with indomitable spirit in spite of a stroke from which he had not yet fully recovered. Only months had passed since the terrorist attacks of September 11, 2001. I watched him with a discerning eye, as if his process to recovery might offer clues to the future of America. I learned that this man of eighty-one years, his right side still weak with paralysis, believed that he would once again be everything he was before.

Impeccably dressed, often sitting with his left hand resting on his cane, he spoke in a declarative tone. When standing, his tall and angular form hunched only slightly. When speaking, his facial expression, self-assured, remained fixed. His piercing gaze took in everything and revealed little. The image of an aristocrat came to mind. It felt improper to do anything but respectfully defer to whatever he said. Amusing, but not surprising, throughout the years he owned two director's chairs—one for his home and the other for his yacht—with his "name" embroidered across the canvas backing: *Lord James.*

James William Bayless

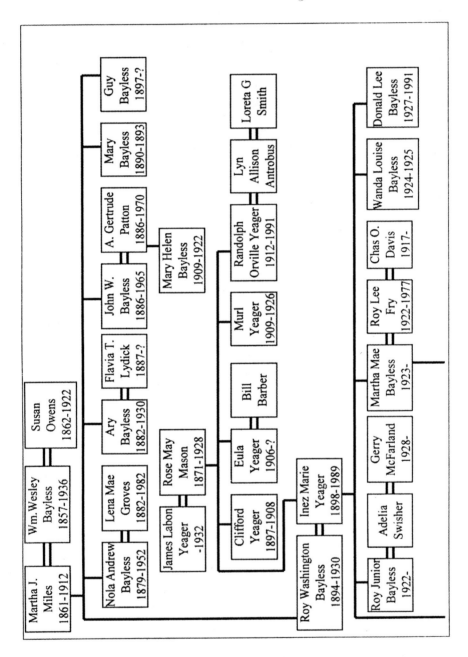

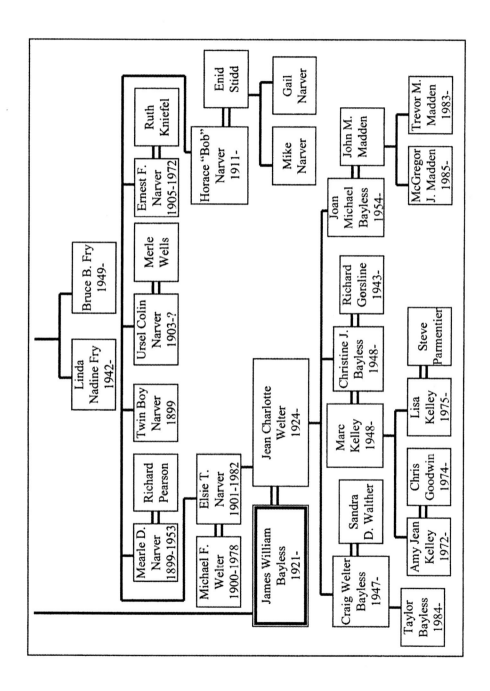

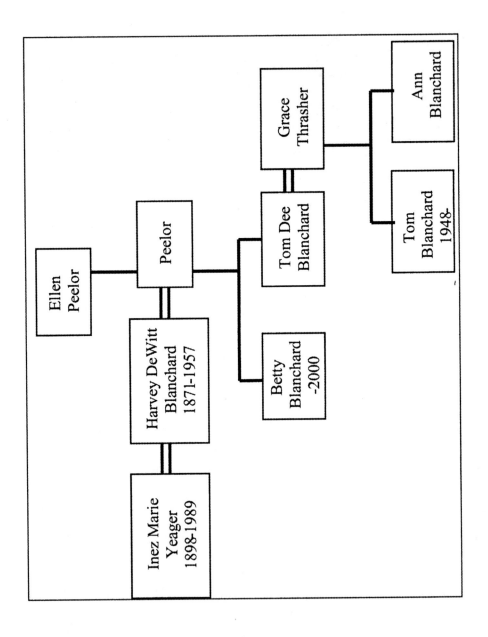

x

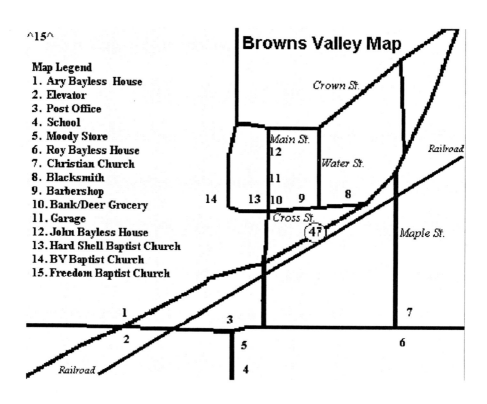

^15^

Map Legend
1. Ary Bayless House
2. Elevator
3. Post Office
4. School
5. Moody Store
6. Roy Bayless House
7. Christian Church
8. Blacksmith
9. Barbershop
10. Bank/Deer Grocery
11. Garage
12. John Bayless House
13. Hard Shell Baptist Church
14. BV Baptist Church
15. Freedom Baptist Church

Browns Valley Map

Crown St.

Main St.

Water St.

Railroad

Cross St.

Maple St.

Railroad

Chapter One

Everyone called him James William.

"The use of nicknames is sinful," Aunt Gertrude said. Inez Marie Yeager Bayless shuddered at yet another reproof from her sister-in-law. The Baptist community agreed with Gertrude, however, so Inez addressed her children by their full Christian names: James William, Roy Junior, Martha May, Wanda Louise, and Donald Lee.

James William came into the world on January 27, 1921. He was named for his two grandfathers: James Yeager and William Bayless. Born at home, on the north side of town, in a house too small for a growing family, he never entered it again after that first year of his life. Certainly he saw it often, a block from the home of Uncle John and Aunt Gertrude and the bank—typical of the farmhouses around town, tiny and painted bright white, a portion of the roof peeking over the front door. He knew every public structure in the township of Browns Valley, Indiana, as well as he knew the fingers on his hands—for there were about as many: three churches, a grain elevator, a smithy, the bank, a barbershop, and a four-room schoolhouse, a post office, two grocery stores, and Uncle John's garage, which repaired the area's farm machinery. Tufts of farmhouses for twenty-odd families dotted the community. Population: 125.

Highway 47 angled its way northeast to southwest through town. The track of Penn Railroad paralleled the highway to the east. Most businesses could be found north of the tracks, but living on one side

1

of the tracks or the other didn't mean that anyone had more right than his neighbor to puff up his feathers.

Inez Bayless blamed her inexperience for the "sickly and difficult" state of James William's health during his first two years. Mother Yeager lived fifty miles away in Mulberry and the thought of asking a neighbor for help deeply discomfited her. Inez preferred to struggle on her own rather than approach the bossy Gertrude. Although fragile with a slight build, James William "was so bright," Inez said. He looked like his father, but he would be her only child with the spirit of a Yeager. After he "finally" began to walk at seventeen months, "he never slowed down—and still hasn't," she said in her 1986 biography.

All memories for James William begin in the Bayless' second home, where his brothers and sisters were born, one after the other. "Roy Junior and I are twins eight days out of the year," says Jim today—who long ago set aside the formal version of his name. Martha May followed on the tail of Roy Junior. Then came Wanda Louise. Four years later, Inez gave birth to Donald Lee at their third home, "the porch house."

During the first seven years of her married life, Inez lived mostly in "maternity wrappers," dresses edged on one seam with hooks that attached onto whichever row of eyelets best accommodated her ever expanding and contracting body.

Inez Marie Yeager first met Roy Washington Bayless in the fall of 1919. About to turn twenty-one, Inez taught the third and fourth grades at Browns Valley School. Once a month, she took the train to visit her parents for the weekend. Sometimes she went to the home of her teacher friend, Maude, who lived near New Market, six miles north of Browns Valley. One Friday evening, the young women stood at the train station in New Market, waiting for their dates to arrive. For some reason—"a communication mix-up, perhaps"—the young men didn't show. As Inez and Maude crossed the street, heading to a diner for something to eat, Guy Bayless, the youngest and perhaps the most handsome of five brothers from a local, prominent family, drove up.

"You girls need a ride?" he asked.

Maude and Guy had attended school together. "Hello, Guy," she said. "You remember meeting Inez at your brother John's home, don't you?"

After a brief chat, it was decided that Inez and Maude would have their dinner first. Then, yes, Guy's offer of driving the two "girls" to Maude's home, a few miles away in the country, would be greatly appreciated.

When Guy returned, he was in the passenger seat. His brother Roy sat behind the wheel of his new Model-T Ford roadster. A WWI veteran, Roy had recently returned after seventeen months in France with the Army Medical Corps. Guy and Maude slipped into the back seat and Inez into the front.

With their high cheekbones and long, thin noses, there was no mistaking the two young men were brothers. They combed their hair straight back in slight waves. Roy's half-mast eyelids suggested an even-tempered disposition.

Inez found Roy "polite, intelligent, and easy to talk to," she recalled years later to her biographer. Dinner and a movie the following weekend began a series of dates. By January, the young couple—he, soft-spoken and thoughtful; she, quick-tempered and impulsive—knew they were in love. Mother and Dad Yeager approved of Roy as "just right."

On Valentine's Day, 1920, Roy smiled at Inez a long while after dinner. It was his smile she loved the best. She felt again that "little thump" in her heart. Then Roy pulled out a small diamond ring. "Yes! Yes!" she cried out, failing once again in her practice of demure expression.

Over the following days, she stared for hours at her left hand. The "singing" in her heart told her she had chosen the right man. True, the diamond wasn't as large and flashy as the one Lewis Whiting had given her. She had met Lewis in letters through her soldier cousin, John Moss. Both men were stationed at Fort Sill, Oklahoma. Shortly after Lewis visited Mulberry, he and Inez became engaged. In the weeks to follow, noticing that her heart didn't "sing," Inez broke off the engagement.

In the glimmer of Roy's tiny diamond ring, Inez envisioned a lifetime of happiness.

But the 1920-1921 economic depression brought hard times for everyone, including the Bayless family. As well, Inez lost her teaching job when the district decided to shorten the school year due to insufficient funds. Wishing to marry and raise a family, Roy and Inez needed more money than Roy's pay as a railroad worker. If Roy had wished to pursue a medical education based on his war training, the Rehabilitation Act of 1919 offered a monthly assistance allowance only for veterans disabled in the war. Roosevelt's GI Bill of Rights would not come into being for another twenty-four years.

Roy received a job offer with an increase in pay at a tire factory in Akron, Ohio.

"How wonderful!" Inez said. The Lord had answered her prayers. She hadn't liked the idea of marrying an itinerant trainman.

Roy's face clouded. Inez studied the brown eyes of her handsome fiancé. "What is it?" she asked.

"It's a good opportunity, of course," he said, managing a smile, "but the thought of leaving behind Dad and Aunt Sue, my brothers…" His father and "Aunt" Sue, his stepmother, owned a farm just outside of Browns Valley.

The thoughts of Inez drifted to her own family. How could she leave behind her frail mother, always such a comfort with her kind, Quaker ways? And her father—although cloaked in stern, Baptist fundamentalism—she loved him all the same. Thoughts of Grandma and Grandpa Mason brought a loving smile. And no, she couldn't leave behind her dear sisters, Eula and Murl, and oh!—little Orville, just seven years old. A tear came to her eye when she thought about Clifford, the older brother she had adored. He had died of typhoid when she was ten, and she often visited his grave. Could she leave him behind?

Inez tenderly touched the cheek of her husband. She knew she'd found herself a fine man, one who cared above all about family.

"But of course we'll go," Roy said brightly. He brought Inez' palms together. "We have the promise of our own family to think about." His words brought a quick laugh of delight from Inez.

Ready to commit to one another for better and worse, but preferably for richer than poorer, the young couple married on March 31, 1920 so that Inez could accompany Roy to Akron. They would

4

live with the Yeagers in Mulberry until their departure date. Roy sold his roadster to finance the trip.

When the newlyweds were packed and nearly out the door, Roy's brother John phoned to announce he planned to quit his job as Browns Valley mail carrier and devote himself fulltime to his trucking and garage business. Would Roy want the job? "You can live with Gertrude and me until you pass the Civil Service exam," John said.

"A government job? Here in Browns Valley?"

Inez ran to Roy's side, her fists and smile tight with excitement. She nodded fervently.

Although not eager to begin her marriage under the same roof as her difficult and critical sister-in-law, Inez agreed to the plan until they saved enough to rent or purchase their own home. She regretted she could not help financially by seeking a teaching position. The policy of Indiana schools—similar to the rest of the nation—prohibited the hiring of married women. School boards felt that jobs providing a second income to a family should be saved for heads of households who were out of work.

Inez and Roy Bayless rented their first home, the white farmhouse where James William was born. While pregnant with James William, Inez operated the local phone service from the house. With the prospect of a growing family—and the fact that no self-respecting wife and mother worked out of the home—she quit that job and took on the fulltime work of family caregiver.

Although Roy's job paid poorly, frugal ways allowed them in 1922 to rent a larger, two-story house on a couple acres northwest of town, not far from the Freedom Baptist Church. Roy's father, William Wesley Bayless, moved in after his wife of six years, "Aunt" Sue, died. Inez gave birth to Roy Junior, and in 1923, Martha May came along. The family now totaled six and, in spite of Grandpa Bayless' contribution, put a severe strain on Roy's pocketbook.

But no one in the Bayless household sensed they were poor. They seemed to live more or less the same as any other family in the small farming community of Browns Valley. Besides, they were extremely happy. "Those early years of my marriage," wrote Inez, "when my children were babies, were exactly as I thought my life should be…absolutely perfect. I had my strong, handsome husband and…beautiful, healthy children. I was blest and I knew it."

Roy felt the same way. While Inez and James William were sleeping hard after a difficult birth, Roy burst into the streets, blustering with his good news. An old woman who had known Roy "since the day he was born" commented, "Why, Roy is just as proud of that baby as he was of that pair of red-topped rubber boots he got when he was five years old." When Roy Junior and Martha May joined the family, Roy's proud grin never waned. And to his way of thinking, the birth of Wanda Louise on October 22, 1924 completed the perfect family of two boys and two girls.

Chapter Two

The morning following the birth of Wanda Louise, James William, age four years and nine months, sat with his thin arms stretched to accept his new responsibility. He talked softly into the eyes of Baby Wanda as he held her. According to Inez, James William would amuse and attend lovingly to his little sister over the next seven months.

Jim Bayless doesn't remember exactly the eyes and flesh and bones of Wanda Louise. Instead, thoughts of his sister recall the presence of something dark and ominous at his back that would visit him often in the years to come. In late May, Wanda Louise fell into a coma. Medical specialists from Indianapolis conjectured that the infant suffered from spinal meningitis. Fearful that the other children might contract the infectious disease, Inez and Roy sent James William and Roy Junior to the home of John and Gertrude. Martha May, who had just celebrated her first birthday, stayed with Roy's brother Nola. He lived in Crawfordsville with his wife, Mae, and their four children. Wanda Louise died three months later.

For children so young, months away from home pass as years. During the funeral, James William stared at his parents, listless with grief. His mother's touch felt mechanical and his father's gaze, cold. Years later, Inez confided she had shed all her tears during the months she kept vigil at the bedside of the baby. James William experienced only her numbness. It was a time of loss. Inez lost her child and James William felt lost from his mother. Yet no one cried that day.

Inez continued to mourn the following year, performing her duties as mother the best she could. Her attentions felt empty to the children. They wanted their mother back. They eagerly brought her bouquets of flowering weeds. She accepted them without joy. Even Inez' deep faith didn't seem to help her. A mention of the Lord and visits from the pastor of Browns Valley Baptist Church brought no light to her seemingly soulless eyes. Then Inez' sister Murl, eleven years her junior, came to help out, and laughter returned to the Bayless household. Murl played with the children and life flickered again in their mother's eyes.

One day, Inez and Murl and their middle sister, Eula, appeared to the family with their long locks—six ounces each—bobbed. Cutting their hair had been Inez' idea. When Eula hesitated, knowing their strict and conservative father would be furious, Murl urged, "But this is the first time I've seen Inez excited about anything since Wanda died. Let's do it!"

James William liked his mother's new look. He smiled shyly as he ran his hand up and down the stubble on her neck. Roy and Grandpa Bayless said, "You look beautiful, Inez." Grandpa Yeager, however, found the appearance of his daughters "unwomanly." He treated each of them with cold silence, and then addressed them as "Bob." He'd say, "Pass the butter, Bob" or "Open the door, Bob, and chase the flies outside." The children would giggle. James William thanked the day Murl had come to live with his family.

Then in April, 1926, in the middle of the night, a thud from upstairs awakened Inez. Thinking Roy Junior had fallen out of his bed again, she went to investigate. He and James William were sound asleep in their featherbeds. Upon checking the room of Martha May and Murl, Inez found her sister on the floor unconscious. She screamed for Roy. They shook the girl's limp body as the three children stood around bewildered. Roy phoned Dr. Ball.

Murl had been lethargic lately, eating too much and making frequent visits to the outhouse, Inez told the doctor, but they'd presumed the symptoms weren't anything serious. Dr. Ball, however, suspected diabetes. A few years back he had read how, in 1921, a Canadian doctor named Banting and his medical student had saved little Leonard Thompson by injecting him with the fluid from an animal's pancreas. Dr. Ball gave Murl a shot of insulin, but it was too late. Three hours after he had whisked her away, he phoned with the news that she had died in a diabetic coma.

James William felt lurking behind him the dark presence he had sensed when Baby Wanda died. He raised his shoulders to keep it at bay and refused to turn around. Look forward, he told himself. Recalling the stoic demeanor of his parents at Wanda's funeral, he didn't cry. He simply listened to the absence of Murl's laughter.

Aunt Gertrude sobbed at Murl's funeral. Jim looked up at his mother for an explanation.

"She had a daughter about the same age as Murl who died just after you were born," Inez said.

"Oh."

Life went on. The family bought a house on four acres at the south end of town, across a pasture from the schoolhouse.

As a matter of routine, the children—ages 3, 4 and 5—would take a nap after the noon meal. Then they'd eagerly await the arrival of their daddy from delivering the mail. James William loved to pass the time in the back seat of his father's car, a Model-T Ford with isinglass curtains. In 1943 Richard Rodgers and Oscar Hammerstein would write the popular *Oklahoma* tune, "Surrey With the Fringe on Top":

> *The wheels are yella, the upholstery's brown,*
> *the dashboard's genuine leather,*
> *with isinglass curtains you can roll right down*
> *in case there's a change in the wea—ther...*

James William would ride with his father and grandfather to buy or sell cattle—sell two and buy one or vise versa. Uncle John transported the cattle in his truck. They'd make only five or ten dollars in this ongoing process James William never did quite understand. It is one of the few activities he remembers doing with his father.

A faint image of a gaunt, smiling face comes to mind. Jim sees his father playing with the erector set his parents purchased from the Montgomery Ward catalog. His father amazed him. He could build anything.

9

In 1927, the government eliminated the post office at Browns Valley, so Roy lost his job. James William had just turned six. Roy refused a transfer offer to Ohio because any American farmer could sniff in the air the impending crash of the country's economy. Although the Roaring Twenties suggested national prosperity, the mechanization in factories created a huge class of unemployed men in the cities. Like other farmers, Roy planned to cling to his land. He had a home and could grow food to sustain his family, a situation far better than that of city dwellers.

Roy reasoned that he needed a cash flow only for the mortgage, and for shoes and tools and such the family could not make, grow, or do without. He took a position at the Kroger grocery store forty-five miles north in the "big city" of Lafayette (home of Purdue University) and came home on weekends. When the management cut personnel to a minimum, Roy again lost his job. "Last hired was first fired," said Inez.

Shortly thereafter, the Lagoda Building and Loan Co. foreclosed on the house mortgage and left the Bayless family homeless. Dr. T. Z. Ball, who brought all the Bayless children into the world, offered them a rent-free house in Crawfordsville, eleven miles away.

"It's just sitting there, vacant," Dr. Ball said.

Roy looked at a dour Inez. "We'll be neighbors to Mae and Noleee," he said, playfully. The family pronounced *Nola* with a long *e* sound at its end. Roy respected his brother, older by fourteen years and a hard-working farmer who raised corn, chickens, and Hampshire hogs. Roy smiled as he thought about helping Nola wash the pigs before sending them off for sale.

Inez looked at the children. Roy took his wife's hand. "Don't worry about them." He snagged six-year-old James William and threw him into the air before lowering him to his lap. The boy laughed. "As long as they're with Daddy and Mother, they don't give a hoot where they live—isn't that right, boy?" he said, throwing James William into the air again.

Roy secured a job selling disability and life insurance for Prudential at the Ben Hur Building, named in honor of Lew Wallace, Crawfordsville's son. Wallace wrote *Ben Hur: A Tale of the Christ*, a novel classic about a Jewish aristocrat who battles Rome for the freedom of his people during the lifetime of Jesus.

But Roy had difficulty with sales. When money is scarce, people buy food, not policies. "Sell or clean out your desk," bellowed Roy's boss. Desperate to hold on to his job, Roy purchased disability and death insurance for himself.

Day after day, he worked the streets of Crawfordsville, trying to sell insurance. He blamed his fatigue on the fact that he had a cold he couldn't seem to kick. He knew he wasn't eating right, but then, he rarely felt hungry.

"You're losing weight, Roy," Inez said with great concern. Roy muffled a cough. "And you've had that cough for months! I'm worried."

"We can't afford a visit to the doctor," Roy responded softly. "Don't worry. I'm fine, honey, fit as a fiddle. Just have a little cold, that's all."

In October, the cry of a new baby filled the house. Not "Phyllis Eileen," as Inez had hoped to name the child who would not replace, but sit in the space of, Wanda Louise. It was Donald Lee who arrived, a snub-nosed, sprightly infant with bright-blue eyes—a child so unlike the brown-eyed, quiescent babies that came before him, thought Inez.

James William and Roy Junior would watch as their mother divided her attention among Baby Donald, Martha May, and her chores. When she sat quietly a moment at the dinner table, Inez focused with worry on Roy as he coughed periodically into his napkin. The boys vied for her attention, and Inez was forever scolding them for quarreling. Roy Junior says of his big brother, "He was always punching me. We weren't close. Never have been." Their father roughhoused with them when he had the time, but James William doesn't remember that very well.

He wanted something from his mother, although today he cannot find the words to describe what exactly it was. "She didn't have much time for us," he says, nodding with understanding. "That's the way it was then."

On a cold December night, James William awoke to the high-pitched alarm of his mother's voice in the next room. "Dad. Get up," she called to Grandpa Bayless. "I need you. Roy is awful sick!"

11

Roy had coughed less that night, and Inez felt hopeful that his cold had improved. She slipped quietly out of bed to allow him a few more hours of sleep. No sooner had she closed the bedroom door than she heard the burst of a choking cough. She found Roy staggering, trying to reach the bathroom. He coughed again, spitting blood down his nightshirt and across her robe.

He leaned on Inez for support as his body quivered. Resting his one arm over her shoulder, she guided him back to the bed. She changed his nightshirt and tucked him in, noticing how desperate he looked. His eyes pleaded for her to help him. The image came to her of James William on the day he split his lip in a fall. She thought, I've never noticed before how much they look alike.

Inez had just returned the receiver of the wall telephone to its cradle when Dad Bayless entered the kitchen, adjusting the suspenders of his overalls. The drawn lines on his forehead accentuated it.

"Dr. Ball is on his way," Inez said, her knees buckling. She sat down.

Dad Bayless looked helplessly at his daughter-in-law. An undemonstrative person and uncomfortable during emotional traumas, Dad Bayless grabbed the coal bucket and headed to the basement with plans to get a fire started.

Inez said a silent prayer and found her strength again. She scurried about to keep busy. After changing Donald Lee, she rousted the other children from their beds. When they were dressed and seated at the kitchen table, she placed before them bowls of the steaming oatmeal they detested.

"Oh, yum, oatmeal," said Dr. Ball when he finally arrived, laughing at Roy Junior's sour face. Within a few minutes after examining Roy, he announced, "Probably a stomach ulcer. Get all the milk down him you can."

The next morning Roy coughed up more blood. Dr. Ball performed tests. Two days later, he stood before Roy and his wife with his upper lip in the grip of his lower teeth. Focusing on Roy, he said, "You've got advanced tuberculosis—probably got no more than six months to live."

No, Inez told herself. She sat down, looking first at Dr. Ball and then Roy. "No," she said, refusing to accept the prognosis. No.

"Daddy's very sick," she later told the children. "We must all be strong and help him get better."

When Roy left for the Veteran's Hospital in Dawson Springs, Kentucky, 250 miles away, Inez stood at the train station with her three children at her side and Baby Donald Lee in her arms. "Smile," she commanded as Roy passed them on a stretcher. "Don't let him see you cry."

Within a few weeks, the hospital phoned. A voice said, "Come at once if you want to see your husband alive." Inez frantically made a call to Roy's brother John. Her sister, Eula, agreed to care for the children. Inez and John headed to Dawson Springs.

Roy had improved by the time they arrived. Praise the Lord, thought Inez. By March, with a treatment of rest and good ventilation and diet, the disease was in remission. Inez would take Roy home, not to Crawfordsville, but to their *real* home in Browns Valley. The disability policies Roy had purchased—not out of foresight but desperation—proved a salvation for the Bayless family when they couldn't have needed it more. Prudential gave them a lump sum—enough to buy back their house—and the promise of $185 a month in benefits.

Inez observed how the children gathered happily around their father's wheelchair when he arrived home. Yet it is difficult to know what ranged in the head of James William—a spark of happiness, perhaps, and the weighty feelings that come when a seven-year-old mind tries to figure out issues surrounding loss and responsibility.

The next month, Roy coughed up blood again. The doctors had advised Inez to expect a recurrence. After all, they knew of no medicines to treat the bacterial infection eating away at Roy's lungs.

Inez and John drove Roy to a Veterans' facility in Dayton, a hundred miles away. The hospital permitted only Inez to visit.

A doctor told Inez tenderly, "Your husband needs hospital care—a proper diet and ventilation."

Inez refused to abandon Roy on the hospital's "Death Row."

The doctor shook his head. He warned her about the highly contagious nature of tuberculosis. "You must isolate the children from your husband," he told her.

But Inez had no intention of keeping Roy away from his family. She would take him home. John and Nola screened the back porch of the Browns Valley home. Confining Roy to that area would allow him the requisite fresh air and the opportunity to live amid his family while remaining a safe distance from his children.

Over the next few weeks, while the men turned the porch into Roy's living quarters, Inez periodically drove herself and the children the fifty miles to Mulberry to see her ailing mother. A sense of the inevitable filled the thoughts of James William. Then in late spring, 1928, a week before Roy came home, Rose Mason Yeager died of kidney failure at the age of fifty-eight.

James William hadn't known Grandmother Rose well. He stared at his mother's grief, at her tears. He'd never seen her cry before. Dressed in a tie and suit jacket, James William thought a moment about Baby Wanda Louise and Aunt Murl. Then the seven-year-old stood stoically as he watched his third funeral in as many years.

Clockwise—John, Guy, Ary, Roy, Nola

John Bayless in front of Browns Valley Baptist Church

Clockwise—Roy Junior, Martha May, James William, Donald Lee

Jim as a toddler

Second Browns Valley Home

Young James William and Roy Junior

Clockwise—Roy, a nurse, James, Martha May, and Donald at
Rockville Sanitarium

Chapter Three

For a second time, Roy had fought back the tuberculosis. His brothers Nola and John brought him home. Adults surrounded him on the porch while his children stood, as instructed, in the doorway.

James William would play with his erector set in the living room and watch his father. At first, Roy's form appeared hazy to the young boy because his vision had "turned poorly of late." Although the Bayless budget could barely manage another unexpected expense, Inez bought James William spectacles. The clarity with which he could then watch his father sleep and read and listen to the radio startled him. He'd lose himself in a stare until his eyes would sting. Roy rang a bell if he needed anything. James William would find his mother.

The skinny, eldest boy would reluctantly stand in line with his brother and sister to accept a daily spoonful of cod-liver oil. His mother prayed that the "nasty, evil-smelling stuff" (she said only to herself) would keep her children inoculated from TB. "She thought it a cure-all," Jim says at age eighty-one. "Maybe she was right! Look how long I've lived."

Inez made sure her children attended church regularly. Grandpa stayed home with Roy. Three times on Sunday and once in the middle of the week for a prayer meeting, Inez, the boys, and Martha May walked across the railroad tracks to Browns Valley Baptist Church, on the west corner of Cross Street.

Every hand had to work the farm in order for the family to survive. Five-year-old Martha May stood on a stool to wash the dishes. Her mother ran a meticulous household, and Martha May adopted her ways. When a neighbor from across the street came to the Bayless home to help, Martha May politely refused. "I wouldn't let her because she had no order to her washing."

The boys focused on helping their grandfather with outdoor tasks. Seventy-one-year-old Grandpa Bayless took over as head of the family. Now more a father to the kids than his own son could be, Grandpa Bayless showed a tenderness with them he didn't reveal to adults. Once when James William had an earache, he swept his grandson to his lap with one arm. At the age of seven, James William was still a mere slip of boy. Grandpa Bayless rocked the boy and gently blew warm smoke into his ear.

Concerned the cigar smoke might aggravate Roy's condition, Inez set down the rule of no smoking in the house. The toothless, old man walked around gumming his cigar.

The farms in Browns Valley grew mainly corn until soybeans came along. Many farmers switched, but the Bayless family stayed with corn. Roy Junior and James William planted it, hoed and shucked it. Farmers also harvested wheat to feed and bed their animals. After a big steam engine threshed the wheat, the boys carried drinking water to workers as they gathered sheaves into shocks for drying.

The farmers hauled their harvest for market to the grain elevator. James William often watched the transfer of corn and beans from the silo structure to a railroad car. His gaze followed the train as it departed for places he couldn't yet begin to imagine.

Uncle Ary, angular like Nola, and the only one with a hook to the long Bayless nose, lived across the road from the grain elevator. That's where James William heard his first radio. It was an old crystal set. He listened with earphones to distant voices that didn't answer back. Not like those on the telephone. The Bayless' had a telephone, but no electricity. James William studied by burning lamps, playing with the wicks so they didn't emit black smoke and foul the air with the stink of kerosene.

James William worked hard, taking to heart the responsibility of being the oldest. He rose at 5 am to help milk the cows, feed the hogs, and clean the manure from the barn. He loved helping his grandfather in the vegetable garden, taking great personal pride in the cabbage, green beans, garden peas, carrots, radishes, lettuce, and parsnips they grew.

The family regularly raised fifty chickens, six hogs, and six cows. They sold nothing but milk. Roy Junior and James William would deliver six quarts daily in a carrier to homes in a three-block radius.

James William brought soured milk into the house that Inez heated until clabber formed. The children poured the mixture into mesh flour bags they suspended above bowls to collect the whey. Then the boys fed the whey to the pigs while Martha May and Inez mixed the curds with milk, salt, and pepper. "So yummy!" Martha May says today. "I still buy dry curds—if I can find them—and mix my own cottage cheese."

Churning butter was hard work, but all the children helped turn the wooden handle. After butter formed, they used a wooden paddle to press out the remaining moisture. The buttermilk they used for biscuits, or they drank it.

James William would always love the taste of buttermilk. Today, a swallow takes him back to his childhood, to the hard work he somehow understood, even then, was forming a man of strong character. As a young father, he would trick his children into drinking buttermilk.

"Wow, did you see that?" he'd say to divert their attention. Then he'd switch one of their glasses of milk with this own of buttermilk and enjoy a playful laugh as the young face soured at the taste. Once his amusement subsided, he'd envision a connection, a blending of time and experience between his past and their present, their childhood and his own.

James William loved nearly everything about the chickens—not feeding them and certainly not the smell of their poop—but he loved their eggs, the eating of and even the collecting of them. Martha May and even Roy Junior preferred to avoid the angry pecks from setting hens on their nests, but James William had mastered the art of relieving a hen of her lay. The act required a no-nonsense attitude, he figured. An unspoken understanding existed between himself and his hens: *You're here to lay eggs and I'm here to take them from you. That's life. Accept it.*

22

He also loved consuming the chickens themselves—the tender, young "fryers" that had not yet matured into the sassy "layers."

His mother excelled at frying chicken in a cast-iron skillet. No pleasure of farm living could surpass the smell of a fresh fryer cooking in lard. Perhaps Inez had heard about the chicken recipe of the Indiana resident and cook Harland Sanders, who lived in Henryville. Colonel Sanders would later move to Kentucky where he perfected his world famous Kentucky Fried Chicken recipe. Like *The Colonel*, Inez "stretched" her chicken dinner of one bird for a family of six with lots of biscuits and gravy.

Butchering a chicken required a special occasion that usually came on Sundays. "James William, go bring me one of those chickens," Inez would say after church. "I've invited the preacher to dinner."

James William would catch one of the precious fryers and "wring its neck" by twirling it by the head. The headless chicken flopped around until it died. James William watched as his mother plucked and cleaned the hapless creature. "Mother," he'd caution respectfully, "some of our 'layers' aren't producing much these days. I'm worried about our supply of eggs. I think it best we save some of our young hens for the roost instead of the frying pan."

Her son's serious and mature manner would catch Inez off guard yet again. She'd smile in wonderment at this child she created and say, "We'll be fine, James William. Don't you worry now."

The slaughter of a hog remains a strong memory to James William. Grandpa Bayless would gore its throat and let the blood drain. The first few times, James William winced at the sight.

John Wesley Bayless stopped and stared at his grandson. "James William, you're going to have to learn that some things just have to be done. A farmer needs to do what needs doing and get on with it."

James William managed to open both eyes. He watched as Grandpa Bayless tied the hind legs of the animal and used a pulley to suspend it above a huge iron pot of boiling water. Grandpa then scaled the carcass to make easier the process of scraping away the bristles. Next, he butchered the meat. Under his supervision, James William packed the hams and bacon in salt.

Making sausage proved more fun than work. James William and Roy Junior helped their mother and Martha May form the patties. Inez would do the frying and then pack the patties in quart jars and add the cooking grease. After boiling the jars, all three children stood them on their lids to cool. By turning them upside down, they prevented bacteria in the air from entering the jars as they sealed.

"I turned over fifteen," James William would say.

"Twenty for me!" Roy Junior would respond, not to be outdone.

"You ever goin' to learn how to count?"

"Don't punch me!"

Martha May paid neither one any mind as she adjusted each jar to form straight lines. She loved her brothers and followed them around whenever she could, but she also could find them annoying. On one occasion, they coaxed her to follow them across a pile of ashes. They were all barefoot on orders that they kick off their shoes the minute they arrived home from school. "The shoes have to last the year," Inez always said. The boys laughed with bravado as they darted in leaps across the smoldering cinders while Martha May stepped with characteristically prudent caution. She burned her big toe.

In the summer, every Saturday it seemed, Roy Junior and James William killed flies. The sticky flypaper hanging from the ceiling couldn't handle the thousands that would make it through the door. It didn't matter that everyone religiously hit the screen before going in or out. The boys stunned flies with a flyswatter and then smashed them between newspapers, making it easier to count them. Inez paid a penny for every hundred they killed in the house. On a good day, each boy stepped onto the porch with two pennies jangling in his pocket.

Martha May remembers how her grandpa would walk down the road to Moody's Store every Saturday night for his weekly supply of cigars. She and her brothers swarmed around him when he returned, trying to find which pocket held the horehound. It was a candy of mostly sugar, brewed with tea from the horehound herb and used in the treatment of cold symptoms. Seated next to the kitchen stove on Grandpa's lap, Martha May would savor the candy with slow licks long after her brothers had finished theirs. A large kettle simmered with water for the weekly bath.

Grandpa and the boys would carry in the #2 washtub and place it in front of the heating stove. James William happily yielded to the rule of "ladies first," which meant Martha May bathed first. He preferred his bathwater cool.

James William and Roy Junior had a daily paper route. They also sold the Sunday *Indianapolis News* to people after church. Their hard work won them a red wagon.

It was a Dan Patch Master Wagon, an early example of merchandise for the promotion of sports celebrities. In this case, the sports icon was Indiana's own racehorse legend, Dan Patch. The horse's life resembled that of James Bayless in more ways than one. The mare was born a scraggy-looking thing. Neighbors shook their heads when the owner went on to train the mare for racing. Not even the locals made bets on Dan Patch. When the mare achieved the status of world champion, the story that she came from hard-luck beginnings in small town U.S.A. sparked her image.

The boys competed to earn money for their mother by performing odd jobs in the neighborhood. They'd give her their paper route money and whatever else they earned. She'd buy a pound of sugar or one of the five-cent, frozen rabbits stacked outside Deer Grocery Store. Although already gutted, the boys had to skin the rabbit. The Bayless family ate every part of any animal they butchered for food. Even the brains. James William still remembers how delicious pig brains tasted. Inez would fry them in lard she collected in a cast-iron kettle. She used that lard again and again.

Young James William knew one thing about life: it was a lot of hard work. But he never complained. He finished his outside chores and then did what he could to aid his mother. He'd knead the bread and help with his father's care. Everything his father touched had to be disinfected, boiled, or burned. James William kept the coal stove fed, and he stoked the fire to burn his father's used sputum cups. His mother boiled Roy's bedding and clothing and then transferred it to a smaller tub. James William and Roy Junior carried one end of the tub to the washroom near the kitchen where their mother used a washboard and Fels Naptha soap in Lysol-laced water to do the scrubbing.

One day while hanging out the wash, James William overheard a neighbor joke to his mother, "James William will make someone a fine wife." Not minding a bit what foolish things people said, he finished his task.

Washing the clothes and scrubbing the floors happened on the same day. Inez would save the wash water in the #3 tub to use for mopping. After James William gathered in the dry clothes from the line, he and Roy Junior would hang the rugs. Everyone took turns beating them. The endless list of chores didn't really bother any of the children. They didn't know any different.

Clothes and pillowcases, tablecloths and napkins were starched. James William noted how his mother avoided the task of ironing with her "sad iron." Sad was indeed the way Inez felt when transferring the pressing tool of weighty cast iron between the stove and ironing board. When her one iron cooled, she'd use the detachable, walnut handle to take it to the stove and retrieve a second iron, now hot and ready. Because an iron took a long time to warm and it cooled so quickly, at least three irons were set to heat at one time on the stove.

Usually, as the irons heated on the stove, Inez swept the children off to bed. More often than not, they went without even a bedtime story or a few relaxed minutes with their mother. From the perspective of the children, Inez gave any spare moment to Roy. But often in the late, quiet evenings, she thought about her children, about how they were faring during these hard times growing up without their father. She worried about Roy Junior who would have to repeat second grade. Was the problem because she started him in school too soon? She had chosen to enroll both January-born boys in school a few months before they turned six. Yet James William was doing fine.

Inez sighed, her feelings about James William an odd combination of pride and concern. That boy will always be fine, she thought.

One day, he said to her, "My father's going to die, isn't he?" Inez nodded. "Yes. Yes, he is." James William looked at her matter-of-factly. "Well, I wish he'd hurry up."

He thought his remark smart and practical, never noticing the pain that broke across his mother's face.

Come autumn, James William helped his grandfather store some of the vegetables in the cellar and bury the more hardy types below the frost line. Inez and her two eldest made straw tick mattresses from the fall harvest, which provided a little cushioning, but the straw caused itching and was noisy.

During the winter, he and Roy Junior assisted Grandpa Bayless with the task of draining maple syrup from the trees and boiling it. Since the chilling Indiana weather discouraged anyone from hiking to the outhouse, metal slop jars were set under every bed. James William had the chore of emptying them in the morning. Sometimes Inez and the older boys made feather mattresses, which helped ward off the chill but offered no support. Worst of all, the feathers smelled like the chicken coop.

Once during an electrical storm, Inez told the frightened children to gather on a featherbed mattress to protect themselves from the lightning. "Feathers don't conduct electricity, you know," Inez said. No, they didn't know, but they followed her advice. Martha May and James William recall that they sat happily on the featherbed during the storm, feeling quite safe.

How precious such moments were, basking in the comfort of their mother's attention. She was usually all business, with little time for anything but the physical health and welfare of her family. Martha May says, "We never went hungry, but we went without a few things...warm cookies after school.... I missed a lot of hugs."

The children often stared at their mother. Because they needed her, not because of her beauty, says Jim. "Women weren't beautiful in those days, dressing as they did in farm dresses and corsets with garters." Inez had let her hair grow again. Bobbing one's hair was, after all, a religious taboo and Inez was a deeply religious woman. She'd twirl her auburn locks around and fasten them plainly at the back of her head.

A weighty sadness had darkened Inez' beauty. Her life had not turned out the way she had planned. Roy became sicker. The children laughed little and played less. Roy Junior and James William did catch fireflies in jars, but except for the erector set, no toys ever scattered across the floor. Inez regretted how misfortune had robbed them of their childhood, of friendships with other children. True, James William did visit a boy down the road who owned an electric train. He liked to watch that electric train go round and round. But he doesn't remember the name of the boy who owned the train. He says he never really had a childhood friend. Not even as an adult would he ever have a truly close friend. Maybe understanding the concept of friendship requires practicing it as a child.

Overall, it was a sad and difficult time for Inez and her children. Roy was "awful sick," and Death, it seemed, had found a comfortable chair on the Bayless porch. To this day, a grayness crosses the face of James William when he recalls those days: "I remember so many funerals."

Chapter Four

Roy lived twenty-six months on the porch. James William has preserved a mental snapshot of his father lying there in the distance. He's the only one of his siblings who remembers Roy Washington Bayless much at all.

Only once did Roy touch his eldest son during those two years. James William needed discipline for some infraction—perhaps for bickering with Roy Junior or for leaving the Dan Patch wagon out where Inez could trip on it. The scolding of his mother's words echoed from one ear to the other: "What if I'd broken a leg? Who would care for this family?" In a moment of poor judgment, Inez sent James William to his father, flat on his back, too weak to even sit. Roy took James William's ear and twisted it "real hard," Jim remembers.

The boy in him didn't see the sadness that filled his father's eyes, knowing he would never see his eldest become a man. James William had no idea of the pride that had welled in Roy the day his first son was born. Nine years ago, Roy had strutted the streets of Browns Valley, his happiness telling everyone that James William was the best thing he had ever done in his life.

Roy knew he had little time left on God's earth. It shocked him when he heard that Ary went first. On Monday, February 10, 1930, Ary Bayless died at home, from a "serious illness" that had befallen him, states his obituary. His granddaughter, Dolores Bayless

29

Epperson, however, says that Ary was a diabetic who died during an appendectomy.

James William had often visited Uncle Ary's home near the railroad tracks. He enjoyed standing next to this man who had his father's eyes. They'd watch for hours as railroad cars filled with corn and beans from the grain elevator.

Roy's strength continued to fail over the rest of the winter and into spring. On Martha May's birthday, May 27th, Inez allowed her daughter to approach the bedside of her father. He couldn't speak. With a wrist so thin Martha May thought sure it might snap in two, Roy raised his bell and rang it softly in Martha May's ear seven times in celebration of the day. "Perhaps that's why to this day I have a passion for bells," she says.

One month later, Roy told a visiting minister, "Well, Rev, the Big Man is counting me out." He died in the arms of his wife.

Two men from the funeral home carried Roy away on a stretcher. From a distance, James William watched his father's face—eyes closed, apparently asleep, as he often was. The next morning, the two men returned with a casket. Inez directed them to place it in the living room, a room the family rarely entered, next to the piano they rarely played. A casket was hardly unfamiliar to James William, yet he lined up with the other children, full of curiosity as their mother opened the lid. James William stared into the strangely serene face of his father. The boy's eyes widened at the dark blue suit. He could not recall the last time he had seen his father in his *church-goin'* clothes. Only memories of bloodstained nightshirts came to mind.

People drifted throughout the house over the next two days. According to Baptist tradition, Roy would be buried on the third day. Until that moment, he would never be alone. His brothers—but mostly Inez—took turns throughout the night sitting at his side.

The Browns Valley Baptist Church held the service. Reverend H.H. Elmore presided with the help of the "Boy Preacher," Rev. Francis McCarty. Inez sat huddled in the front pew with her children: James William, age 9, Roy Junior, age 8, Martha May, 7, and Donald Lee, 2. A funeral procession north to the Freedom Cemetery, about three miles out of town, followed immediately. James William rode with his mother, brothers, and sister in a borrowed, convertible touring car across the flat, open prairie. A soft breeze passed through the grasses and across his face. James William looked ahead to Freedom Church, a typical House of God with its doors beneath the peak of an A-frame roof. Four narrow, stained-glass windows adorned each side. He believed in that moment what his mother had said, that God was with them that day. As a tall steeple blinded James William in the sun's glare, he imagined Him there, waiting.

The Veterans of Foreign Wars stood at attention as a bugler played "taps." The uniformed men fired a 3-gun salute. Roy and Martha May winced and covered their ears. Impressed by the display of honor, James William watched closely. The pallbearers lowered the casket into the ground near the tombstone of Uncle Ary and next to the marker for Wanda Louise.

"I was used to death," Jim recalls about that time in his life. "Death didn't scare me. I've never been scared of anything. Learned that from my mother. I have her Yeager blood. I've never doubted that my life would turn out just fine. *Not always right, but never in doubt.* That's me."

Inez stared at the pile of debts with dark, brooding eyes. Then she straightened her carriage and smoothed her hair as she considered a way to both work and keep her family together.

Teaching school appealed to her the most. A decade had passed since she had last set foot in a classroom. It seemed longer somehow. Perhaps a school board might hire her now that she was head of a household. Inez considered how she might work again in spite of how "tongues would wag."

She learned that the teaching certification requirements for Indiana had changed. The Terre Haute Normal School where she had received twelve weeks of training now required a two-year program of study. State "normal schools" dedicated their interest to educating teachers who would work in the "common" or public school system.

Since education cost money, Inez' dream seemed out of the question. She prayed that when the death benefit from Prudential arrived, she could pay off the debts and have enough left over to update her credentials at Terre Haute. Unfortunately, the debts absorbed most of the money, and none of the Bayless clan offered her a school loan. A bitterness planted itself as she thought about how she had taken their father into her home, and how he still remained in her care even though she had no real income and four children to feed. Yet a part of her understood why no offer of money came her way. One, she never asked, and two, social protocol expected a woman with young children to put her energies into finding a man rather than a job.

Another blow came that month making any possibility of going to school out of the question. In February of 1931, the tuberculin skin tests the children took every three months came back positive for all four children. The memory of Dr. Ball's prognosis for Roy exploded in Inez' ears: "Six months."

Dr. Ball sent the children to the waiting room and shook Inez by the shoulders to break her hysteria. "Here, girl," he said. "Get a hold of yourself. I said that the tests were positive, *not* that the children were sick.... Snap out of it! You'll scare 'em to death if you keep looking like that."

He offered to explain the situation to the children and how they'd have to enter a sanitarium for "at least" a year.

"I'll tell them myself," she said coldly, irrationally blaming him for handing down a death sentence to her children.

In the hallway outside of Dr. Ball's office, Inez took Donald Lee in her arms and said, "Roy Junior. Martha May." She looked last into the penetrating gaze of her eldest son, who was just a month into his tenth year. "James William." She swallowed. "Dr. Ball says that a tiny part of the sickness your daddy had is now inside each one of you. But if we all pray real hard to the Lord Jesus, that sickness will go out of our lives forever." She almost believed her own words. She set Donald Lee down and held his hand. Scanning the faces of each one of her children, she added, "You'll do that with me, won't you?" They nodded.

The children had to wait until vacancies opened at the sanitarium. Roy's veteran benefits would pay for their treatments.

In the meantime, Inez spent what little money she had fixing up the house, hoping a makeover for her home might brighten her mood. It didn't. Melancholy about how poorly her life continued to fare, she sought comfort in the Church. Inez knew that only the Lord could sustain and perhaps strengthen what little hope she had left. As well, only church activities welcomed widow ladies into their social circles.

She continued to teach Sunday school as she had since turning sixteen. Her children accompanied her to the mid-week prayer meetings.

That summer, the Christian church across the street from the house had a visiting evangelist who preached every night for two weeks. James William walked over one evening and watched, mesmerized as the preacher ripped his collar from his neck and dramatically tore it in half. The scary dramatics of this evangelist reminded James William about the hell and brimstone craziness of the "hard shell" Baptist Church, located across the street from the bank and Uncle John's garage.

The evangelist called out, "Stand, I say, and give yourself to Jesus!"

Ten years old, at an "age of accountability" his mother called it, James William stood and made a promise that he would become baptized. Two weeks later, the preacher at Browns Valley Baptist Church immersed James William into the waters of Sugar Creek and the boy was "saved."

Today, when recalling his baptism, Jim chuckles. "I always say that dunking in Sugar Creek is what eventually brought on my diabetes."

A visitor played the violin at one of the Wednesday prayer meetings. The soothing sound made James William feel he was taking a nap with his eyes open. After the meeting, the children scurried around playfully as Inez mingled among the adults.

"Children," she said, "come here, please." She was standing next to the violinist. "I want you to meet Mr. Curtis Elliot." Inez directed her gaze at James William. "He's a missionary."

James William studied the instrument. He didn't care for the way the man looked at his mother. Mr. Elliot's harelip formed a twisted grin.

In April of 1932, two vacancies opened in the sanitarium, a compound for tuberculin patients about three miles out of Rockville and thirty miles from Grants Pass. Lush lawns surrounded the two-story, rectangular brick building that stretched almost a block long. It provided dining and separate living quarters for the male and female children. A schoolhouse sat in back.

33

Inez delivered James William and Martha May first. As the children watched their mother back away from them, her gaze shifting nervously between the car and her children, Martha May cried. James William stood stiffly when Inez lurched forward to hug him goodbye. His look of cold accusation stared after her as she drove away.

"I don't think I really *blamed* her," Jim said sixty-five years later to his mother's biographer. "I just never trusted or felt close to anyone again until I met [my wife] Jeanie."

Donald Lee arrived at the sanitarium next. Roy Junior followed in May. The children would line up each morning, opening their mouths like baby birds to accept a spoonful of cod-liver oil. Martha May never saw her brothers except occasionally in the hallway and when Inez came to the sanitarium on weekends. Roy Junior became increasingly withdrawn, choosing to interact little with anyone, including his older brother.

During her visits, Inez talked with fresh excitement about the Bible. She'd quote a string of freshly memorized verses and recall the World Fundamentalist Convention in Columbus, Ohio, she had attended with Roy Junior shortly before he entered the sanitarium. "We ran into Mr. Curtis, didn't we, son?" she said the first time. Scanning the faces of her children, she added, "You children remember him. The violinist who played at church."

Curtis Elliot's name came up often in connection to a faraway place called Oregon. The Oregon Christian Center (OCC), located near Murphy, offered refuge for missionaries on sabbatical and for Christian widows and orphans. The Reverend R. Ward Lamkin and his wife, Minnie, wrote to Inez, beckoning her and the children with open arms.

On one occasion, Inez drew a breath and announced with practiced calmness, "Children, I have something to tell you about Grandpa Yeager."

James William looked coolly at his mother. "He's in heaven with Grandmother Rose."

"And Daddy," said Martha May.

Inez sighed. "Yes. Yes, that's right." She blew her nose. "I'm sure they're all together…" Her smile seemed forced. "…with Baby Wanda."

James William glanced unhappily at Martha May who sighed and, like her brother, pushed away her feelings. She had no more room. But she wanted to be like her mother who was praying. Martha May closed her eyes and told the Lord she loved Him. Roy Junior stared into his hands. Four-year-old Donald Lee took the opportunity to crawl onto his mother's lap.

Adjusting the toddler into a sitting position, Inez smiled with the news that her little brother, Orville, nineteen years of age to her thirty-three, was coming to live with her. Orville became her project. She felt it her Christian obligation to convert the boy whose interests revolved only around music. To her relief, Orville joined a group of men at the First Baptist Church in Crawfordsville who "testified" in song under the guidance of Pastor Barney Astrobus.

"Orville is smitten by the pastor's daughter, Allison," Inez said brightly. A lightheartedness infused her visit that weekend she shared the news.

In late 1932, Inez gathered her children during a walk outside the sanitarium. She shivered a bit from the cold, but they seemed comfortable enough. They were used to the chilling air since their caregivers constantly herded them outdoors during the day and made sure they slept on the screened porches at night. Life at the sanitarium had put color in their cheeks and flesh on their slender bodies.

"Children," she said into their expectant stares," I've sold our house in Browns Valley."

Inez had made an agreement with a family to make monthly payments of eleven dollars and pay a final lump sum of $500.00 in approximately three years. James William didn't know what to say. The doctors had told him he would go home soon, and he had an idea what that meant. He held a snapshot in his mind of where he used to live, of the henhouse and the kitchen, of his room upstairs and the garden he had tended with Grandpa Bayless. He would recall their house with a porch, though it no longer existed. His mother had hired a carpenter to enclose it and make it part of the living room. She did it to erase the memories of Roy's death, but James William remembered.

"Where will we live?" he asked.

Sarah Zale

"Here in Rockville," she said, smiling. "Once we're all together again, we'll move to Oregon, to the Christian Center I told you about."

"Oregon," James William repeated, although the word evoked no images to hold onto during the next two months.

Chapter Five

In early spring of 1933, James William and Martha May left the sanitarium, moved into the tiny house their mother had rented nearby, and waited for the release of Roy Junior and Donald Lee.

"Where's Grandpa Bayless?" James William asked.

Inez hung her head. James William couldn't read the emotions battling within his mother. On one hand she was eager to leave all memories of the Bayless family behind her. She wanted nothing more than a new life for herself and her children. Only her fondness for John gave her any regret about leaving Indiana. Then there was Grandpa Bayless. She felt guilty about abandoning him after he had played such a prominent role in her family. He had been there to help her run the farm. He had given the children a male figure to turn to as their father lay inaccessible, dying.

"He's living with Uncle John and Aunt Gertrude," Inez said softly. "We'll visit him soon."

Inez bought some baby chickens. James William planted a garden, this time without his grandfather. But he heard Grandpa Bayless' coaching words and at times sensed his presence. Life goes on, though. James William was the man of the family now. He felt no regret about the past nor questioned his mother's wisdom about the future she had set before them.

At the end of June, a thunderstorm drowned most of the chicks. James William gathered them in a gunnysack without a thought that

37

they had once been alive and that he had fed them. Once the ground absorbed some of the rainfall, he buried them. He now accepted death with the same steely resolve that allowed him to swallow the spoonfuls of cod-liver oil without a thought. Death was a natural part of life, unworthy of serious contemplation.

The seed of a practical man had been planted. The thoughts and future plans of James William took root without effort as naturally as anything that grows. Within that seed were difficult beginnings, and other things that would decide the man he'd become. First, there was the Montgomery Ward catalog. James William would read it as he sat in the outhouse, making a mental wish list: a bicycle, fine clothes, cars. He possessed no doubt that one day he'd have the money to buy them all.

Second, an image germinated in the boy in the form of his next door neighbor. Head of the Browns Valley Bank, Edgar Pitts always wore a suit with a hankie in his breast pocket. He and his wife, Pearl, had no children of their own and always welcomed the Bayless children into their home. James William admired that Edgar Pitts always dressed nicely—even when the bank failed in 1929 and he had no reason to wear his tie. Roy Junior and Martha May called him Uncle Edgar, but James William always thought respectfully to himself: *Mister* Pitts.

Roy Junior and Donald Lee came "home" to the Rockville house in early July of 1933. A week later, Inez' sister, Eula, married Bill Barber. At the end of the month, the newlyweds would accompany the Bayless family to Murphy, Oregon, paying their way as drivers of the used automobile Inez had recently purchased. The Bayless family readied their non-essential belongings for auction.

On the day of the auction, James William, with ledger in hand, documented the sales and wrote receipts for the money he collected. After the last of the buyers drove away, he approached his mother on the porch with an exhausted sigh. "Here, Mother," he said, handing her the cigar box of money. "This should be enough to get us to Oregon."

She smiled, noticing how her son's shoulders stood nearly even with her own. She realized she hadn't looked closely at him in a long time.

What the family didn't sell, they loaded onto the two-wheeled trailer attached to the automobile. Inez took special care packing her precious Haviland china, patterned with green and brown leaves on a white background. The troop began their journey that very afternoon. The three oldest children commandeered the back seat, and Eula sat between Bill and Inez in the front. During the first few hours of travel, five-year-old Donald Lee climbed many times between Inez and the chatter of his brothers and sister before finally falling asleep across his mother's lap.

The two Barbers, Inez, and the four Bayless children weighed down the vehicle. James William, who loved cars, remembered it as a "Whippet," made by Willys-Overland.

His mother said, "No, son, I'm sure it wasn't."

James William's eyes sparked. He didn't like being wrong.

"It was a Plymouth," she added. "A 1927 Plymouth."

In later years, James William learned more about cars—especially those manufactured by Chrysler-Plymouth. He discovered, but respectfully never said to his mother, "The first Plymouth didn't roll off the Chrysler assembly line until June 11, 1928."

So it could have been a Plymouth—albeit not a 1927 model—but James William is sure it was a six-cylinder, touring Whippet, modeled after the Overland. Whether a Whippet or Plymouth, the vehicle suffered two to three flat tires a day. By the third day, the boys became a "practiced pit stop crew."

Roy Junior was particularly skilled. He'd always shined when it came to mechanical tasks. That's why, James William reasoned, their father passed on his watch to his namesake rather than to him—Roy Junior could best maintain it. But unlike his younger brother, James William would never have lost the watch somewhere in Kansas.

The troop traveled from early morning until the bedtime of Donald Lee. They stayed in auto courts, the predecessor to motels: housing structures approximately 200-square-feet with an attached overhang for a car. Two rooms cost Inez three dollars each night. Their diet consisted mainly of hamburgers and cheese sandwiches. The children sang hymns such as "the Old Rugged Cross":

> *On a hill far away stood an old rugged cross,*
> *The emblem of suffering and shame;*
> *And I love that old cross where the dearest and best*
> *For a world of lost sinners was slain.*

They sang popular songs such as "K-K-K-Katie." The children broke out in hearty laughter when Inez would improvise: "*M-M-M-Mama, beautiful Mama—she's the only g-g-g-girl that I adore...*" They played road games that required finding a white horse or letters of the alphabet on signs.

Inez recited the work of "Hoosier Poet," James Whitcomb Riley. She repeated "The Bear Story" until Bill good-naturedly cried out in protest. To the delight of the children, Inez' Indiana farm dialect came off dramatically well:

> *W'y, wunst they wuz a Little Boy went out*
> *In the woods to shoot a Bear. So, he went out*
> *...An' purty soon he heerd somepin' go "Wooh!"*
> *...An' he wuz skeered,*
> *He wuz. An' so he runned an' clumbed a tree...*

On one occasion, Uncle Bill took over.

> *...Up higher—'way up higher in the tree*
> *Than the old Bear kin climb, you know.—But he—*

Roy Junior broke in with an exaggerated shake of his head. And James William, not to be outdone by his brother, chimed loudly in unison.

> *He can't climb higher 'an old Bears kin climb,*
> *'Cause Bears kin climb up higher in the trees*
> *Than any little Boys in all the Wo-r-r-ld!*

"Okay, boys," Inez said, laughing, her hands over her ears. She finished the poem about how the boy in the story eventually killed one bear, then another. She raised her voice as she arrived at the poem's close.

> *Yes, an' killed*
> *The other Bear ag'in, he did - an' killed*
> *All boff the bears, he did - an' tuk 'em home...*

Everyone, even Donald Lee, joined in on the final line.

> *An' cooked 'em, too, an' et 'em!*

Near Wendover, Utah, they were driving at night because the days had grown too hot. Bill drove as everyone else slept. When another inner tube of a tire blew, he pulled over as far as he could next to the ditch and slipped outside quietly to repair the flat alone.

A rear-end collision into the trailer jolted everyone awake. Eula screamed, "Bill, Bill, where are you?" The children flew out of the car behind the two women. Bill was nowhere to be seen.

The driver of the other vehicle appeared. "What are you fools doin' parked on the road with no taillights?" he yelled. When the faces of only women and children looked back at him, he added, "Is ever'body okay? Ain't you got no man with you?"

In response to Eula's ongoing cries, Bill had started crawling from the ravine on his elbows. He had seen the headlights of a truck approach dangerously close and dove over the trailer hitch into the ditch.

"Bill!" Eula screamed, as she saw his head at her feet.

"I'm fine," Bill said, more dazed than hurt. Everyone took a piece of him and helped him stand.

The truck driver took off his hat and nervously smoothed back his hair. "Now looka here, young feller. You can see for yourself there ain't no taillights, and you wuz parked clear out in the road. There just weren't no way I could keep from hittin' you."

"Of course we don't have taillights *now*," Inez said angrily.

Bill shooed the women and children back into the car. Shortly after, as the truck took off down the road, Bill announced, "The fellow will send a tow truck from Wendover to haul the trailer in."

Repairs required more money. Hamburgers in town cost an unprecedented twenty-five cents. Later, as they crossed Nevada and another mealtime approached, Inez gazed down into her purse as if her wishing might produce a roll of bills. The children stared for hours into the monotony of the desert landscape and begged for more burgers and drink.

Just miles from the California border, the group treated their diet to some peaches from a roadside stand. When the guards at a California agricultural inspection center disallowed the peaches to cross the border, the two older boys mischievously suggested, "Let's eat them all!" Not even the adults had any argument with this plan. No sooner had they emptied the bag than stomach cramps and diarrhea overcame everyone.

Happily—from the perspective of Inez' pocketbook—food now held less appeal as a form of comfort. It was a quiet ride to Sacramento and north on California's Route 99 to the Oregon border. The road angled west and followed along the Rogue River. Inez' purse held less than five dollars when Martha May read the sign, "20 Miles To Grants Pass," a southern Oregon town situated, according to Minnie Lamkin, six miles north of the Oregon Christian Center. Inez sighed with relief that they would make it after all.

Then the familiar pop of air burst from a rear tire. James William assured his mother, "That'll be the last one, Mother. Don't worry." He opened the door and jumped off the running board to help Bill and Roy Junior fix the flat.

Inez smiled at this unflappable son of hers, trying for a moment to figure if she really knew him. At twelve years of age, nearly thirteen, he possessed a maturity that announced to the world he didn't need her any longer—didn't need anyone, really. James William frightened her some, as he always had, with his self-possessed ways. She worried about him even though everything about his demeanor told her she had no cause. Bowing her head, she said a prayer for him— something she'd do again a thousand times or more in the years ahead.

Chapter Six

The children stuck their heads out the window of the automobile into the hot, dry air to gawk at the rolling hills looming above them.

"The Siskiyous Mountains," Bill said, smiling at the brown-mopped Martha May.

"The Siskiyous," James William said, articulating each syllable carefully. He tossed his head. "They're not much. 'Member the one we saw last week in Colorado, Uncle Bill?"

"Pikes Peak," said Bill.

"Yeah. Pikes Peak," James William echoed. He remembered how Bill had called it a *fourteener*. "Yes, sir, fourteen thousand feet, give or take a foot," he had said.

"Fourteen thousand feet," Jim said now, with a knowing nod to his sister.

Bill turned north and the car crossed Caveman Bridge into Grants Pass. It was Monday, August 12, 1933.

The town began as a stagecoach stop along the Applegate Trail. The 1851 discovery of gold in the rivers brought miners and the timber industry. The region flourished. A road crewmember suggested naming the area "Grant's Pass" after the Union general, and in 1883, the town and name became official. Eventually the apostrophe disappeared, its use in later years a red flag to any local that a tourist had come to town.

43

The kids hung out the windows like panting dogs as they gawked at the block after block of attached buildings. Pedestrians nodded and smiled. Martha May read the street names, "M, L..."

"Somewhere around here thousands of people are hiding," murmured Eula. Even Donald Lee looked at her and waited. "I saw a sign back there—*Population 5000.*"

Inez read from the most recent letter sent by Minnie Lamkin that provided directions to the town. "*Stop at the first tall building after the bridge.*"

Bill turned off 6th onto K Street at the Del Rogue Hotel. James William squirmed along with his brothers and sister when their mother disappeared into the hotel.

"Where's Mama?" Donald Lee asked.

"Making a phone call," Bill said over his shoulder. "Who can find the letters A, B, and C?" he added, hoping to distract the younger children.

Inez returned shortly, smiling. "Friendly people here," she said, climbing into the back seat. "Head two blocks that way, Bill. We're going to pick up some hamburger at the Piggly Wiggly Market."

Bill looked at her with a slightly raised eyebrow.

"Mr. Curtis will meet us and serve as our guide to the OCC." Inez searched her purse, pulling out nickels and pennies. James William patted his pockets, hoping but knowing he had no money.

The children burst out of the car and into the market like monkeys released from a cage.

"Six cents a pound," the man in the bloodstained apron told Inez.

"Three pounds, please," she said, looking into her hand. "And James William, run over there and grab a tall bottle of Orange Crush."

Martha May carried the hamburger as the boys fought over the Orange Crush. Inez felt around for Donald Lee's hand.

"Who's that, Mama?" Martha May asked.

Inez followed the line of vision from her daughter's finger to the car. Curtis Elliot stood with one foot on the running board, talking to Bill and Eula. He smiled with his crooked, harelip grin as Inez approached.

"Thank you for meeting us." She looked away, uncomfortable with his obviously smitten interest in her. "Go with Mr. Elliot, boys," she said, ushering James William and Roy Junior into the front seat of the truck. She gave a tug to Donald Lee's arm and hurried him into the back seat of the car. "Come along, Martha May."

Bill followed on the tail of the pick-up, seven miles south on Williams Highway. They passed Murphy General Store and then crossed a bridge over the Applegate River, the largest tributary of the Rogue River. Inez tried to hold Donald Lee still in her lap. The road veering sharply to the east caused Inez to lean into Martha May. The little girl giggled.

Inez smiled, then craned her neck around Donald Lee to take in the scenery. She thought the flat, lush farmland of the river valley beautiful, but she was already second-guessing her decision to bring her family to this strange land. The air felt dry and unfamiliar. She stared in awe at the endless sprawl of blackberry bushes.

Two miles from where they had turned east, a fine, white farmhouse held her attention on the left when Bill made a sharp right onto a narrow path. Dust scattered from the wheels of the pick-up and hung in the light of the lowering sun before coating the windshield. "Thick underbrush lined the track and evergreen trees rose tall behind the bush," Inez wrote later. "Yellow-leafed oak and maple trees crowded the roadside. In some places, their branches joined to make an umbrella-like covering."

Bill shifted into low gear as they snaked up the path not much wider than the car. The sun shot sporadic, blinding flashes through the trees. Then the car abruptly stopped on the tail of Curtis Elliot's truck. The two older boys sprinted for the only solid structure, a small cabin with peeling bark. Bill and Eula opened their doors and stepped out simultaneously.

Inez stared from the back seat at the clearing. Three tents stood near the cabin. Tarps extended from the roofs of two automobiles parked near a dry stream. James William and Roy Junior explored the area like puppies sniffing out new territory. Bill's characteristic, unreadable smile inched across his face. A cow slowly turned its head to look at Inez, and then took a halfhearted nibble from the dry, uncut grass.

Inez stepped weakly toward the Lamkins, her mind unbelieving as it repeated, *But where's the Center?* She had imagined a two-story, brick building similar to the Rockville Sanitarium.

"Please call me Brother Lamkin," said the elderly preacher over his wire-rimmed spectacles. "And my wife here…" he added, placing his hand at the back of a squat, white-haired woman.

Smiling kindly, the woman said, "Call me Aunt Minnie."

Inez looked about, her eyes wide. She glanced back at the car, at the visible few feet of road that had brought her to this wilderness, and saw all the bridges she had crossed and then burned.

Brother Lamkin spoke incessantly as the sun set behind the mountains. "And don't worry," he assured her. "You will have a house soon." He hesitated. "That is, of course, when the Lord provides the material and the workers."

That first evening, the Bayless clan slept on cots in the cabin. Thereafter, tents served as their quarters. Bill and Eula had their own.

Good, Inez told herself. *The night air is good for the children. The doctors at the sanitarium would approve.* But then she shuddered fearfully at the screeching of a northern spotted owl. She thought it sounded indeed like a cougar—not that she'd ever heard the cry of that particular cat.

James William, too, felt afraid. Maybe his fear began with the timorous words of his mother as she questioned people about the cougars. Perhaps the sounds of "cougars" entered his dreams in spite of the fact that Brother Lamkin assured everyone that cougars no longer inhabited the area.

The following Friday, the Ward Hyde family, who lived in the "fine, white farmhouse" Inez had seen on Williams Highway, hosted a social gathering for the community. She learned from others how in 1930 Ward Hyde, an alfalfa farmer, had donated twenty acres of his land for the purpose of establishing non-denominational religious programs in Applegate Valley. He contacted the American Sunday School Union (ASSU), which sent the missionary D.D. Randall to organize Sunday schools in the area. Soon after, Brother Lamkin assumed Randall's position. Other businessmen, "pillars of the community," included Joe Gray and the "attractive" Harvey "Dee" Blanchard, who had "snapping blue eyes," according to Inez.

Picnic tables lined the mowed lawn between the house and barn. Across the alfalfa fields, the Applegate River slowed to a walk, passing white oaks and canyon maples. The children took turns cranking the handle of a wooden ice cream churn to freeze the cream before Mrs. Hyde would add the blackberries.

Inez took pains to avoid Curtis Elliot.

"Whatever happened to Mr. Elliot?" James William asked a few weeks later. "I don't see him around anymore."

His mother blushed. "I don't know for certain. Other matters seem to have called him away."

As the cooler weather approached, Inez worried about finding suitable living arrangements for her family. Joe Gray offered her a rent-free, two-room cabin, situated north of the Ward Hyde property and across the Applegate River not far from the Blanchard ranch. Although the cabin had no electricity and no running water, Inez gratefully accepted.

James William, Martha May, and Roy Junior started school in the fall. They walked two miles to the two-room Murphy schoolhouse at the sharp easterly bend of Williams Highway. Although Donald Lee could have started first grade, Inez thought the walk too strenuous for the six-year-old, especially once the deep snows filled the roads.

James William didn't mind school, even though he never received the highest grades. Later in life he decided that people who made all A's rarely succeeded in business and at life in general. "Sometimes a person can be so smart, he's dumb," he says. "I had a business partner like that. Had no common sense."

Inez slept in one bed with Donald Lee and her daughter. Martha May would sleep with her mother until the day she married. Roy Junior and James William each had their own cot.

An Oriental carpet brought from Indiana held at bay some of the cold air leaking through the cracking floor. Members of the community loaned Inez a shelf, a wood cook-stove, a table with four chairs, and a cupboard for the Haviland china she treasured. Family life centered around the round, oak table. It was where the children did their schoolwork.

Neighbors donated wood. The handsome widowed neighbor, Dee Blanchard, who owned a large ranch down the road, showed the boys how to use a double-bitted axe to cut kindling and how to start a fire in the stove using pitch. He supplied the family with milk. In October,

Bill and Eula Barber left the church community and moved on to Michigan, home to Bill's relatives.

Money was scarce, even as Inez and her children continued to receive the eleven dollars a month payment for the house in Browns Valley. Inez sold her car. She found work cleaning a house for one dollar a day. In November, she started "pinning" turkeys on Dave Snively's turkey farm, a half mile north of the General Store, again receiving one dollar for a day's work.

Before she could remove the birds' pinfeathers, they needed butchering. Men strung the live creatures from their feet across a wire. The turkeys' mouths gaped as they gobbled in terror. One man had the task of thrusting a knife into their throats and then brains, often failing in his attempt at "instant" death. Inez would cower and turn away. She prayed her children would never see, much less perform, such a gruesome activity. Young boys would then pluck the turkeys, leaving the stubborn pinfeathers for Inez to remove.

Mrs. Snively gave Inez a butchered turkey with a deformed breast for her Thanksgiving dinner. It mysteriously disappeared after she hung it on a tree outside the cabin. Inez figured that a cougar absconded with the bird. She didn't really mind since the appeal of eating turkey left her the first day on the job. The boys, however, learned that Joe Gray's kids had stolen the turkey as a prank. The children reclaimed the creature and quite enjoyed their Thanksgiving feast. Inez never ate a bite.

The Baylesses settled into their new home. The children adopted Oregon ways of speaking and doing things. Everyone stopped addressing the boys by two names. But James would forever, with affection, call his sister Martha May.

Betty, daughter of the widowed Dee Blanchard, came to the Bayless cabin in search of a mother figure. "May I call you Mother?" Betty asked. Out of compassion, Inez said yes. Both eleven-years-olds, Martha May and Betty became best friends—and thirteen-year-old James had his first girlfriend.

They walked together to school and to church, which were housed in the same building. James and Betty would ride in the back of her father's car holding hands. They kissed.

Chapter Seven

Life in Oregon had revived a sense of optimism in Inez. Only the gossip about herself and Dee Blanchard prickled her spirit. The desire to teach, not catch a man, directed her focus. If life continued without any more ugly surprises, she might get her dream.

Then came a series of blows. First, someone alerted the community about the Bayless children's history of exposure to TB. Neighbors signed a circulating petition demanding that Inez take her family back to Indiana. Inez resented the fact that no one had asked if the children posed any real threat to the community. Next, a nurse from the Josephine County Health Department scolded Inez for housing her children with their weak lungs in a drafty cabin. Inez wondered, Does this nurse know anything about the treatment for tuberculosis?

Inez fumed but said nothing, and she advised her children to do the same. Being the topic of community gossip irritated her greatly, but her pride counseled her to appear indifferent. James followed his mother's lead and ignored all the fuss. He had no intention of returning to Indiana.

Then Inez received a letter from Gertrude Bayless in Browns Valley. "You should never have left here," Gertrude wrote in sharp rebuke. "Leave that place where you are unwelcome and get home where you belong." How in the world? thought Inez—how did Gertrude learn about our troubles with the OCC community?

Then the petition disappeared. The nurse never returned. The neighbors apologized, confessing they didn't know the children had received a clean bill of health from the sanitarium. Inez smiled with understanding. She knew the fear the word tuberculosis generated. Fifty years later she would comment that TB in the 1930's "was almost as frightening as AIDS is today."

People stopped giving each Bayless family member a wide berth when passing by. Inez later learned that Ellen Peelor, mother-in-law of Dee Blanchard, had been the instigator of the trouble. When Dee discovered the petition, he had used his influence to put an end to the entire matter.

That winter, Roy concocted a get-rich scheme. He and James would become trappers and trade the furs. Traders made "millions of dollars" in the early days, Roy assured his mother. Inez gave her sons money to buy a few traps. The boys alternated turns checking the traps for game, but they never caught anything. The business ended the day Roy tried to free a skunk. Over the next two days, he sat in the tin washtub in a fruitless attempt to drown the offensive odor.

Come spring, Ward Hyde and some other men from the community built the Bayless family a two-room frame home overlooking the Hyde farm. Inez thankfully paid a meager rent. Then the kindly Mr. Hyde offered James and Roy an edge of his alfalfa field to grow peas, cabbage, carrots, beets, and various leafy greens.

The hot, dry summers of the Applegate Valley required that the boys learn about irrigation. They took turns going with their mother—often in the middle of the night—to make sure they received their allotment of water. Once each week, various canals, ditches, and lumber chutes called flumes carried water from Applegate River to a main ditch. Farmlands were flooded via ditches according to a schedule set by the State.

As Inez and James walked to their garden at the Hyde farm, she would raise her kerosene lantern to the trees in search of cougars. James wasn't sure whether he believed his mother or Brother Lamkin about the existence of cougars in the area, but he kept his mind open to the possibility. He decided that if he saw one, he would take the lead from his mother and head in a "dead run" to the open fields.

Inez wrote often to her brother, Orville. She started calling him Randy. "Randolph Orville Yeager is his God-given name," she said, obviously proud of her little brother.

Uncle Orville had married Lyn Allison Antrobus, daughter of the pastor at Crawfordsville's First Baptist Church, just as Inez had hoped. With his every accomplishment, she would beam. She called him a "broad boy preacher," meaning a young evangelist speaker of bold effect. Her intuition told her Randy would accomplish great things in the Church, and she was right. In 1977, he would publish *The Renaissance New Testament* and constantly make revisions and additions over the next eight years. The work received a citation of appreciation from the Laymen's National Bible Committee in 1988 for outstanding service to the Bible cause. The 18-volume set of 600 pages per volume was the product of fifty years of meticulous labor. It included, among other things, a translation and commentary, an exhaustive Greek/English concordance, and a lexicographical analysis.

"The Lord has great plans for Randy," she'd say to James. Inez believed her persistent direction responsible for her brother's good standing with the Church. She hoped James might give his life to the Lord as Randy and others had done. "Remember Francis McCarty, the boy preacher at your daddy's funeral?…Then there's that new boy preacher I've been hearing about—little Billy Graham…"

James wrote some religious "tracts" of scriptures that kids passed around like greeting cards, but the idea of becoming a minister never appealed to him. He copied scripture, but he also wrote lists from the Montgomery Ward catalog of what he would like to own. He studied the pictures of water faucets when the Hydes were installing a new water system. James wished he could buy them the best faucet the catalog had to offer. He was learning that although the Church would always be important to him, money seemed to be the guiding star for the life he was beginning to envision.

In the fall of 1934, James attended a high school sponsored by the Oregon Christian Center, but a few months later, the school went broke. James transferred as a freshman to Grants Pass High School, hitching a ride in the rumble seat of Trombly's Model-A Ford. Fellow student Ellwyn Wilson rode along with them. Every day after school and into the evening, James waited while the boys shot pool. Critically eyeing their roguish behaviors, he plotted how his life would steer clear of the path those two had chosen. He figured Trombly and Wilson would one day find themselves in prison—which Jim believes is exactly what happened. Wilson, he recalls, passed bad checks.

The thirteen-year-old James found himself a job in Grants Pass. A man and his wife, who both worked, hired the boy to perform various duties. In exchange for room and board and a weekly salary of $1.25, James mowed the lawn, washed the dishes, and performed other household chores. He saved his money and bought a bicycle—not exactly like the shiny two-wheeler in the mail-order catalog he had dreamed about, but a used one—for six dollars.

He returned home again the following summer and worked odd jobs with Roy. They deposited their pay into "Mother's College Fund." That fall, the family planned a move to Ashland, forty-five miles southeast of Grants Pass so Inez could attend Southern Oregon Normal School and receive a teaching certificate. The boys took advantage of a program offered to prospective college students by Montgomery Ward. They distributed order blanks with their mother's name printed at the top. The mail-order house sent a percentage of every customer's purchase to the Normal School to defray Inez' expenses.

It rained little the summer of 1935. The lacy tips of ungainly cedars turned brown and the pines dropped their needles. The personality of the shrubs faded as their greenery withered.

When a forest fire broke out west of the Christian Center, Inez told the children to pack what they could and place it in the farm wagon. She quickly stacked her Haviland dishes in a tin washtub. The Baylesses escaped down the narrow, winding road to the Hyde farm with James and Roy trading off the reins of the frisky, old horse leading them. James glanced periodically at his mother, sensing that her whispered prayers had mostly to do with her dishes.

The farm wagon arrived amidst a flurry of young Marshall Hyde and other neighbor boys trying to smother the sparks that had landed on the roofs of the barn and chicken coop. James and Roy grabbed wet gunnysacks to help. Inez fed the workers who spent all night fighting the fire. She smiled when during a break she checked her china and saw that it had arrived without a single chip.

In late summer, the family lived in a tent west of Grants Pass, downriver, so they could pick hops, the largest agricultural crop in Josephine County. The plant with its cone-like flowers grew on vines wired to tall poles. Pickers dragged mesh bags down long rows. Inez claimed she didn't know farmers sold the flowers to breweries to make beer, but James says, "Mother knew as well as we did. Being so religious, I'm sure she just didn't want to admit it."

Inez understood how public opinion could tarnish a person's reputation, and four pairs of watchful eyes noted how adeptly their mother avoided making herself the target of gossip. James, for one, although disparaging on occasion about his mother's pretentiousness, paid heed to her examples. He would come to adopt her belief that appearances are important.

The farmers paid the pickers by the weight of their mesh bags. Inez praised the boys for their hard work. She wondered why they grossed two and a half times more than her eighty-four cents. "The reason is simple," says Jim today. "We put rocks in our bags."

At the end of August, Inez received the $500 final payment for "the porch house" property in Browns Valley. She borrowed an old truck from Ben Jess, a neighbor, for the forty-mile move east to Ashland. Donald and Martha May rode with their mother in the cab. James and Roy sat in the truck bed. A tarpaulin covered the few worldly goods the family kept for this new phase of their lives. Betty Blanchard demurely waved goodbye to James. He nodded in response, not really feeling bad about leaving. He stretched from the waist and looked out over the tarp to the road ahead.

The Baylesses found a little house to rent in Ashland with three rooms and an outhouse in back.

"Look, Mama," said Martha May, "our house is on Indiana Street."

"A good omen," said Inez.

Just a coincidence, thought the sensible James. Convenient, though, because the various schools for everyone radiated within a few blocks from the house. Inez enrolled Don in second grade and Martha May and Roy at the junior high. James started his sophomore year at Ashland High School. The Normal School was just a short distance away on Siskiyous Boulevard.

James liked the town of Ashland. Although not as large in population as Grants Pass, it had two attributes: the Southern Oregon State Normal School and Lithia Park. A fine auto court—or auto park it was called—resided within the park, as well as the Chautauqua Tabernacle.

Ashland's world-renowned Shakespearean Theatre had its beginnings in 1893 when the town erected the Chautauqua Tabernacle to hold community lectures and local fairs. In 1935, the year the Baylesses arrived in Ashland, college professor Angus Bowmer noticed that the condemned building, if the roof were removed, appeared strikingly similar to an Elizabethan theatre. Workers built a stage within the shell of the old Chautauqua arena, and college students performed plays, a tradition that evolved into the Oregon Shakespeare Festival, an event Jim enjoys attending today.

James found a job in Ashland almost immediately. He awoke each morning at 4:30 and rode his bicycle to Heard's Dairy. After milking the cows, he separated out the cream, and then bottled the milk and added caps. He rode on the back bumper of the milk truck, delivering milk just as the first milkmen did in 1860. New England farmers started delivering their extra unrefrigerated and unpasteurized milk to their local customers right after the morning milking and before the sun caused it to spoil. James did the same.

He fast-pedaled his bike home by 8 am with milk for his family. Everyone had already started the day by then. James changed his clothes in an empty house and ate oatmeal or Cream of Wheat that had hardened in the pan. He never took the time to re-heat it. By nine, he arrived at school and slept through his first class.

It was The Depression era, but James had no real sense of being poor. He just figured that's how life was.

Nevertheless, he had heard about President Roosevelt's inaugural promise on March 4, 1933 to exercise "broad executive power to wage war against [the Depression]." The administration and Congress created the New Deal, a slew of federal programs to bring about relief, recovery, or reform. The farmers in Murphy had talked about the Agricultural Adjustment Act (AAA), supposedly a relief measure for farmers. At the time, James puzzled over paying farmers to *not* plant crops. He liked the idea of the Tennessee Valley Authority (TVA) bringing electricity to everyone; he'd never lived in a house with electricity. Fellows he knew participated in the Civilian Conservation Corps (CCC) that hired unmarried men 18-25 on relief rolls to plant trees, build parks, roads, and fight soil erosion on federal lands.

"The AAA, CCC, TVA and the like—Alphabet Agencies," Jim recalls, "intended to help the needy, I realize now. I have never expected anyone but me to put any money in my pocket so I didn't pay much heed at all to the whole business."

It would be a few years before James came to appreciate the concept of helping the poor get on their feet. The financial assistance of two men would get him started on his path to success. Jim would become an ardent supporter of Roosevelt. Although he didn't like how the New Deal formed a foundation for a welfare state, it was the New Deal that led to one of Jim's favorite quips: "Give a man a hand, and then get out of the way."

Roy started work at Herbert's Grocery. Martha May took over the cooking and housework and the care of Donald. James worked at the dairy, did his schoolwork, and became involved at a local church. The Bayless family joined the First Baptist Church on Hargadine Street, down a block from the Shakespearean Theatre. Built in 1911, its Mission Revival style with round, wooden doors and numerous stained glass windows accounted for its beauty. No longer a church today but the Oregon Cabaret Theatre, it houses a successful company that produces musical and dinner theater. The Primavera restaurant operates out of the basement where Inez taught Sunday school.

"Our family attended church, as we always had, four times a week," says Jim. "I continued to live an active, Christian life." But at this point, a very subtle change began in James' relationship with the Church. He certainly made no intentional decision to alter his fervent commitment to his religion. It just happened.

Following his Sunday morning duties at the dairy, James rode home on his bicycle, washed up and dressed in a suit, and then pedaled to the church service. He tried to make Sunday School, which followed soon thereafter, and another church service in the evening. A prayer meeting convened mid-week. James didn't always make it to both Sunday services as well as Sunday school. After all, cows didn't care what day it was. They expected to be milked in the morning and at night. James didn't miss his church obligations often. Just sometimes.

Work, church, and classes monopolized James' life. One job or another kept him from engaging in extracurricular activities or social events. He had no time for close friends, but he never really felt isolated or lonely. Even at fourteen, a practical mindset directed his life. He had little time for frivolities.

Never having had time for sports, James failed to acquire an ease with physical games. His children would one day sum up their father's attitude about sports as "the pastime of children." In high school, when James found he had a little extra time on his hands for an extracurricular activity, he picked the debate team rather than a sport. Fate played this hand, guiding James in a direction he could not yet see. It seems she whispered in his ear: *The debate team? Quite useful for the grooming of a successful man.*

Sophomore year, James argued in favor of the Unicameral Legislature—a topical subject since Nebraska had recently decided to eliminate their House of Representatives, making it the only state with a single body legislature. James' team traveled to five local high schools. He honed his skills of argument with each debate. People at school started calling him Jim.

In the spring of 1936, Jim started sleeping at the dairy on a cot in the backroom. He still helped out his mother with the household expenses, but in his mind, he had basically moved out of the house. A guiding voice spoke to him that his brothers and sister did not hear—a voice serious and knowing of people and worlds beyond anything his siblings, or even his mother, could imagine. His life would soon branch off in a divergent direction. He could feel it.

In the meantime, early workdays, school, and helping out his family occupied him. Then one especially dry and hot day, Jim decided, on a whim, to attend a swim event at the park. Once there, he couldn't imagine what had prompted him to come. He had never, in fact, allowed himself to laugh and play with abandon. That he couldn't swim embarrassed him. The kids poked fun because he wouldn't join them. "I can't, you know," he said, taking off his eyeglasses. "My eyes. They're a problem. The water hurts them."

His own lie stung him. *Why did I say that?* It felt ugly inside. He would try never to do that again.

That fall, a junior and "temporarily" living back at home, Jim again served on the debate team. He purchased an Ashland High School red and white sweater with two bars across the sleeve and attached his debate pin, placing it where a sports letterman would put his letter "A." The pin meant a great deal to Jim. Why should only athletes get recognition for their skills? This act was the first time Jim scratched the itch of his present day pet peeve: The minds behind the scenes, those who build and keep this country running, don't receive the acknowledgement that Hollywood stars and athletes do.

Instead of returning to the dairy, Jim took on two other means of employment. He accepted a job re-shelving books in the school library. Anything with numbers came easily for him. He did well with the Dewey decimal system.

He worked his second job mornings before school at an automobile storage center called Lithia Garage, not far from the Lithia Hotel. He would open the garage so people could get the vehicles they had stored for the night. Occasionally he'd drive a car to someone waiting at the hotel.

The name "lithia" was common in Ashland. Long before the first Europeans came to this part of the country, indigenous tribes believed in the medicinal qualities of the springs. They imagined the escaping carbonic gas as the "breath of the Great Spirit." In the late 1800's, an entrepreneur tapped and bottled the spring water, claiming it would "minimize the effect of hard liquor." Inez shook her head at that claim. "Better they should suffer," she said to Jim.

In 1908, the Woman's Civic Improvement Club asked the City Council to create a park. The voters approved the proposal. In 1913, Bert Greer, a journalist incited talk about Ashland becoming a health resort and healing center. The following June, a city ordinance passed, stipulating that $110,000 would be used to bring soda, sulfur, and lithia water to Ashland. They paid John McLaren, designer of San Francisco's Golden Gate Park, $65,000 to landscape the park. The town adopted the motto: "Ashland Grows While Lithia Flows."

Tourists came to taste the mineral waters that flowed nowhere else in the world but around the heart of Ashland. For the life of him, Jim couldn't imagine why any fool would drink water he could smell. Bitter, nasty stuff! he thought.

Jim watched the park grow. He liked walking the trails that followed the river. All the different trees fascinated him. There had been very few trees where he grew up in Indiana. The native alders, conifers and madrones grew in the Murphy area as well, but the dogwood with white flowers in the spring and brilliant red and yellow fruit in the fall; the silver maples, their leaves bright green on top and silvery beneath; and the black oaks, with their bitter acorns, were new to him.

His mother's graduation ceremony took place in the park. She stood a moment at its entrance beneath the ailanthus tree, wearing her cap and gown. "They call it the *tree of Heaven*," she said, smiling. The trunk of the tree was nearly as wide as Jim was tall. After the war, he would see that same tree on the cover of a book titled *A Tree Grows in Brooklyn* and recall that warm day in late August 1937. He'd see his mother—perhaps the happiest he had ever seen her—and each of his siblings, as if posing for a picture, smiling.

The image didn't seem real. He shook his head, blurring the vision.

Chapter Eight

The day after Inez graduated, the family moved back to Murphy. Inez had secured a teaching job at the school for an impressive seventy-five dollars a month. They rode in Jim's car, an old Model-A Ford he had recently purchased with his own money. Pulling a borrowed trailer full of their belongings, Jim drove the forty miles to Murphy. When the tongue of the trailer hitch cracked in the Applegate Valley, Jim and Roy used their ingenuity. They cut an oak limb with their double-bitted axe and used it as a splint. Jim drove slowly but safely on.

The family rented a three-bedroom house off Williams Highway on a knoll above the Murphy General Store. While Inez admired the fireplace and the new linoleum floors, the children stood amazed at the sight of their first real bathroom.

Don had his mother for fourth grade. The older children rode a school bus seven miles to Grants Pass High School. Jim sold his car and took a job after school behind a soda fountain at a restaurant on 6th between D & E Streets. He rented a room for six dollars a month from Mrs. Burton, the cook at the restaurant.

Scooping ice cream evoked an odd pleasure in Jim. He thought about how his Uncle Nola lived in Crawfordsville near an ice cream parlor. Never did Jim or anyone in his family set foot in that establishment. It wasn't the Baptist way. No dancing, no music, no ice cream. As Jim scooped the vanilla, chocolate, and berry scoops, he watched with self-conscious awkwardness as people partied and engaged in lighthearted foolishness.

The soda fountain's name, the Cave Shop, related significantly to the history of Grants Pass. In 1874, a deer hunter discovered the caverns of colorful hanging stalactites and rising stalagmites. Spelunkers continue to use the walls with distinctive bumps of "popcorn" as a trail of crumbs for finding their way out. Tiny calcite crystals also line the passages. Due to their look and feel of cottage cheese, the crystals received the name "moonmilk," a medicinal product that quickly cures infections. Ranchers smeared it on livestock to heal injuries. Moonmilk is of the same type of bacteria used to make today's antibiotics.

The citizens of Grants Pass good-naturedly exploited the endless network of underground caves in the area to bring tourists to town. In 1922, businesspeople began a tradition, which continues today, of dressing as "Oregon Cavemen." They wore shaggy animal skins to welcome visitors. Although no scientific evidence suggests that prehistoric humans ever walked the "marble halls of Oregon," the Cavemen pay tribute to the mythology.

Jim wore his Ashland "letter" sweater when he worked behind the soda fountain of the Cave Shop. A carload of kids from Grants Pass— unmistakable "athletes"—hassled him about misrepresenting himself with the sweater. Jim smiled and pointed to his pin.

One boy leaned on the counter in Jim's face. "Yeah, and so what?"

Jim again flashed a smile as if to say, Isn't it obvious? The boy looked at his friends and shook his head, saying, "Let's get out of here."

On another occasion, a crowd came into the Cave Shop after a football game. Some kids surreptitiously pulled flasks from their coats and poured liquor into their cokes. When everyone had left the shop, Jim and a couple of waitresses sipped the melting ice cubes that still retained a hint of hard cider. It was the first time Jim ever drank alcohol.

After graduating from high school, Jim worked all summer at the Cave Shop with plans to attend the University of Oregon in Eugene the coming fall. A business career repeatedly entered his thoughts.

Although college seemed a wise next step, Jim didn't have enough money. One day he crossed the street at the Cave Shop Restaurant and entered the 1st National Bank.

"I'd like to borrow some money," he said, as if a calm and clear articulation of his wish was all it would take to receive a loan.

Jim walked out of the bank with a shrug. He'd find another way to come up with the tuition. As he walked along the Rogue River to think, the beauty and the power of the river that rambled through town impressed and mesmerized him. Except for giving himself to the Lord in a baptismal ceremony, Jim's exposure to water had been minimal. He knew people traveled from great distances to enjoy this river that literally coursed outside his back door.

Deciding he wanted to feel comfortable around water, he signed up for swimming lessons offered by the National Park Service. He showed up at one of the swimming holes where the Rogue River flows through the Oregon Caves National Monument, 488 acres of forest and marble caverns. Young kids laughed and played in the water. As in the past, Jim felt embarrassed that he didn't already know a little about swimming. No one else his age enrolled in the class. He quit after two or three lessons.

Come September, Jim registered at the University of Oregon. College seemed the right place for a young man who wanted to become someone a bank would happily loan money. He joined Pi Kappa Alpha fraternity and registered for mostly business classes. When not in class, he worked four jobs.

Seymour's Restaurant hired him as a "soda jerk." Jim accepted the title with amiable disregard. He liked the fun-loving atmosphere of a soda fountain. On weekends, he worked in a grocery store. At the fraternity house, he collected the boys' laundry and dry-cleaning for a commission, and he waited on tables to cut his dues payment in half.

Then his feet started hurting. Bad. He could hardly stand. Crippled, he couldn't work. That meant he couldn't pay his tuition. So after one fall and winter term, he quit school and returned to his mother's home in Murphy.

Not one to be discouraged, Jim told himself he'd find another way to learn about the business world. In the meantime, with his brothers and sister in school and his mother teaching, Jim took over the household chores. He washed the clothes in big boilers, ran them through a wringer, and hung them to dry.

In the summer, he started work at a cannery, cutting up green beans on the night shift while sitting on a stool. With fall came the job offer of digging up gladiola bulbs. Jim could work on his knees, collecting the bulbs to save for re-planting in the spring.

One afternoon, after hours of digging, Jim stretched his back and his legs and took notice how dirt soiled his clothes and formed a veneer across the sweat of his skin. He examined the grime under his nails and shook his head. I need a plan, he thought. Doing odd jobs like this the rest of his life would simply not do. Nor did he want to work at a storage garage or behind a soda fountain, in a library or at a grocery store.

He needed to find a way to walk. A foot specialist in Grants Pass designed a pair of arch supports for him. Jim started walking reasonably well again. He never put on a pair of shoes again without inserting those same arch supports he had specially made in 1939.

With that problem solved, he made plans to attend business school. He talked to Betty and Tommy Dee Blanchard about the plan. If he could come up with the money, he could move to Medford, a town located halfway between Grants Pass and Ashland and enroll at Medford Business College. J.R. Calvert, an insurance businessman in Grants Pass and the father of Ray, a young man Jim knew from high school, made Jim a loan of one hundred dollars. Tommy Dee, who was working in a sawmill in McCloud, California, near Mt. Shasta, offered Jim fifty.

Jim's jaw dropped. Then he considered, *Well, he does work. Has his own car.* Jim shook the young man's hand, eyeing him with sincere gratitude. "You'll get it back," he said.

With more than enough for tuition in his pocket, Jim packed his bags and hopped a bus to Medford.

Medford Business College was tiny. It occupied one room on the second floor of a junk store in an old building downtown. Jim learned shorthand and typing. He paid attention this time when repeating an accounting course he had taken in high school. After six months, a man named Jim Wallin from the General Insurance Company offered him a job with the Harold Brown Agency in Medford. "You'll start at forty dollars a month," said Mr. Wallin.

At nineteen years of age and looking fifteen, Jim dressed in a new suit for his first day of work. He cleaned his eyeglasses before studying his appearance in a small, chipped mirror. His slightly wavy, brown hair, slicked back like his father's, needed one more draw of the comb. Jim smiled with approval at his reflection.

He augmented his beginning salary by operating an elevator in the Jackson Hotel. When he closed the door on his small, ten-dollar-a-month flat for the final time, he felt quite pleased with himself. Next stop: a spacious rooming house.

At the agency, Jim took dictation in shorthand, kept the books, wrote and typed the policies, and made sales. Harold Brown handled outside sales, but he had a drinking problem and didn't often work. Jim took on an ever-increasing amount of responsibilities. James William Bayless, the businessman, was on his way.

When Jim received a raise to sixty dollars a month, he repaid J.R. Calvert for the hundred-dollar loan. He also settled his fifty-dollar account with Tommy Blanchard.

"I'll always be grateful to Mr. Calvert," Jim says today. "He changed my life. He gave a poor, know-nothing kid a chance." He sighs with gratitude and respect. "And that Tommy Dee. He certainly didn't have that money to spare."

On March 18, 1941, Inez married Tommy's father, Dee Blanchard, in the living room of the Oregon Christian Center. Dee didn't want a fuss made about the affair. Reverend Lamkin performed the ceremony. Martha May and Tommy's sister, Betty, sang from the hymnal:

> *Blest be the tie that binds*
> *Our hearts in Christian love,*
> *The fellowship of kindred minds*
> *Is like to that above.*

Of the Bayless children, only Donald attended. Mrs. Lamkin came, as did a grim Ellen Peelor. In spite of the good Christian that Inez was, she never quite forgave Ellen for circulating the petition to send Inez and her children back to Indiana—but the woman, after all, was Betty's grandmother and "family" to Dee. So Inez held her tongue about Ellen's presence.

Inez would have liked her boys there, but she possessed little hope they could raise the extra money it would take to bring them to Murphy. With a casual phone call, she told Jim about her plans to remarry.

"Mother, I don't think…" Jim started to explain.

"I understand, son. It's not anything. Just a quick, legal formality," she lied.

On Sunday, June 15th, Betty married a man named George Buck on the same day Martha May married Roy Fry. Although best friends, each girl wanted a separate ceremony. Betty and George married in the morning after church, Martha May and Roy at two in the afternoon. The guests experienced a "double feature" of sorts in the living room of the Blanchard ranch. Dee wouldn't contribute a cent for any costs accrued due to frivolous festivities. Inez began to see clearly Dee's no-nonsense, "penny-pinching" ways.

Jim arrived for the weddings. He brought no gift, but he knew no one expected him to. Although employed, he didn't really have an extra "penny to bless himself with," said Inez. She and his "sisters" appreciated the simple fact that he had come.

A genuine smile of goodwill crossed his face as first Betty, then Martha May, walked down the aisle, even though he had moved on from so many of the connections that bonded the people in that living room. He wondered if he appeared to them as he saw himself: no longer a farm boy and more worldly than anyone present.

A distinguished, gray-haired Dee Blanchard gave away both brides. Jim admired his stepfather's stride. The two men were alike in many ways. Neither one ever took much to farming. Dee had trained as a bookkeeper. A photographic memory and an acuity with numbers suggested to Jim a fine intelligence.

That November Jim couldn't make it to the marriage of Tommy Dee Blanchard and Grace Thrasher, the woman who would one day write the biography of Inez. Her father had recently acquired the Murphy General Store. On the day of the Thrasher-Blanchard marriage, Jim made a mental toast to Tommy Dee, thanking him again for the loan that helped launch his career in business.

Any thought of his own marriage hadn't yet entered Jim's mind. Young, with a promising job, Jim was enjoying himself in a somewhat jaunty fashion. He'd had a few girlfriends that were more casual acquaintances than anything. "No one special," he'd tell people, although today he's quick to say with a twinkle, "What girl *isn't* special to a young man of twenty?" Then Oren, a friend from the telephone company, told him about a nice girl named Peggy who lived in Jacksonville, a few miles west of Medford. Jim called her up immediately.

They got on well and dated a few months, although Jim saw other girls as well. Then Peggy invited Jim to visit her in California, where she was staying with a relative. A few days after Christmas in 1941, Jim made the drive to Pasadena. He had a new car—well, new to him, but six or seven years old. With the help of a small loan from Harold Brown, Jim had purchased the Chevy with white-walled tires for $150. Once a month at the garage, Jim hoisted up the car on a lift and painted the white tire walls to a spotless gleam. Every Sunday he washed and polished the body and admired it with a wide grin. That mysterious place under the hood, however, eluded Jim—that was his brother Roy's area of expertise—but he knew his Chevy looked mighty good on the outside.

US 99 took Jim pretty much all the way from Medford to Peggy's relatives in Pasadena. He drove to Ashland, across the California border near the Siskiyous Summit and through the Cascade Range, past Mt. Shasta to Sacramento, through the San Joaquin Valley to Bakersfield, and finally to Pasadena. The two-lane route went through the center of every town, complete with stoplights. He usually drove late into the night. When Jim stopped for some sleep, he'd stay at a Millner Hotel, a chain of cheap flophouses.

During the long, slow drive, Jim reflected on the family motor trip with Uncle Bill and Aunt Eula from Indiana to Oregon. Certainly the farm boy in his memory was someone else. As he straightened and pictured himself now behind the wheel, he imagined the smartly-groomed Uncle Edgar, who had lived next door to the Baylesses in Browns Valley. *Mister* Pitts. Jim caught his own eye in the rearview mirror. He grinned and nodded. "Hello there, *Mister* Bayless." He felt rich with dreams of his own possibilities.

Jim planned to take Peggy to the Rose Bowl Stadium. Oh, he knew there'd be no football game there that year. The Japanese had seen to that when they attacked Pearl Harbor a few weeks earlier. For security reasons, Duke University would host the Rose Bowl game in Durham, North Carolina, and the West Coast venue would sit silent.

Peggy and Jim drove to the stadium on New Year's Day. Jim liked the idea of going "just for the lark of it." The thought of being alone with a girl at the Rose Bowl Stadium tickled him more than being at the game itself.

It was Oregon State College's first trip to the Rose Bowl. Bets were on Duke to win. When the radio announced the winning 68-yard pass from Oregon State's Bob Dethman to Gene Gray, Jim was driving along in his spit-polished Chevy with a pretty girl at his side. Life is good, he thought.

The Army drafted Jim in September of 1942 and instructed him to report to the induction station in Portland. He'd never been on a train or to Portland. The train stopped in Grants Pass. His mother and Dee Blanchard met him at the station with a large box of fried chicken for the trip. Jim studied the couple before him as if they were strangers. His mother seemed to love Dee, the way she'd look up at him and smile for no particular reason. But Jim did not recognize that smile. Never—except in church as she stood next to his father—had he seen her stand so close to a man, their shoulders occasionally touching. Jim turned his head slightly and thought about how many years had passed since then. When Dee Blanchard called him "son," Jim winced inside. But yes, he liked Dee Blanchard, the straight-speaking, fundamentalist Christian man who knew the value of a dollar.

After a quick kiss to his mother's cheek and a strong handshake from Dee Blanchard, Jim got back on the train. The couple waved from the platform as Jim's northbound train chugged forward. Their faces blurred through the wavy glass. Jim sensed himself observing the passage of time—his past slipping behind him and the train's engines accelerating him to a new and unimagined future.

Chapter Nine

At the military Induction Center, Jim ran into a fraternity brother. Already serving his country, the young man saluted, then with a wide grin, gave Jim a vigorous handshake. "So Uncle Sam managed to find you in that hick town you're from, eh? What is it again—Ulysses something? Gettysburg? Bull—"

"Grants Pass," Jim said with a chuckle.

"I'll take care of you, Jim Boy. Pi Kappa Alpha forever and all that. I'm going to see that you're assigned to a post in Portland." He recalled how Jim left school due to a case of bad feet.

Although not sure what his buddy meant, Jim thanked him and returned to Medford for the standard two-week furlough. He put in an application for Officers' Candidate School and awaited orders to report for boot camp at Ft. Lewis, Washington. To his surprise, he was told to return to the Induction Center for duty. He hopped a train to Portland and never went to basic training. No one ever showed him how to fire a gun. No one even demonstrated an official salute.

Jim stood on the sidewalk at the corner of SW Alder and 11th, across the street from the Elk's Temple. He looked up at the five-story, brick building the Army had leased for its Northwest Induction Center. To the right he noticed a dirty white hotel with a scalloped roofline. Stalling, he walked nearly to the corner of 10th for a better look. "The Governor Hotel," he said aloud. Assessing next his 125-pound frame, from the spit-polished shoes to his Army-issued sleeves, he added, "You're in the Army now, Private Bayless." Then he angled across the street toward the entrance of the Elk's Temple.

Jim drew rations and quarters, which meant he received pay for living on his own. His responsibilities at the Induction Center included picking up new recruits—mostly for the Army, but an occasional Navy man too—at the train station. They came from Oregon and southern Washington. Jim put them up at a hotel and handled the cost of their meals. He was promoted to a corporal.

Every time Jim glanced at the new "chevron" stripes on his sleeves, his confidence gained more momentum. He talked more, laughed more. New to casual socializing, however, even he thought his attempt at humor sounded like wisecracks. Nevertheless, for the first time in his life, he had the time to be "one of the boys"—and more. Jim got the distinct feeling his buddies—*sometimes*, anyway—looked up to him.

Officially, Jim took orders from a colonel. "He thought he was running things," says Jim. "Truth is, I was in charge."

Every three months, Jim renewed a contract with the Imperial Hotel to house all the new recruits for their overnight stay. He lived at the hotel as well, which was a six-block walk northeast of the Induction Center. A monthly rent of twenty dollars included maid service. Only half of the Imperial's former self still exists today. The part facing South Washington Street, which included Jim's room, is now part of the Plaza Hotel.

The Army fed the new recruits on the first floor of the Induction Center. Since Jim signed the meal tickets, he ate there all the time at no charge to himself. For supper, Jim walked with his buddies to the USO George White Service Center where free food was served. So, rarely did he reach into his pocket to cover a meal. For an enlisted man, he found his standard of living quite agreeable.

The "battle of Broadway," however, annoyed him a little. Nearly every day Jim went by foot or bus the fifteen blocks north on Broadway to Union Station where all the draftees arrived by train. He'd march the whole crew of them down Broadway, through the stoplights, and right on Alder to the Induction Center. Traffic would stop and honk. Pretty girls waved from the sidewalks. No one minded delaying their day to enjoy a patriotic moment. Nothing mattered but the war, and these men were soldiers.

In collusion with his peers stationed at the Induction Center, a conniving Jim told the draftees who had opted to go directly to Ft. Lewis without a two-week furlough—"redballs," they were called—that they had to fork over their unused food and gas ration stamps. So Jim had extra.

"It was quite the life," he says today, with a smile. "I withdrew my application to Officers' Candidate School when I saw how good I had it at the Induction Center." If called to the front, Jim would gladly have gone, but until that time, the Induction Center suited him just fine. He didn't know how much of a role his fraternity brother had to do with his landing that soft assignment, but Jim mentally thanked him many times over the years.

The food stamps allowed the purchase of liquor. Jim had grown to enjoy a drink or two on occasion. The Blitz-Weinhard Brewery, just a few blocks north of the Induction Center (an area later called the Pearl District) gave free beer to enlisted men. Jim often stepped into the taproom for a glass with Jack Patton and some other fellows he knew from the Center.

"So, Jack," Jim said, emptying his glass as they stood at the bar, "are those wedding bells I hear?"

Jack faked a punch. "Yeah, yeah," he said, smiling. "Looks like it's going to happen."

"Beverly's a nice girl."

"Yes, I got lucky. And what about you and—?"

"Another beer here," Jim said to the bartender. Looking straight ahead, he said to Jack, "Nah, not going to happen."

Jim also frequented Jantzen Beach Amusement Park, named for one of the park's investors, Carl Jantzen of Jantzen swimsuit fame. The summer before, in July of 1942, journalist Clara Shepard of *The Spectator* had called Jantzen Beach "The Coney Island of the West." She wrote:

If a young man about town says 'dancin'' to a girl, he might just as well say Jantzen Beach...for they are synonymous as far as she is concerned. The golden-canopied ballroom features the sweetest swing in the country every night of the park's season, with a parade of 'big name' dance bands moving across its boards...in engagements of a night to a fortnight.

When the forty-acre park opened on May 26, 1928, fifteen thousand people waited at the gates. Almost twice as many came the next day to enjoy the merry-go-round, fun house, Big Dipper roller coaster, the ballroom, five swimming pools, and picnic grounds—and, of course, the music of bands like Tommy Dorsey.

Jim loved the sound of the big bands. Young ladies urged him to dance as their feet kept time to the jazzy beat, tapping like bombs ticking. Finally he yielded and walked among the jitterbug gyrations of a thousand people, sure no one would notice he had never before danced. But within the throng of voices and horns, he heard his mother's disapproving voice. He imagined her standing beyond the dance floor, shaking her head. With a smooth glide, he turned his back on her and danced.

The popularity of Jantzen seemed linked to the Big Bands themselves. The park peaked during the 40's, and then declined in the 50's. By the 70's, no one went any longer. Today the popular amusement park is a shopping mall. A wood wall sculpture hanging in Jim's home reads *Dancin' at Jantzen.*

They had been working together at the Induction Center a year before Jim really noticed her. Jean was a civilian, a typist, a very sweet and attractive girl with a petite frame, a bright smile, and brown hair that hung to her shoulders in loose curls. Jim had seen her around, but he already had a girlfriend by the name of Dorothy Abel. He'd even purchased a ring—not necessarily for Dorothy, but "just in case." He found the ring in a hockshop called Semler's. "Got a great deal," he told people. "Just couldn't pass it up." Then Dorothy dumped him, told him that her old boyfriend, George, had returned from overseas. "Goodbye, Jim," she said, extending her hand. Jim thought, *Your father likes me.* But of course, what did that matter? Businessmen like Mr. Abel understood Jim—it was the girls that gave him trouble.

Then one day he found himself talking to Jean Welter. "Let's have breakfast tomorrow morning," he suggested. "I'd like that," she said, her wide smile stretching beneath high cheekbones. They met at the

Jolly Joan, a restaurant inside the Morgan Building down the block from where Jim lived. He could see it from his bedroom window on SW Washington Street.

Before a second date, Jean had her wisdom teeth pulled. Pain forced her to refuse Jim's invitation to a movie. She fretted to her mother that he might think her excuse meant she didn't like him. "He'll call another time," her mother comforted. "Oh, he won't. He won't," Jean moaned, her worry causing her more distress than her extracted teeth. She knew then that she was falling for the guy.

They started dating, often taking the trolley or walking to the cinema, followed by dinner at the Jolly Joan. Jim soon learned that Jean Charlotte Welter, a Catholic girl and native of Portland, was the only child of a mechanic and housewife. The Welters moved to Timber, just west of Portland, until Jean entered the eighth grade. Then they returned to Portland.

Jim found it easy talking to Jean. Maybe because she did most of the talking. She spoke at an articulate pace, placing emphasis on unexpected words and syllables as if rehearsing for a play. Jim liked her dramatic flair. She always watched him attentively when he spoke, and she laughed easily—certainly not because he possessed an amusing sense of humor, but because she seemed to know a secret about being happy. He felt happy with her. He thought her beautiful. Most of the time he hardly noticed the "lazy eye" problem called strabismus that caused her left eye to turn inward.

Thanksgiving, 1943, Jim took Jean home to meet his mother, brothers, and sister. As the bus neared Grants Pass, Jim—"the sophisticated soldier sitting next to the unsuspecting ingénue" (according to Jean)—said loudly, "Where are you getting off? How would you like to come with me?"

Startled, Jean froze, noticing that "an old motherly-looking woman" wore a weepy look of concern. Regaining her composure, Jean took her young man's arm and said, "I think I would like that very much." She sensed wide eyes and slackened jaws at her back as she stepped with Jim to the front of the bus and out the door.

Jean liked Martha May, but her relations with everyone else in the Bayless circle remained distantly cordial. She wasn't impressed with farm living. Although from a modest background, she possessed, according to Jim, "classy" sensibilities. Using an outhouse made her uncomfortable.

She told Jim she dreamed of making a success of her life. Her smile spread across her face in slow motion, as it often did. "One day I'm going to have all the things I've ever wanted," she whispered breathlessly.

Jim nodded. He had the same plan. It began the first time he sat in the outhouse looking at a mail-order catalog as his father lay sick and dying. With the passing of years, he felt the itch of all possibility in the palm of his hand.

He considered a response to Jean and then swallowed it. People always laughed when he announced his "fancy pants" dream, as his mother had called it. He didn't wish to spoil the evening with this young lady he had grown to like quite well.

"Tell me, Jim," Jean encouraged, gently.

He glanced at her and then away. "I plan to become a millionaire one day." Jim looked back when he heard no response.

Jean was smiling. "I believe you," she said.

Jim smiled back at this woman. At that moment, she appeared more beautiful than ever. She believed he could make a success of his life. She didn't laugh. A new faith in himself planted its feet.

At seventeen, newly graduated from high school, Jean had taken a summer job at the Induction Center. She had planned to attend the University of Oregon in the fall of 1942, but when everything in the world seemed about the war, Jean's enthusiasm about leaving the Center to take college courses in Eugene paled.

When she first met Jim, she thought him a smart aleck. After he asked her out, she found she liked how she felt on his arm. He oozed confidence and pizzazz. She began to notice that he actually ran the Induction Center and that he would be that kind of person the rest of his life—a person in charge, she thought, one people listened to because he made sense.

In the living room of her parents, he said casually, "What would you say if I asked you to marry me?"

She should have said, "Now don't go too far out there on that limb!" But she didn't. For months she had daydreamed about every phrase he might say that sounded anything like a proposal. Never did she think he'd get down on one knee, take her hand, effuse how much he loved her and could not live without her—but she secretly hoped. "I'd say yes!" she said in a burst of happiness, each succeeding word louder than the one before it.

He smiled with relief. From his suit pocket he drew the engagement ring he had purchased at Semler's hockshop and placed it awkwardly on her finger.

His feeling of satisfaction began to melt as Jean proceeded to talk gaily about starting a family right away. His shoulders drooped in thought.

Then a plan took form and his thin frame straightened. He found again his "take charge" demeanor. "But we must be out of the Army first. I have to establish myself in business before—"

"Oh yes!" she said, nodding in complete agreement with the reasonableness of his plan. She felt inside the visit of something very soft and sweet. Like angels. Jim made her feel safe. She smiled at him and he kissed her.

Jean's uncles, on her mother's side, thought their seventeen-year-old niece too young for marriage.

"I don't think you've looked closely lately," she told Uncle Bob, spinning around, her full skirt opening like an umbrella. She explained to him how living with the war every day at her job matured a young lady fast. She felt up to the task of being an equal partner for the serious and ambitious, twenty-three-year-old James William Bayless.

Only occasionally did she think about the plans she had made before meeting Jim. She had hoped to study speech and drama in college. It was her skills in these areas that helped her become Bethel Queen at Mt. Hood Masonic Temple. Although the reign of most queens took place during the high school years, Jean was crowned for a six-month reign following graduation. Her tiara sat on the dresser in her bedroom the evening Jim proposed.

June 4, 1943, Jim attended a Masonic meeting with her. At that time, unaffiliated individuals were allowed. When the leader politely asked if any guest had something to say relevant to the proceedings, Jim stood, and with all the dignity of the Grand Master himself, said, "My name is Jim Bayless, the guest of your Bethel Queen, Jean

Welter. I wish to announce that I recently asked her to marry me. Happily, she accepted." The room applauded.

Jim and Jean married February 19, 1944 in the sanctuary of Portland's majestic First Presbyterian Church. Since Jean was Catholic and Jim Baptist, they compromised and adopted a denomination somewhere in between. Dr. Paul Wright, a good friend of the Welter family presided over the ceremony. The old, downtown church, perhaps Portland's loveliest, had its beginnings in 1854. Some of Jim's buddies from the Induction Center attended. Cpl. Jack Patton, who examined the vision of the draftees, served as best man.

Gail, the daughter of Jean's Uncle Bob, walked the aisle as flower girl. Jean asked Jack's new wife, Beverly, whom she knew from work, to be her matron of honor. The bride wore a long, v-neck, faille gown of simple design, gathered at the bosom and with lace at the neck. She carried a white Bible with a spray of white orchids. A crown of seed pearls held in place her net and lace veil. Sixty years later, that very veil would rest on a life-size statue of a dog during the wedding of Jim and Jean's fun-loving granddaughter, Lisa.

Jim's brother Roy, serving his country as a hospital orderly overseas, couldn't come to the wedding. Martha May, Jean imagined, felt shy about coming without her husband who was also in the war. Both Martha May and her stepsister, Betty, had toddlers to think about. Don, the youngest brother, only sixteen and uncomfortable around his older brother he didn't really know, also bowed out. Besides, he was a teen having problems adjusting to his new stepfather. Dee, a strict fundamentalist, had no time for the shenanigans of a boy who had never known a father's discipline. Before the year was out, Don would persuade his mother to sign the underage form permitting his enlistment.

Inez came alone since Dee thought all the fuss around weddings amounted to a waste of time and money. Since Inez was working at the time, teaching school, she paid her own way. Dee reasoned that if she worked, she could pay for activities that didn't concern him. As well, she paid half of their living expenses—even when they fed the parking meter on a trip to town.

Jim observed his mother's floor-length, elegant dress, one unlike he had ever before seen her wear. She had a corsage on her lapel:

three large flowers, one beneath the other. When she smiled at Jim, he could tell she felt proud of him.

Jim still held the rank of corporal when he married, but received a promotion to sergeant shortly following the ceremony. The photographer asked Jim if he'd like an extra stripe painted on his uniform for the wedding pictures. Jim looked incredulously at the man. "Of course not!"

Mr. and Mrs. James Bayless spent their first night as husband and wife in their own "City of Roses." Jim booked a suite at the Multnomah Hotel, one of the grandest accommodations in the Pacific Northwest. With its chandeliered ballrooms and marbled staircases, it was the preferred hotel of kings and queens, celebrities, presidents, and Portland's most esteemed social circle. Jim didn't want the hotel to make a fuss over the fact that Jean and he were bride and groom. Hopefully, everyone would assume the couple frequented such hotels often. "Act casual," Jim said. "They'll never guess." But while checking in, Jim removed his Army hat, spilling rice everywhere. He smiled sheepishly. The man behind the desk smiled back, and Jean laughed.

Once in their room, Jim told Jean how during his boyhood in Browns Valley and Grants Pass everyone would gather around and plan a "chivaree" for the newlyweds. He confessed with a laugh that he had "chivareed" many a couple in his time by making annoying noises on the first night of a marriage and then quietly listening for the bed to collapse because someone had sawed the bed slats nearly through. Jean smiled politely, but said a little thank-you prayer to God that they were far away from people who did that sort of thing.

The next morning, Jim and Jean took a train to Seattle and then a ferry to Victoria, British Columbia. They stayed at the 460-room, Empress Hotel, nicknamed the "Jewel of the Pacific." As Jim danced his new bride across the ballroom, dazzled by the light reflected in the prisms hanging from the chandeliers, he shook his head slightly in disbelief at all the grandeur about him. He loved the British feel of the Edwardian style. It was so much more than he had ever imagined. People actually lived like this! Every day. He wouldn't have a penny of savings when he returned to Portland, but no matter. He laughed. Jean looked up at him and laughed, too.

They stayed three nights. The Army had given Jim only a five-day furlough. The colonel insinuated Jim might receive orders at any moment to report for active duty. Back in Portland, Jim and Jean rented a one-bedroom studio on SW 15th and Taylor Street at Lownsdale Apartments for $37.50 a month. They slept on a pull-down, "Murphy" bed.

"Remember our room at the Empress?" Jean said dreamily as she snuggled next to her new husband.

Jim put his arm around her and pulled her close. "There will be many Empress nights in our future, Mrs. Bayless. I promise you."

Jean took a job as a receptionist at the Equitable Savings & Loan Co. For an evening out, the couple often went to fifty-cent movies. Jim persuaded Jean to start drinking alcohol in a moderate fashion. The purchase of a pint of whiskey, dinner, and two tickets to the movies cost Jim no more than five dollars. Restaurants didn't sell alcohol by the glass. People brought in their own liquor.

Jim continued his responsibilities at the Induction Center. When the supply of available draftees dried up, Jim was put in charge of WAC recruiting. Most of the other servicemen assigned to the Induction Center were called up. Jack Patton was assigned to a base in San Diego.

That summer of 1944, Jim started experiencing increasing pain in his sacroiliac. The Army sent him to Barnes Hospital in Vancouver, Washington, where doctors diagnosed Jim with progressive arthritis. Over the next three or four months, Jim walked about in a full back brace. In November of 1944, the Induction Center closed. His exit papers from the Army read: "Special Service, WAC Recruiting. Medical Discharge."

He found a job almost the next day. His old boss, Harold Brown out of Medford, offered him a partnership in his agency. First, however, he suggested that Jim get more company experience at the Portland main office of the General Insurance Co. They would pay him $200 a month.

Two hundred dollars sounded nice enough to Jim. He stepped in the door of the Board of Trade building and looked for a sign to double-check the location of "The General." *6th floor.* Right, Jim said to himself. Off in the corner, a gentleman was buying a pack of cigarettes at the smoke shop. It was Jim Wallin, the same fellow who had hired him right out of business school to work for Harold Brown. As Mr. Wallin tapped a cigarette on his pack, he noticed Jim. "Well, how are you doing, kid?"

"Good. Very good, sir." Jim extended a hand in greeting. "I'm on my way to work for the main office."

"I see. Not there any longer myself." Wallin took a long drag.

"Really," said Jim, a bit curious.

"I hired on with a man by the name of Dooly. Like Harold Brown, he's an agent for the General. Third floor. You should stop by and see Mr. Maurice Dooly. Tell him I sent you."

Jim nodded a thank you to Mr. Wallin as the elevator door closed. "Third floor," he said to the back of the elevator operator. Why not? Wallin had steered him right the first time.

Mr. Dooly agreed to see Jim without an appointment. Jim liked the man instantly, the way he looked, impressive in stature, bulk, and demeanor. His affable but business-like manner clicked with Jim's image of a good boss, though it wouldn't take much to outshine the tippler Harold Brown.

"What's Brown paying you?" Mr. Dooly asked.

"Two hundred," Jim said.

"I'll give you two fifty. You can start tomorrow."

The offer appealed to Jim beyond just money. He knew Jean didn't like the idea of leaving behind her parents and her mother's relatives. She adored her uncles. The whole Narver-Welter clan differed from the Bayless family the same way the bustling and exciting Portland differed—according to Jean—from the "humdrum" Grants Pass. If Jim worked for the Harold Brown Insurance Agency in Medford, he and Jean would live only thirty miles from Grants Pass.

"I was young," says Jean, "and familiar only with the ways of my own family. They were close and affectionate while Jim's family came across so remote, aloof...Inez' domineering ways frightened me. Uncle Bob hugged you when you came in the room and hugged you again when you left. I didn't want to have to deal with figuring out how to be married and lose my family too."

A childlike smile fills her face. "A Narver was always excited about one thing or another. If something was happening in your life, you were the center of attention. You were the star. I liked that, and I wanted to hold on to that."

Jim took the job at Dooly. His back problem miraculously improved, and he removed the brace. Jean continued working at the Equitable Savings & Loan Co. They bought a car. Since the war had brought a halt to the automobile industry, they found a used Desoto to Jim's liking. It cost him five hundred dollars.

He thought occasionally about his mother and other family back in Grants Pass. But the line had been drawn, separating Jim from his past. He had entered the corporate world of big-city life and had no intention of ever returning to his roots—except to visit.

Chapter Ten

"There are very few people I'd call truly *nice*," Jim told his wife one evening, "but Mr. Dooly is one of them." On the Board of Directors for a number of companies, including the General Insurance Company, Maurice Dooly was respected by the Portland community. The most esteemed social circle welcomed him. After meeting Mr. Dooly, Jean called him "an old-fashioned gentleman."

His brother, now retired, had started Dooly & Co. thirty-four years earlier in 1910. The firm now totaled about twenty-five employees. Everywhere felt dark and murky with the Philippine mahogany doors and wainscoted walls. Galvanized iron pipes hung from the ceiling. While policy prohibited women to smoke in public, every man, it seemed, took advantage of this inalienable right. Where the sun managed to enter, the rays gathered the particles of smoke to form a ghostly blanket. Private offices lined up behind the receptionist. The desks of women assistants and spittoons dotted the open areas.

Ethel Pugh, who Jim noticed "didn't seem one bit interested in men and never even dated," worked the switchboard, tangling with the "ropes" for incoming calls and plugging them into a vertical board of connectors to employees with telephones. Later she worked in casualty insurance. Her quick wit always made Jim laugh.

A woman named Michael Wyckoff showed up one day saying Chuck Evans had told her to report for work. No one knew about this hiring and decided against asking Mr. Dooly if he knew what his son-in-law had done. They discretely gave Michael the vacant secretarial

79

position handling fire insurance policies. Eventually her competence landed her the position as head of her department.

In the early days, the bane of Michael's existence was her stapler—certainly the first one ever invented. When attempting to attach an expiration notice to the daily report, she would struggle with the weighty gadget that created a staple from a feed of a wire roll. Long after other secretaries owned modern staplers, Michael "was stuck with her ageless wire wonder," said Ethel, until either due to murder or suicide, it met its demise with a fall to the floor.

Both Ethel and Michael worked with Jim until he retired. They remember the birth of Jim's first born. They co-hosted a party when he was promoted to regional director after thirty-five years with the company.

Mr. Dooly's two son-in-laws worked in sales. Five senior partners, including Mr. Dooly—all at least thirty years older than Jim—ran Portland's largest insurance firm. Claude Lilly, a kindly old gentleman who had been at Dooly forever, handled small accounts, thereby receiving only a small percentage of the profits as a partner. Ed Thomas, who was "all business," made Jim bristle when he called him "son" or "boy." The other two partners, Harry Grannatt and Ferry Smith, could often be found at the smoke shop on the first floor, rolling dice. The shop's owner would "shake you" for money or anything else. Jim, however, wasn't the gambling kind.

Jim closely studied Harry Grannatt, the top salesman at Dooly because he had astutely recognized the potential for newspapers as clients for strike insurance. But Jim disliked the eccentric Grannatt, in spite of the fact that he was successful at what he did. Jim's daughter Christie says that "the Bayless children learned at their father's knee that a businessman must dress conservatively, be clean shaven and early to appointments, keep his desk neat, and pay attention to detail." According to Jim, Mr. Grannatt fell short of meeting these requirements.

"Besides," Jim said, "he's so smart, he's dumb." Grannatt read medical books in the restroom and repeatedly started fires in wastebaskets with the butts of his cigarettes. He developed a formula for computing percentage payments to the salesmen that Jim found unacceptable. The formula did not reward the person moving uphill in his career and did not punish enough the person heading downhill.

In addition, Grannatt wrote a book of poetry in 1939 titled *The Pied Typer of Shrdlu-Etaoin*. Although the book had rhyme, the reason for writing such silly verse eluded Jim. "Foolish!" he said, and offered the final poem as evidence to support his opinion of the man.

> *I think that I shall never see*
> *A poem lovely as a tree;*
> *A tree that's swallowed at a gulp*
> *Into a vat of sulphite pulp—*
> *Alas, how many lovely trees*
> *Are used in printing poems like these*!

Jim began early in his career with Dooly & Co. as a salesman. If the war hadn't left the business world short of men, he may have started out on a lower rung of the ladder. But after only a few weeks, Dooly handed him policies. "Can you get 'em to renew, Jim?" Then a few old accounts came Jim's way through the trust departments of various banks. He went out and got new ones. Dooly had put him on a horse and he was out the gate.

Although Jim liked Mr. Dooly a great deal, he realized that his boss didn't do much around the firm. He arrived late and mostly sat around smoking cigarettes. When he came in, Jim often went back into his office to talk for ten or fifteen minutes. He wanted his mentor to hear his ideas and to fully realize his commitment. Mr. Dooly would offer a little guidance, thereby "grooming" him for success. Then he'd step out of the way. A "gentleman's gentleman," Jean said, amending her first assessment of him.

During one of his conferences with Mr. Dooly, Jim bragged about the "large sum" of money he would net upon receiving his percentage for the premiums he had collected. "I'm really growing in this business, sir. I'm worth $1000."

Mr. Dooly looked with admiration upon the ambitious young man. He smiled and said, "The first thousand is the hardest you'll ever make in your life. The next thousand will come a lot easier."

Liquor appeared from desk drawers that first Christmas season in 1944. Sam, the mailman, stopped in for a nip—as he would every holiday season for the decade to come—and usually "reel out of the building much later, cap askew, with a very carefree grip on his mailbag," said Ethel. The official Christmas party, held on the 24th, Michael added, was no more than a "water glassful of booze and a handshake from the boss." But by then, the employees were already on their way to a Christmas Eve hangover—the "unofficial" party had started at lunchtime.

At the close of six months, Harold Brown contacted Jim and said, "Okay, it's time to come back to Medford and be my partner."

Jim assessed his situation. Maybe he would be better off as a partner at Brown than a mere salesman at Dooly. But then Jean's ill feelings about moving to Medford prickled his neck. She'd certainly cast her vote for Dooly & Co. Well, maybe she was right. Jim began to see Dooly & Co. as a big pool in which a little fish could learn how to swim.

"Jean, I talked with Harold Brown today," he said.

Jean watched him and waited.

"He still wants me as his partner."

She showed no expression. Already she had learned: It had to be his decision.

"I told him I plan to cast my lot in Portland."

A smile crossed her body. She extended her arms into the air as she walked toward her husband and hugged him.

Feeling confident about his potential in the business community of Portland, Jim took steps to climb the city's social ladder. He joined the prestigious Multnomah Athletic Club, located next to the Multnomah Stadium. The club today boasts over 20,000 members. Jim established a membership mainly for the social activities, although he also used the weight room on occasion.

Still living in their rented studio apartment, Jim thought it time he owned a home. Because of his status as an Army veteran, Jim had priority for building materials. The Bayless house would be one of the first new homes in Portland since the start of the war. Although VE-Day recently marked the end of the war in Europe, the United States still battled Japan.

The bank agreed to loan money to the young businessman now established with a reputable firm. "What do you think of that, 1st National Bank of Grants Pass?" Jim smirked. He purchased a lot for $360 on SW Martha Street just off Sunset Blvd, near where Jean's Uncle Bob lived with his wife and two small children. Jean was pleased.

Jim hired Van Evera Bailey, a notable modern architect, to design their two-bedroom home. The innovative design included a spacious dining room, kitchen, a living room with large windows, and a carport—a drying yard, as well, since the first fully automatic clothes dryers wouldn't appear on the market for another two years. The middle section of the roof rose up at the front of the house but extended flat on either side. The house would cost seven thousand dollars.

One of Jim's clients came on the job as general contractor. The workers began in late summer and managed to finish the house rather quickly. Their services weren't in demand from customers because few others besides Jim had the money or access to materials. *Architectural Forum* and *House Beautiful* wrote feature stories about 2145 SW Martha Street. No one had ever seen such a house before. Never mind that the blueprints called for electric radiant heat in the ceiling that didn't work. The wires imbedded in the plaster would break. Jim had to have electric heaters installed.

On VJ-Day, August 9, 1945, in an uncharacteristic display of emotion, Jim walked over to Jean's office a few blocks away and kissed her in front of everyone. Jean blushed but secretly enjoyed the attention. Although Jim felt bad that the dropping of the bombs on Hiroshima and Nagasaki killed so many civilians, he believed the move necessary to save American lives. "I don't think the Japanese were ready to surrender. I justified the bombs in my mind," says Jim today. "If I had been President of the United States, it's what I would have done."

Everyone in the Bayless family returned from the war basically intact, although Martha May's husband, Roy Fry, suffered injury on Guadalcanal. He recovered and found a job delivering soft drink. Don, who married his girlfriend after his mother signed the underage enlistment papers, had received a "Dear John" letter and came home divorced. When he visited Portland, Jim gave him money to attend the University of Oregon. Shaking his head, Jim scoffs, "Don took the money, returned to Grants Pass and re-married. He never attended college nor did anything worthwhile with his life."

Jim's brother Roy married Adelia Swisher. The marriage didn't last a year. He immediately married Geraldine "Gerry" McFarland, a woman who didn't mind grease under her fingernails. Together they started Bayless Auto Parts, the perfect business for the boy who had always excelled when tinkering with mechanical things.

Jean and Jim traveled to Grants Pass for Thanksgiving, a tradition they'd continue in the years to come. The Baylesses were "family," a holy concept Jim's mother, as if reading from the Bible, had always preached. As an adult, the *James William* in him heard the call and returned to his family once a year, even though the company of his mother, Martha May, Roy Junior, and Donald recalled bitter experiences of his childhood he wished to forget. *Look forward,* he would remind himself as he bowed his head for grace before the Thanksgiving meal. As everyone ate, if anyone said, "Remember when…," he'd say, "I never look back."

James William returned to Grants Pass mostly to see his mother, the woman with a fierce will who had created Jim in her own image— "two peas in a pod," claims Jean. *Jim*, the businessman who lived in the big city of Portland, created a new definition of family that had little to do with his past, except for one thing: It was driven by the same fervent commitment he had witnessed in his mother.

In 1946, Jean's desire for her own family had heated from a simmer to a full boil. She had been married almost three years with the prospect of a family nowhere in sight. Certainly something must be very wrong with her. To soothe and brighten his wife's dismay, Jim let Jean pick out a floppy-eared cocker spaniel—even though he disliked dogs. She named it Peter.

In August, Jim and Jean took their first vacation. On the recommendation of Jean's Uncle Bob and Aunt Enid, they traveled to Lake Creek Lodge, located on the east side of the Cascade Mountains. They stayed in a romantic knotty pine cabin. Two months later, Jean felt certain her angels had answered her prayers.

Jim and Jean were about to see a movie at the Newsreel when Jean announced she was pregnant. "Is it a boy?" Jim said, excitedly. People around smiled. "Well, I'm not sure," said Jean. "It's a boy," Jim declared. "I think we should have a boy first."

Jean laughed. "I'll tell the doctor."

In late 1946, Jim bought his first new car, a Plymouth. Never again, he vowed, would he purchase a used one. He drove to the Portland Junior Chamber of Commerce he had joined to acquaint himself with the city's business community. He became very active in the organization in the years to come. Often, he took charge of fund-raising projects. One year he suggested that the Chamber erect bleachers and charge people to view Portland's Rose Festival. The project proved successful.

He also served as chairman for the "Merrykana Parade" and worked closely with Francis "Frank" Smith. Jim says, "We put on a hell of a show downtown and in the stadium with horses and Indians and dancing in the streets." The two men became good friends. Frank's wife, Nancy, actually met Jim first. She had worked for the Red Cross when Jim was a sergeant at the Induction Center. When Frank and Nancy decided to adopt a baby, Jean was pregnant with her first born. Frank asked Jim to accompany another friend of theirs to pick up the infant boy. Jim accepted the honor and helped deliver Baby Norman to his new parents.

"Perhaps our children will be friends," said Frank.

And they were—as infants, anyway, says Nancy. The boys went with their parents to the beach. "They would fall asleep snuggled together in the same playpen."

In the years to come, the Smiths and Baylesses socialized together. When Jim purchased real estate, Frank served as his attorney. Over a six-year period after Jim retired and until Frank died, the couples vacationed together in Alamos, Mexico.

On May 5, 1947, Craig Welter Bayless entered the world, perfect in every way.

A miracle, thought Jim. *And a boy*—just as he had "ordered." A special child destined to make a unique mark on the world should have a unique name, he thought. A fellow he knew by the name of

Craig Finley worked in the mortuary business. Jim had never heard the name Craig before meeting Mr. Finley and liked it. Jean suggested that Welter, her maiden name, fit nicely in the middle of Craig and Bayless.

When Craig was about a year old, a neighbor asked Jean to drive her to a department store in downtown Portland because she wished to enter her son, Donny, in a photo contest. Perhaps Donny would win the first prize of a year's supply of baby clothes. Jean thought, Why not enter my darling Craig as well? Craig turned on his charm that day and took home the big prize. "Dad," he says today. "I've been self-supporting since my first year of life."

When dressing Craig in one of his new outfits, Jean's eyes misted with joy as she held her son. "I want a big family, Jim. I want a *group* to surround our lives."

Jim touched the cheek of his baby son. Then he looked at his wife as if he had mentally checked his list and could now confidently move to the subsequent item. "Next, we'll have a baby girl," he said.

On November 26, 1948, Jean came through. Not one to ever show much emotion, Jim "wept with happiness at my bedside," recalls Jean. "We had a blue-eyed, curly-haired little girl to go with our brown-eyed little boy. She was precious with her heart-shaped face and a dimple in her left cheek. Apparently I had done everything perfectly."

A fan of Buz Sawyer, the comic strip superhero who gained military experience during World War II, Jim wanted to honor his daughter as the namesake of Christy Jameson, the woman Buz finally married after enjoying exotic exploits around the world.

What? Jean thought, but knew that a tactful approach would serve her better. She persuaded Jim that a nickname would not do—How about Christine? And for a middle name, they both liked the name Joan. How about Christine Joan? Jim agreed to the compromise, but he always called her Christy. Everyone, of course, followed suit. They spelled her name with a –y until the spring of 1958, when she adopted the more hip spelling of Christi with an –i. When thirtysomething, she added an –e.

Jim and Jean brought Christie home to her brother—but no Peter. The poor cocker had run into the street and was struck dead by a car. A few tears welled in Jean's eyes as she told Craig that Peter had "gone to heaven." Jim deposited Peter at the vet, glad to be rid of the worry about a puppy running about the house.

A photographer came every month to snap pictures of the children. Jean's parents, Mike and Elsie, who lived a short distance away on NW 23rd and Pettygrove, became permanent babysitters. They dined at the Bayless home every Sunday. "Their lives joined ours," says Jim. He didn't seem to care that his in-laws didn't own a home—and never would. Christie says, "My grandparents lived in a rented apartment in an unclassy neighborhood on the wrong side of town. Yet they were completely accepted, adored, and enjoyed by my parents."

Jean's father, Mike, a mechanic for Bingham Pump Company, helped Jim with house projects. Every weekend they had a new one. As workers constructed the Bayless home, Jim and Mike built the furniture. Weeks before Craig's birth, they constructed a plywood crib.

Craig called Mike *Bobop* and Grandmother Elsie *Gramuz*. The names stuck as affectionate nicknames used by everyone in the family, with *Gramuz* soon taking on the shortened form of *Muz*. "A sedate British mother and stern German father" Christie would later say about her mother's parents. Jean generally agreed, but would add, "He wasn't really so stern, and she was a little cutie." Elsie Narver Welter, slight and porcelain fragile behind her glasses, cast a contrasting figure next to the muscular, chisel-faced German with slicked-back hair.

Jim would address Muz's brother as "Uncle Bob," even though the man was but ten years Jim's senior. Bob's friends would sing out with a snicker, "Uuuuncle Bob" until he finally said, "Jim, would you mind just calling me Bob? I'm not your uncle, in case you haven't noticed." Then he gave Jim one of his big hugs.

A close relationship with Jean's family changed Jim. He learned to both give and receive an occasional hug. Even if his words didn't exactly say *love* often enough, or he didn't embrace his children with ease, they knew he loved them. As he played with them, he would picture himself a young boy in Browns Valley, sitting at the doorway that marked the line he was forbidden to cross, watching as his father lay dying in the distance. He'd promise himself time and again that his children would never know that same desperate loneliness.

Chapter Eleven

In the early days of insurance, all agencies were either board or non-board. Non-board agencies, with their independent agents, were more competitive and less restrictive, and they always paid a dividend to policyholders. It was required that an agency have only all board or all non-board clients. Dooly & Co. was a non-board agency.

General Insurance, one of the non-board companies Dooly represented, owned the reputation of being the first insurance company to assure lower premiums. It also offered the financial stability and security associated with an investor-owned stock company (an accepted philosophy until the scandals of large, public corporations in 2002). Jim clearly saw the vision of General Insurance.

After hearing once again Jim's praise of "The General," Claude Lilly said during a meeting, "Don't you like money, Bayless?" His eyes twinkled as he took a kindly stab at humor. Like the other senior partners, Claude had been doing his job the same way for a very long time.

"Maybe he likes clients," Harry Grannatt interjected, with his typical offhand wit. "Ethel says the switchboard is all lit up with calls from widows and retirees who can't wait to get their hands on you now that premiums have risen to six dollars."

Claude smiled sheepishly.

Jim believed that lower premiums to the customer, in spite of the resulting lower commissions to the broker, could ultimately pay off for an ambitious producer like himself.

Jim often ate lunch alone at Al Morrell's lunch counter on the first floor of the Board of Trade Building. There were no booths—just stools. He would order the Shrimp Wiggle—melted cheese and shrimp on toast. More often than not, he'd grab the sandwich and head back to his desk to work.

Sometimes he ate with Alan Green, Jr., who in 1947 joined the firm as a salesman. Jim enjoyed the robust character with the booming voice people called "Punch." Although Punch soon left Dooly to take over the Irwin-Lyons Lumber Co. when his father-in-law died, the two men became life-long friends. A Stanford graduate in political science, Green went on to become the consummate backroomer, the man behind the Oregon campaigns of Gerald Ford, Ronald Reagan, George Sr. and George W. Bush. Other backroomers affectionately called him "Mr. Republican."

One afternoon in late 1948, as the snow fell outside the windows of Al's lunch counter, Jim reached into the breast pocket of his jacket to pay for his Shrimp Wiggle and coffee. He felt the bulge of cigars he'd use as a segue to talk more about his new daughter.

"Here, have another cigar, Punch."

"Thanks, Jim-boy. Don't mind if I do."

"Fortunately, she looks like her mother."

"Is that so?" Punch grinned across the rim of his coffee cup. "Thank your stars for that Jim-boy."

Back at the office, the salesmen gathered for their end of the year meeting. Senior partner Ferry Smith announced that Mr. Dooly would further ease his way into retirement. His release of twenty percent of the company would allow the firm to bring in three new partners in 1949.

"Gentlemen, let's welcome our new junior partners of good standing—Rudy Rimback, Warren Munro, and Jim Bayless."

"Here, here," came the response, with the raising of water glasses.

As Jim headed out the front door of the Board of Trade Building that evening, he stopped to buy more cigars. Truth was, he didn't like the things, but this recent habit of passing out cigars told him things were going well for him. Darn well.

Although only a junior partner, Jim easily assumed a leadership role in the firm. He generated sales second only to Harry Grannatt, and he monitored the productivity of the whole company. According to company procedure, everyone recorded his sales in the "New Business Book." Mr. Dooly checked the book daily, as did Jim. Ethel accused some of the salesmen of documenting new business one day only to cancel it the next. No one kept track of cancellations, so unless Ethel bent the boss' ear, Mr. Dooly believed all his salesmen were producing. But Jim knew the truth.

One day while eating alone at Al's, Jim straightened his posture on the stool, nodded in acknowledgement to a Dooly secretary, and then glanced around the room, smiling. A perfect family waited for him at home, his health was good, and nothing blocked his view to his goal of becoming a successful leader in the firm. One day he'd own all the worldly goods of his dreams.

His eyes darted about the counter in excitement as he made plans. Next step: He wanted a new house, one that would reflect his rising position in the business community, one that would announce to the world an optimism about his future. It would have to be a very special house at a spectacular location. Not an average structure, of course, like those burgeoning through the soil of the new subdivisions everywhere around the city.

He drove around Portland, looking. Where should a successful man live? Mr. Dooly owned a home in Portland Heights. That's it. He'd find a location overlooking the city. Yes, on top of a hill.

One day he found himself making his way on winding roads within a thick forest. He drove up a very steep hill to the highest point of a development and gazed lovingly from a thousand feet above the city—a location higher than the home of Mr. Dooly. The developer, Jim Hessler, wanted $4500 for the lot.

"It has a magnificent view," Jim told Mr. Dooly.

"Don't buy it yet, Jim," Mr. Dooly said, thinking the lot might come down in price.

Jim couldn't see letting the perfect location slip through his fingers. After signing the deed, Jim drove to the wooded lot where his family's new home would soon stand. He looked north (Perhaps the living room will go here) to the Willamette River as it bisected the city. Mt. St. Helens, still a perfectly symmetrical cone of white, stood straight ahead. To the east rose up the imposing Mt. Hood. As Jim panned the view, he identified Mt. Rainier, Mt. Jefferson, and Mt. Adams.

"Lots of windows. Huge—" he said into a fierce wind. Jim huddled into his pockets and the collar of his winter coat.

At the Junior Chamber of Commerce, Jim met an architect with Williams & Smead and hired the firm to design his new home. He sold the house on Martha Street. The Bayless family moved into the Binford Apartments as one of the first homes in Hessler Hills took form.

Dr. Paul Wright, pastor for the First Presbyterian Church who married Jim and Jean and christened five-month-old Craig Welter Bayless, baptized Christine Joan on April 2, 1950. The Bayless family became active members of First Presbyterian Church. They attended the Sunday church service and Jean taught Sunday school.

That August of 1950, Christie and Craig accompanied their parents to Grants Pass to visit Inez and Dee at their ranch. Jim liked showing off his new daughter and his growing son. He wanted to talk about his promotion.

Everyone, of course, cooed over the baby about to walk and talk. They admired how fast Craig was growing and laughed at how he called his grandmother Nanny Dee Dee. But everyone had little to say about Jim's success that was readily apparent by the dress of his family and the car he drove. Although he had told his mother about his promotion in a phone conversation, she never mentioned it during the visit. Jim had to announce it on his own.

As usual, Inez talked about Uncle Orville. "Randy is doing so well for himself in the Church." She caught Jim's eye. "He just spoke at another Bible conference. Let's see, was it in Illinois or Iowa?"

Jim knew his mother would never forgive her oldest son for pursuing business rather than seminary training—"like Randy"—and for not going to Wheaton College—"like the boy preacher, Billy Graham." No matter what Jim did in life, she would only see that he had fallen short of her mark.

91

As Craig sat on his father's lap on the tractor and Jean posed behind them, Inez snapped a picture of the three. Jim looked lovingly at his son but thought about his mother focusing the viewfinder. He knew her devout Christian heart told her to love and feel proud of her son, and so she did, in her way. It was enough for Jim. For the rest of her life, he would visit her at least once a year. Why? "Just a son's feeling for his mother," he says.

September 15, the family moved into their new home on the hill. Similar to the house on Martha Street, a shed roof on the new home would overlook tall panes of glass—nine this time, twelve feet in height. The glass wall framed the majestic Mt. St. Helens. No one knew the mountain seethed and bubbled within, biding her time for only one more human generation. The roof on each side of the rise lay flat, extending out over three bedrooms, a large kitchen, family room, and two baths. The Oregonian described the "1950's modern" home as one of the best examples of new home architecture.

Towering near the house were the tallest and most massive radio transmission antennas in all of Portland. Radio waves perpetually flooded the house, disrupting most electrical devices. Craig says, "But the view sure was great!"

The family settled into life on 3131 SW Fairmount Boulevard. The two children kept Jean busy. Craig preferred to run, rather than walk, anywhere. Christie, almost two, gave complete focus to Craig whenever he was around. She'd worm in her mother's arms until she was set down. A typical, pear-shaped toddler of mostly diaper, she'd waddle as fast as she could after her brother.

Jim and Jean began ballroom dance lessons on Thursdays at the Arthur Murray studio and enjoyed "practicing" their new steps at the Multnomah Club. Dancing became a social event they'd continue long into Jim's retirement years.

The couple often played bridge on Saturdays. Although they didn't excel at the game, they enjoyed it—particularly the social aspect of getting together with new friends. Jim tried poker, but he didn't approve of gambling—not so much on moral grounds, but because he hated to throw away money. Even when playing his favorite game of Pitch, a card game of bidding and calling trump, he refused to gamble. He didn't even like bingo events put on by the church. "Gambling is a form of taxation I don't have to pay," he'd say.

Jim and Jean socialized with their old friends Jack and Beverly Patton. After the war, Jack became an optometrist and found work at Zell Optical in Portland. He would provide eye exams and glasses for the Bayless family in general, as well as for Jean's special needs related to her strabismus problem.

Clark and Margaret Bullock from church became good friends. They lived on the valley side of the hill. Clark, an accountant, always wore a tie. He drank martinis while Jim sipped his usual scotch.

The other lots in Hessler Hills were sold, but it would be a while yet before the names of neighbors filled the Bayless engagement book. The area began to bloom when H.A. "Andy" Andersen, CEO of Andersen Construction Co and soon to be one of the richest men in Portland, built his home between the Baylesses and the radio tower. Carolyn and Wade Hansen would move in across the street. Dr. Roderick and Mary Begg lived in the house next door. The partner of the doctor, Larry Noall, and his wife, Margaret, would become Jim and Jean's close friends.

Jim stumbles over the phrase "close friends." Although the date books Jean has kept religiously from 1950 to the present abound with social engagements every week with the same names appearing repeatedly over the fifty years, Jim asserts, "I've never really had a close friend. Jean's the same way. Sure, we've had friends, but no one really close."

Craig says, "Mom and Dad collected friends by the dozens. They distinguished little between an acquaintance and a friend. Someone met yesterday was a 'dear friend' by tomorrow."

Christie explains that her father regarded friendships as secondary to raising a family and achieving his business goals. "Friends" were people who appeared in any particular circle where he stood: in his neighborhood, at work or a club, or on the golf course. He had precise ideas about what he valued in people. Christie, a freelance journalist whose description of her father reveals her knack for turning a phrase, says, "Dad reveres self-made men and women who are loyal and well groomed. He honors people who keep promises, are on time and efficient. Seemingly born without a sense of humor, he appreciates those who were, such as Craig and Uncle Bob Narver. He dislikes vague conversation and repetition. Dad wants specifics—and only once. He doesn't admire athletes, teachers or artists, beards or moustaches. And he doesn't like liberals."

If people met his criteria, Jim respected or admired them. But no one, he says, except his wife, has ever made it into his inner circle.

The Bayless family of four celebrated Christmas in 1950 with the Narvers, as they would in the decades ahead. Elsie (Muz) and Mike (Bobop) came—she already gray and thin with a timid smile, and he, looking German stiff, but a Narver by marriage and therefore a "hugger." Elsie's brothers—Bob, Ernie, and Ursel—arrived with their wives and children. They read from the Bible and sang carols at the piano.

"The Narvers were as different from my family as night and day," says Jim. "They were outgoing and moderately successful. City folk. My family was small-town. The Baylesses, with their very religious background, came across stiff and unfriendly. They thought less of me because I partook of liquor, the 'devil's drink.' Think oil and water. The Baylesses and Narvers were like oil and water."

The Bayless Christmas card was a photograph—as it would always be. "Our cards give a visual history of the 1950's and 1960's life and fashion," Craig reminisces with typical humor. "The cards assumed that all Mom and Dad's friends cared desperately at the holiday season to learn what the Bayless family was up to. Since they were so curious, we, of course, obliged."

Chapter Twelve

Jim assumed more leadership in the firm as Mr. Dooly showed up less. The bookkeeper started leaving the employee paychecks on Jim's desk since he would make signing them a priority before the day was out. If a secretary wanted a raise, the management committee discussed it, but Jim gave the final approval.

Jim went with Warren Munro as a guest on numerous occasions to the University Club, a private men's club. As the son-in-law of Mr. Dooly, Warren had greater access to the Portland social scene. Jim's first visit to the club had been the night both men became partners. He liked the feel of the club with its ivy-covered exterior of red brick, slate, and stone in imitation of early 1600 England architecture. Inside, the design exuded elegance and formality.

Jim winced each time he considered how he could never become a member of such a club. Only college graduates were offered admission. *Never mind. There are other clubs,* Jim would tell himself, with a twist of the wrist that caused the scotch to circle his glass.

As Jim made his way toward center stage at Dooly & Co. and in Portland society, Jean created a stage for herself at home. Both strong personalities, Jim and Jean each had ambitions beyond that of simply actors. They wished to also direct the productions of their lives.

As a young child, Jean invented a playmate named Poket. She directed herself and Poket in private productions. In a piece of writing about her mother, Christie imagined the scene: "They impressed critics, charmed audiences, and influenced the powerful." She added, "Early in Mom's marriage, she learned that Dad, although a great guy, just wasn't cut out to be the actor to her stage directing. Fueled by frustration and a creative nature, Mom wore paths in the carpet at night, performing her dramas. With sofas and chairs as her audience, she talked to the drapery. She recited the leading lady's lines as well as those of her handsome and successful, although uncooperative, male star."

Then children entered Jean's life, "Pokets" each one of them. "As babies, we cooed and burped like obedient fledging stars and starlets," Christie wrote. "Mom read stories and the child prodigies listened. She dispensed lists of chores and the good little soldiers marched. These short people were just like Poket: always present, loving, obedient, and unquestioning about who was in charge...."

In the summer of 1951, Dr. Wright announced during church service that Billy Graham would appear at Multnomah Stadium in August. Jim recalled the light in his mother's eyes as she had talked about the boy preacher. Images flashed to him of his own preaching on street corners in Crawfordsville the year his father sold Prudential insurance. "I'd like to see him," Jim told his wife.

"I'll get tickets, dear."

Over 25,000 people filled the stadium. Jim nodded with respect. Imagine: a farm boy who grew up in the Depression able to command the attention of all these people. Beyond admiration, Jim liked what the man had to say. Dr. Graham preached a simple way of life, guided by the same fundamental values that directed Jim's own life: Just be honest with yourself and others. "Tell the truth," Jim would say often in the years to come, "and you'll never have to remember what you said."

That winter, Jean told her husband she'd like help around the house. A "Negro" woman named Mary Nash came to work for them. Christie recalls, "She was shiny black, round and smelled a funny sweetness. We called her MeMe. She had a solid presence. I liked her."

One or two days a week, Jim would drive to the bottom of the hill and pick Mary up at the bus stop. The University of Oregon Medical

School sat in the background. Mary would work all day, and then Jean would take her back to the bus stop. Jim thought Mary nice but didn't really notice her. All he knew is that she lived in the colored section of Portland and had a family. A person didn't inquire into the lives of the help in those days.

But he paid her social security benefits. While employers of domestic help even today have a scandalous reputation for not paying the fees, Jim found such behavior dishonest.

"I remember when Mom and Dad had formal dinner parties," says Christie. "Sometimes MeMe would stay and help serve. She made us hot dogs. I loved her for that!"

"Until I went to college, she was the only black person I knew," recalls Craig.

Christie adds, "My father had a pretty liberal attitude about blacks—or *Negroes*, as we said growing up. But how hard is it to be liberal about a group of people who have no presence in your day to day life?"

In September of 1952, Jim and Jean enjoyed a two-week trip alone to Mexico. It would be the first of many trips to that country. They walked the crowded streets of Mexico City; stared in awe at Taxco, the city of silver; sunbathed in Acapulco; enjoyed Cuernavaca, the holiday choice of Aztec kings; and admired both the familiar and strange in the majestic, universal city of Córdoba.

In November, Jim voted Democrat. His status as a registered Democrat meant, more than anything, that he felt proud he had supported Roosevelt. In 1948, instead of voting for Truman, he voted for Thomas Dewey. "Dad dismissed Truman as a haberdasher who happened to be in the right place at the right time," says Craig. Truman owned a haberdashery before serving as a county judge, a senator, and of course, Vice-President. In later years, Jim would support Truman's ending of WWII. He'd praise him for the Marshall Plan that was introduced under his watch.

In 1948, however, Jim preferred Dewey. He liked his perfectionist, businessman ways. They discussed politics in Dewey's hotel room, and Jim soon agreed to work on the Dewey campaign.

In the 1952 elections, Jim voted for Adlai Stevenson. Better a liberal than a soldier, he thought. All the hoopla about the heroic general named Eisenhower didn't impress Jim. The war was over. Give the Presidency to a man who knows about taking care of business in the civilian arena.

Craig says, "Dad is a FDR Democrat at heart. He is a conservative Democrat more than a Republican." But Jim has faith above all in a good businessman, regardless of his political affiliation. Craig speaks with startled exclamation to emphasize his point: "He voted for Ross Perot!"

According to his son, Jim loves his money but deep down is a populist who believes in capitalism and self-determination. Jim supports the fight for a more equitable distribution of power and wealth. Craig says, "Dad believes that everyone should have a chance at success, and grinding poverty robs them of that chance. He would like to see people get a hand *up*, not a hand *out*." Jim isn't a "true blue conservative." For instance, he believes in gun control and a woman's right to choose. He believes in family, and he values personal responsibility and hard work. "In short," says Craig, "he is tough on the outside and soft on the inside."

Remodeling of the Board of Trade Building began and then never seemed to end. Workers stripped the exterior, built and hung scaffolds. Dust entered the open windows, resting in layers on business letters and jamming the keys of typewriters. Air hammers deafened. Walls came down on the interior and bed sheets hung in their place. The addition of a lunchroom took business away from Al Morrell's lunch counter, so on occasion, Jim would go down and have his Shrimp Wiggle sandwich.

As he left the building for the evening, noise reverberated in Jim's head and the taste of dust lingered in his throat. An offer from Warren Munro for a drink at the University Club always sounded particularly inviting. One evening, as both men sipped scotch—their suit jackets still on with their ties unloosened—Warren said to Jim, "So, think you'd like to become a member here?" He threw down the last of his drink with the same hand that held a cigarette.

Jim swirled the ice cube in his glass. "Don't get me going, Munro. You know that's impossible." Jim finished his drink and stood to leave.

Stopping Jim with a touch to his forearm, Warren said, "Sit down. Let me explain."

Jim hesitated.

"Come on. Drinks are on me."

Jim sat. Warren raised his index finger to the bartender and then circled it above their glasses. He looked at Jim with a smile. "There's a way around that problem. I can submit your nomination as an associate member."

"Really?"

"Really." Warren raised his glass in a toast.

Jim grinned. When the two drinks met, through the din of male voices, Jim heard the ring of fine crystal.

After becoming an associate member of the University Club, Jim started holding meetings of the Dooly partners there.

He accepted posts on the Board of Directors of both the Portland and Oregon Insurance Agents Associations. In 1953, General Insurance, Jim's provider of preference, adopted the new technology of computer-based automation. It now had a tool that would allow independent agents to better compete with direct insurance writers. "The General" gave birth to the Selective Auto and Fire Insurance Company of America (SAFECO). In support of the new company's vision, Jim resigned from both his posts with the Insurance Agents Associations and attended SAFECO's first board meeting in Seattle's old Metropolitan Theatre.

The Pacific coast lies only ninety minutes from Portland. The summer of 1953 began a tradition of a week at the beach. Bill, son of the Dooly partner Claude Lilly, and his wife joined the Bayless family that summer at Surf Tides Apartments in Lincoln City. Jim and Jean knew they'd return the following summer as well. Craig says today, "My friends' parents made their vacation plans a month or week ahead of time. Not my family. The one thing that stands out about all our vacations is that I knew at least one year in advance when we were going, where we would stay, and for how long."

Jim drove his family to Surf Tides that first summer in a new Chrysler Imperial, outfitted with enough chrome and metal to build three cars today. He had officially switched from Plymouths to

Chryslers. White ones. Jim always bought white cars. The Imperial came with power windows, an automatic transmission, and power seats. On Craig's first day of school in September, Jim offered to drive his son.

As they pulled to the curb of Robert Gray Elementary, Jim watched with amused pleasure as Craig powered the windows up and down until his schoolmates gathered around.

"Bet you've never seen this before," Craig crooned.

Every two years when Jim bought a new Chrysler, they'd put on the same show for the kids. Jim seemed to enjoy it even more than Craig.

When not working at Dooly—which Jim did even on Saturday mornings—he immersed himself into projects around the house. Mike Welter assisted his son-in-law in the endless process of maintaining and remodeling the new home on the hill. The to-do list of projects included building a rock wall, greenhouse, and patio; setting poles for a clothesline and assembling a swing set; constructing fences; trimming hedges; and planting and sowing a vegetable garden.

Craig, who had just celebrated his seventh birthday in May of 1954, was helping Jim in the garden. Taking a break from the task of loosening the soil, Jim drew a handkerchief from his pocket and wiped his forehead. He leaned a moment against the hoe to watch his son and recalled himself as a boy in Browns Valley. He was about Craig's age as his father lay dying on the porch. Jim would work in the garden with his grandfather, readying the soil for planting.

Now here he was a father himself. He arced back his head in wonder at how that could be—and that, although he knew little about being a father, he could be a good one.

Craig was building mounds with the trowel to hold the seeds. He hesitated and smiled up at his father before resuming his task. Jim smiled too, at nothing in particular, except at the thought his son would one day surpass any father's dreams. Leaning a moment longer against his hoe, Jim looked out over the valley and wondered what Roy Washington Bayless had thought about him.

In five months, he'd be a father for the third time. He didn't really need another child. Two seemed a perfect number—a handsome set of a boy and a girl. Yet Jean had persisted. She wanted "a group." So Baby Joan was on her way.

Today, Christie suggests that the thought of a third child worried her father a little. His happy world felt at risk. What if the new child happened upon them anything less than "perfect"? Besides, he liked how his two children—his family of four—stood in front of the world's mirror and reflected a sense of balance.

A radio blast competing with the brrrrrr of the electric saws irritated Jim. He had no idea how the construction workers could accomplish anything amid all the cacophony and chaos they created. An hour earlier, Jim had boomed to one of the workers, "How can you hear yourself think?"

The young man turned off the circular saw and grinned. "That's Bill Haley and the Comets, sir. You know, rock 'n roll." He shook his hips with a jitterbug motion.

"Rock 'n roll," Jim said. Of course he'd heard about it.

Jean tapped Jim's arm. "Go," she said gently, shooing him with both hands. "Let the men do their work."

He'd had a suggestion or two to offer the workers, but he relented to Jean's orders. In only a few more weeks the addition of a master bedroom and bath would be finished. When Baby Joanie outgrew her crib, she'd have her own bedroom, as did Christie and Craig.

"Dad, are we done?" asked Craig.

Jim turned to his son with a start, and then took a few jabs at the soil. "No, let's get these seeds planted today."

Craig went back to planting as Jim gave the soil an occasional strike with the hoe. Someone turned up the music.

"Do you know how to jitterbug, Dad?" Craig asked.

Jim smiled. "You should have seen me at Jantzen Beach." He imitated the construction worker's move demonstrated earlier. "Want me to teach you?"

Craig eyed his father curiously, and then blushed. "Nah."

Out of respect when a fellow male lets slip an expression of emotion, Jim turned away. "Muz and Mike will be over tomorrow for Sunday dinner. Bobop is going to help me with some tiling. Can I count on you too?"

Without meeting his father's eye, Craig said, "Do I have to, Dad? David Poppe and I have plans."

Recalling his own work-dominated childhood that allowed no time for friends, Jim said, "Sure, Craig, go ahead."

Craig shot a look at his father to make sure he wasn't upset. Apparently Dad meant what he said. At age seven, he had no trouble reading his father.

"Did you know we're going to name your new sister after Bobop?"

Craig looked up with surprise.

"Joan Michael," said Jim.

"Dad, what are we going to do with another girl around here?"

"I don't know. Seems we're about to be out-numbered."

Craig shook his head. "Should have gotten a dog."

That was the exact sentiment Craig expressed when his father first announced the coming of the new baby. Jim had summoned his two children to the living room. He stood waiting and Jean sat perched anxiously on the edge of the sofa. Rarely did the family spend time in that room except around Christmas and other big events. Something important must be happening, thought Craig.

He didn't quite understand all the words, but he got his father's message: There was indeed big news. He and Christie should feel quite pleased and certainly not upset because the news was good and somehow Mom's doing. Even if they did feel upset, nothing could be done to change the fact that a baby would arrive in seven months, and "Isn't that wonderful?"

Craig took his sister's hand and shuffled out of the living room, muttering, "Big deal. What we really want is a dog."

"I think that went quite well," said Jim.

Jean sighed. "Oh, Jim."

Chapter Thirteen

Before dawn on October 18, 1954, Jim awakened Christie with the announcement: "Get up. The baby's coming."

"What?" Christie said, rubbing her eyes.

Jim said, "I'm taking your mother to the hospital. Then I'll drop you and Craig at Muz and Mike's house."

Jean gave birth to Joan Michael a few hours later at Wilcox Memorial, the maternity section of Good Samaritan Hospital where all three children were born under the guidance of Dr. James Whitely. The next day, Christie skipped into her first grade classroom and announced, "I have a new sister!"

Because young children weren't allowed on the ward, Christie and Craig stood on the street corner with their father and waved to Jean and Joanie at the window.

Will mother notice? Craig wondered.

"Look, Baby Joanie," Jean said during the first visit. "Wave to your big sister, Christie. And see that boy next to her in his new football uniform? (*Yes, Craig, I see.*) Oh, and look at that. Seems now he's lost both front teeth."

Another perfect child, said Jim with a sigh of relief. That first day, he proudly held his third born, wondering only once or twice who in the world she resembled with her dark hair and complexion.

Later, Jean was "resting on my laurels" when a nurse popped in to announce that a demonstration on bathing an infant would soon begin.

"Oh, no thank you," Jean refused politely. "My two children at home gave me all the instruction I need."

The nurse returned moments later. "Mrs. Bayless, may we use Baby Joanie for a demonstration in the nursery?"

Jean threw back the covers and darted from her bed to observe the demonstration. "Yes, she *is* gorgeous," Jean would respond to the oh-and-ah comments. "She's my baby, you know."

Dr. Paul Wright baptized Joanie at First Presbyterian Church the following June. The infant pulled at her mother's large white hat during the proceedings and giggled with delight when she saw Craig and Christie in the front row.

Joan Michael would come to expect the applause of four pairs of hands. When she turned thirteen months, Craig and Christie impatiently coached her in the art of walking, clapping furiously as if their applause could defy gravity. "Embarrassing," the older siblings would mutter as poor Joanie took another spill. After all, neighbors Gretchen Noall and Laurie Lou Schiewe had taken their first steps weeks ago.

Christie's delight with her little sister continued to dissipate with time, perhaps because she resented a certain loss of focused attention on herself. According to one early memory, Christie, a new Bluebird (young Campfire Girl) had just received her Bluebird hat. She proudly pranced around wearing it. Somehow Joanie managed to take it into her crib, and during a nap, wet on it. Both outraged and hurt, Christie's face ballooned and reddened as she controlled a need to scream at her baby sister.

According to Christie, Joanie was different from everyone else—more playful and energetic. Before Joanie, the family "had balance," a perspective probably inherited from Jim. Christie lived with her daddy in a serious and ordered world while Craig emulated the sweet reserve of his mother. The newest Bayless changed the equilibrium of the family. Says Christie, "My sister grew up under the cloud of...*and then there was Joanie.* It was supposed to be funny, but I realize now that the kidding probably hurt her feelings."

Offering a different perspective, Jean's face lights up when she talks about Joanie. "I dreamed about a large family. I wanted babies. I wanted a *group.* After having two children, I wanted at least one more. Joanie made us a *group*. She's noisy and funny and *has a blast,* as she says. Everything she does is a *blast."*

Christie says, "Craig and I were little robots." The two possessed an unquestioning readiness to do the expected. "I have a feeling we were adorable, appropriately dressed and coifed—little stick figures like dollhouse cutouts on popcicle sticks. We were Jeff and Mary in a perfect 1950's television family, not wanting to disappoint anybody, not wanting to rock the boat...and then there was Joanie.... She rocked the boat and my parents loved her, too. That puzzled me."

The 1954 Bayless family Christmas card was a photograph of all three children. The incoming holiday cards replaced photos on a large bulletin board in the family room. Craig and Christie played a memory game to see if they could identify the sender from the front of the card.

The Christmas tree went up, punctually, on Jean's birthday, December 15th. The Narvers and Baylesses gathered during the holidays at Uncle Ursel and Aunt Merle's large, 5000-square-foot home or at the Baylesses. Other times they went to Uncle Bob and Aunt Enid's. The gathering of great aunts and uncles and second cousins exuded warmth and family closeness.

On the morning of New Year's Day, Jim marched around the house like an eager, cheerful drill sergeant dismantling the tree and décor.

"Jim, Jim, please wait!" Jean called out.

It's no use, thought Christie. The words would cross her mind every new year in the decades to come. Dad was on a schedule—tree up on the fifteenth and down on the first. No amendments and no excuses!

With the house remodeled and Joanie ushered in, the projects slowed and then ceased, and Jim discovered golf. The greenhouse was torn down. The garden suffered neglect. In the spring of 1955, begonias and radishes were out and golf was in.

The necessity of going to work on Saturday mornings put a crimp in Jim's enthusiasm for golf, but work always came first. He started bringing Craig and Christie to the office, allowing Jean time alone with the baby.

To Craig's eyes, his father simply moved big piles of paper from one side of his desk to the other and talked into a dictating machine. Dad also wrote his name in a great flourish with the scratch of a pen—like John Hancock, he decided, someone he had learned about at school. Eight-year-old Craig would retreat to a vacant office and practice signing his name in the fashion of his father.

The phones, black and clunky with their slow and stiff rotary dials, served as props for Craig's favorite game: telephone tag. He and Christie would memorize all the office workers' names, initials, telephone extension numbers, and office locations. Starting the game, Craig would sit at a desk and try to figure which extension was the farthest from his sister. He'd shout the name, initials, or number of that office worker. Then he'd dial the number. Christie would have to reach the ringing phone before it rang three times.

The children would look occasionally to check Jim's reaction. He always seemed totally absorbed in his work. Jim possessed a father's second sense, however, and worked comfortably knowing their every move.

Jim considered himself a good father. His rearing philosophy was simple: "Just do as I say." The simple belief that he knew best determined his behavior. He kept a list of phrases at hand that communicated simply and clearly his position. "Dad wasn't one for speeches," says Christie. "Whatever he said, he repeated a hundred times or more. 'Parenting by cassette,' we called it."

While his voice said, *I'm the boss*, his manner communicated, *I dictate with benevolence*. A friendly father, he helped his children with their homework and participated in their games—even hide-and-seek. He romped on the floor with them and laughed for all the times he didn't as a child. Craig says, "Dad loves to laugh. He doesn't tell a lot of jokes, but when he does find a good one, he won't hesitate to tell it over and over and over again. Mostly our family poked fun and acted silly. We laughed a lot at nothing in particular."

Jim perceived his strictness as only a veneer. But the children had trouble, sometimes, seeing through that veneer. They learned early their father's dictum that there is only one way—his way—to think and behave. But they always felt the love that ranged beneath the surface.

And then there was Jean. She brought angels to the household. If a person made a mistake, if the world seemed to jump the track and lose the sense of order their father expected, Jean would talk to her angels. For important matters, she went straight to God. Her angels handled matters of less priority. If anyone had a problem, Christie would tell everyone to get Mom's angels working on it.

As well, Jean knew about that other world—that of the imagination. Stories of fantasy sparked dreams of each child's possibility. Craig says about his father: "Dad does not have a vivid imagination. He's a doer and not a dreamer, a practical person focused on what can be immediately achieved. He did not tell bedtime stories or make up playful characters. He's a no-nonsense person who likes to get directly to the point. You won't find any science fiction or fantasy on his library shelves. He reads non-fiction or biographies. He has a hard time being entertained because he vigorously resists suspending his disbelief. When we would relate a story or watch a movie, Dad's usual response would be *not* how fun the story or movie was but why it couldn't possibly be that way. In Dad's world, Superman never flew."

Jim knew how to create molds and Jean made sure their structure included a gate for escape. She understood about applause and that all children—adults too—require a solo time in the sun. Jean says that when Jim announced to his Grants Pass family that he had been made a partner at Dooly, "his mother congratulated him but then patted everyone else in the room on the shoulder. That was wrong. Jim deserved all the glory then. Another time, another place…they could have theirs."

In the Jean-Jim manor, the children reached out and grabbed everything set before them. No shrinking violet would have survived, but Craig and Christie and Joanie each bloomed: an azalea, an amaryllis, a freesia.

In March of 1955, Muz and Bobop stayed at the house with the children so Jim and Jean could take a road trip. The Oasis Hotel in Palm Springs, a client of Dooly & Co., offered Jim and Jean free accommodations. They thought they had fallen into paradise. Palm Springs had not seen the last of this Portland couple.

In April, Jim took Craig to the father-and-son banquet at the University Club. Craig's initial thrill at accompanying his father to a private men's club dampened as his mother laid out his suit. Dinner in the dark and stuffy, smoke-filled, formal dining room left much to be desired in the eyes of a not-quite eight-year-old. The discovery of a kumquat proved the highlight of the evening. At first he thought it an odd-looking orange. The skin smelled sweet. A bite into the inner fruit, however, made Craig's face pucker and he spit it out. Fortunately, his father didn't notice.

The following month came Christie and Baby Joanie's turn to attend the University Club's father-and-daughter banquet.

"You're going to love it," Craig told the older girl, taking his best stab at sincere mendacity. "Yes, Christie, you're going to have a great time."

A proud father, Jim sat at his table with Christie at his side and Joanie in his arms. And the truth was, Christie had a good time—and an even better time after Jean arrived to take Joanie home. Christie loved being Daddy's girl, doing everything to his pleasure, taking the place of Mom that special evening. In the years to come, however, her enthusiasm for the event disappeared.

"No, they didn't enjoy it at all," says Jim today. "The formality of it all bored them. But I believe above all that a family should do things together, should stand before the world and have their actions say: *We are a family.* As the children became older, they balked about attending the banquets. I just told them they were going. 'Be ready at six o'clock,' I said, and of course, they were."

The summer of 1955, Jim continued to play golf, and he roused everyone within his circles to join him. He organized a golf tournament at work and a golf weekend in his neighborhood that became a biannual tradition.

The Hessler Hills community of fifteen families formed a tight web. Beyond sharing the golf weekends, they played bridge together, went dancing, held block parties, entertained at each other's homes, started an investment club, and built a neighborhood playground. Any parent would give any kid a ride up the hill. The neighbors cared for one another as family.

One afternoon, Christie stepped on a nail protruding from a board. Some kids carried her out of the woods with the board still attached to her foot. Dr. Begg from next door, an orthopedist, came across the lawn with his little black bag, removed the nail, and gave Christie a tetanus shot. She never went to a doctor's office. "Medicine was practiced that way in our neighborhood," says Christie. "Quite a few doctors lived near by. If anyone became sick, a neighborly physician made a house call."

Jim greatly admired Wade and Carolyn Hansen, who lived across the street. Wade, an accountant, worked for Touche, Ross, Bailey, & Smart, known today as Deloitte & Touche, one of the top accounting firms in the nation. The Hansens agreed to become the foster parents of Craig, Christie, and Joanie should anything happen to Jim and Jean.

The neighborhood proclaimed Ira and Loretta Keller the patriarch and matriarch of Hessler Hills. Ira, head of the Portland Development Commission, was playing a significant role in developing the city. He lived with his wife in a sprawling home called "High Point," which served as the community swimming hole and the gathering place for Christmas caroling. "High Point?" Jim would say with a friendly laugh. "Ira, my house is at the highest point in Hessler Hills. How about we call my home High Point and yours Low Point?"

During the summer, Christie and Craig would sit on the milk box in their swimsuits waiting for Joanie to waken from her nap. The Kellers made their pool available at 3-5 in the afternoon between Memorial Day and Labor Day. Only children accompanied by an adult were allowed, and Jim or Jean took the children religiously. Jim only watched, never participating in either a swim lesson or play. Avoiding the risk of appearing foolish in the water plagued Jim his whole life.

Craig liked playing in the pool at the Keller's, but an early experience would forever darken his attitude about the sport. The summer before, after May had announced his seventh birthday, he started lessons at the Multnomah Athletic Club. Soon to be renovated, the "creaky, creepy old place smelled like cigars, liniment, and chlorine." Mostly, Craig hated the instructor, "an old guy with no ability with kids." Swim, he'd order, or be humiliated. Craig passed the course, nevertheless, and received his Winged M—which stood for *Multnomah.* As promised for sticking with the lessons, he was given a football uniform from his father—the one he wore to visit his mom and newborn Joanie in the hospital.

With the coming of Christmas, Jim decided it was time to re-vamp the Dooly Christmas party. This year they'd leave the office and cater the occasion. "Invite your spouses," Jim said, concerned how the men tended to imbibe an excess of Christmas cheer and get a little too friendly with their secretaries. Reservations were made at the Heathman, an upscale hotel with a restaurant in downtown Portland.

Ethel came up with the idea for everyone to draw names and buy a gift. People would buy inexpensive gifts from Goodwill, and Ethel would compose verses that related to both the recipient and the gift. Senior partner Ed Thomas received an oilcan for his squeaky rocking chair. Someone bought "cheater" spectacles for partner Bill Reed. He had just bought his first house and couldn't afford glasses because he was "flat busted," Ethel joked.

Chapter Fourteen

Christie didn't understand why her brother could take swim lessons and she couldn't.

"You have to be seven, dummy," said Craig.

"Oh?" She thought a moment. "Why?"

"You don't grow gills until then," he said, practicing the serious gaze of his father.

"Gills?" Christie said, with a quick feel under her arms—her serious side, so like her father's, confused again by her brother's wit.

In November of 1955, after Christie's seventh birthday, she happily found herself registered for swimming lessons, which would begin after the holidays. Craig resumed lessons as well because his father communicated loud and clear the importance of learning to swim.

Then came the piano and dance instruction. Christie says, "We were given a 'liberal arts' childhood. Not that it was liberal, in the sense that we had any say, but my parents introduced us to a whole array of social activities for kids."

She adds, "We would stand like good little soldiers, always on time for the next event—cheerfully. To demonstrate a proficiency at everything was expected, but no demand for greatness ever pressured us. We were constantly told we could do *anything*. It was never too much trouble to drive us anywhere, to get us involved in anything. We grew up confident."

The children took piano lessons, just as every kid they knew did. Jim encouraged them with, "I sure wish I could play." The kids wondered why he didn't sign up for lessons as well, but they never asked. Neither parent seemed musically inclined in voice or instrument.

It would be a few years before the two older children enrolled in dance lessons, but Christie has embossed memories of dancing in the mid-fifties. While her mother readied for parties at the Multnomah Club, her father, elegantly attired, as usual, would wait for his wife in the living room. He'd place a record on the phonograph and take his daughter's hand. Wearing her pajamas with feet, she would take her place on her father's shoes, and they'd dance.

Jean would enter the room wearing—Christie remembers one time specifically—a strapless, gold lamé dress. Her father pursed his lips as if about to whistle and then said, "Jeeeeanie, you are sooooo b'you-tiful and I am sooooo uh-gly." Craig and Christie rolled on the couch in wild laughter.

Etiquette dictated that Craig and Christie dress up when they later learned ballroom dancing. The foxtrot, waltz, and tango became part of their repertoire. Craig received instruction on how to properly behave around young girls. "We pranced around like little adults," he says. "No wonder our generation rebelled with rock 'n roll!"

Jim loved gadgets. The 1950's ushered in the beginning of labor-saving devices and high-tech toys. Recalling the boyhood hours he perused the Montgomery Ward catalog, Jim now delighted in buying any advertised item he pleased. Besides owning the best lawn mower and an electric lawn edger, the Baylesses had a blender, television set, stereo, camera, and movie and slide projectors. If there was a more modern way to do something, Jim was quick to embrace it and let everyone know that he had one.

When Jim first purchased the electric lawn edger, Craig and Christie grinned. No more clipping the grass with hand shears—and because they weren't allowed to use the edger, they now had one less job to do. But their enthusiasm about the edger soon disappeared. Although the machine could manicure the lawn beautifully, it also possessed the ability to carve an edge into the operator, should it have the mind to do so. Craig says, "It was perhaps the nastiest, most dangerous gadget ever devised. Even unplugged, it looked mean. When stored in the basement, I had nightmares that it would blade its way into the house and devour me. Dad agreed, I think. He operated it as if it were the devil himself."

"Craig!" Jim would call out over the rage of the edger's motor. "Guide the cord out of the way."

"Christie, you gotta do this for me," Craig would plead to his sister.

"Oh no you don't," Christie protested.

"I'm busy, Dad!" Craig would holler to his father. "Christie's coming."

Not about to cause a scene, Christie scurried to assist her father. She did her best, but the edger always managed to "slice and dice" the cord.

In July, the Baylesses decided to give camping another try. The family had experimented on an earlier occasion with living in the great outdoors. After a day of roughing it in the Mt. Hood National Forest, Jean voiced a preference for the civilized convenience of indoor bathrooms and plumbing. "A fire," she announced, "belongs only in a fireplace."

The kids had been enjoying a wild freedom that day: Craig and Christie ran through the woods; Joanie played in the dirt next to a rushing stream. But when it came time to set up the tents and roll out the sleeping bags, Jean packed their belongings. Jim loaded everything in the trunk. "Into the car, everybody," he directed. They drove midway to the summit of Mt. Hood to Timberline Lodge, a historic landmark built in 1937 of mammoth timbers and native stone. The Baylesses closed their eyes and fell asleep between clean, crisp sheets.

Once at home again, Craig told his friends how much he loved camping. He related the details of the fine, outdoor experience his family had enjoyed. When informed that camping involved sleeping on the ground and peeing in the bushes in the dark, Craig's eyes widened with shock. "You didn't go *real* camping," Skip Souther told him. Only momentarily disheartened, Craig felt relieved he had bypassed the experience. Sleeping outdoors sounded like a really bad idea.

Jim, however, succeeded in persuading Jean to give camping one more try. Joanie would stay with Muz and Bobop. He rented a teardrop travel trailer and hooked it to the Chrysler station wagon. Everyone helped loading the gear, and the family set out for Yellowstone Park. Even Jean believed the adventure might be fun. "What more could you want, Mom?" Craig said. "Look there. Our motel room will travel right with us!"

The Chrysler, however, didn't seem to appreciate the weighty tow on its bumper. Losing energy like a weary child, it slowed and then stopped. Craig and Christie wiggled at the same rear window as they watched their father take off the gas cap and blow into the filler tube. After huffing and puffing a while, he called out, "Jean, try starting the car," and it started.

"Vapor lock," Jim said before anyone could ask.

The vapor lock would happen again and again. Jim would return to the driver's seat with a black imprint of the gasoline filler tube around his mouth. The children giggled and Jean joined in. Craig and Christie knew nothing about vapor lock. They just figured Dad loved his Chrysler enough to kiss it.

As they toured the western wilderness of Wyoming, Christie and Craig sat in the back seat reading. Jim pointed out the majesty of the mountain range. Hearing no response, he declared loudly from behind the wheel, "Kids, put down those comic books and look at the Tetons!"

Craig and Christie glanced at one another and shrugged, wondering why it didn't occur to their father that they saw snow-capped mountains every day of their lives. A toupee of white topped Mt. Hood, fifty miles east of their home, all year long.

This vacation, the family stayed in campgrounds. Unfortunately the trailer didn't do much to improve anyone's opinion about camping. The four Baylesses spent a good deal of time hiding in the dark with the trailer door locked while bears rummaged through their campsite. The verdict was in: Camping was for other people. *Let it be known. The Baylesses do not camp.*

They could probably handle picnics, though. One day when the family decided to see how they'd do on a simple afternoon outing at the park, Joanie slipped off the end of a picnic bench. A layer of sand covered her moist skin and sticky hands. As Jim brushed off his little daughter, mumbling, "I hate picnics," Jean started laughing and couldn't stop. Craig and Christie caught her bug. Jean teetered in a pendulum of laughter. When her arms flew up to catch her balance, everyone laughed even harder.

Joanie stood patiently as Jim picked at sand from her face and clothes. With a solemn face, he said, "Messy."

"Methy," Joanie repeated.

The laughter gained momentum all over again.

Jim had come to realize he didn't like doing anything that deprived him of the clean and ordered life to which he had grown accustomed. He had worked hard to acquire the modern conveniences that assured him a comfortable lifestyle. Why ever deprive himself of them? He ventured to the woods a few times as a hunter, but he never hit anything. "Almost shot the dog, though," he says. Dealing with the mess of killing anything made no sense to him. And thank goodness a fine cabin awaited him after his trek into the great outdoors.

The weekend following the trip to Yellowstone, the Baylesses drove up the Columbia River Gorge in Washington to the cabin of Uncle Ursel and Aunt Merle. It lay just beyond Bonneville Dam near Bridge of the Gods. The porch wrapped around the cottage and overlooked Wauna Lake. Jim loved the area and thought some day he might buy property there. Craig loved it, too. "A beautiful place," he says today, "full of sun, picnics, canoes, boats, and all the things a little boy cares about more than anything. Today, when anybody says *cabin*, I think of the times we spent at Wauna Lake."

As Jim watched Craig and Christie swim in the lake with strong and confident strokes, he felt a little envious. For all Craig's whining about taking lessons, he seemed to love the sport. He had lessened his complaints after their talk the second year.

"That old goat is a terrible instructor, Dad," Craig had said. "He can make a fellow feel this big." He left almost no space between his thumb and forefinger.

"Do you want to learn to swim or not?" Jim had responded. He didn't share that he had quit swimming lessons. He didn't say that he, too, had felt humiliated by the experience.

"Yeah, I do."

As Craig walked away, Jim had smiled proudly. *I like the stuff you're made of.*

Joanie sat at the shore of Wauna Lake, taking time out to watch her sister and brother swim. In the Keller pool, as well, she studied their every move. Getting her out of the water at five o'clock was not easy. "Watch me, Joanie," Craig would say. He'd lift himself with straight arms out of the pool, pausing a moment to wait for his lanky, eight-year-old body to round with muscle. "See, Joanie, I'm going home. Want to come with Keggy?" Sometimes this worked. When Joanie refused to budge, he'd say, "Christie, see if she'll follow you."

Christie would make a face at him. "Real funny."

Ever since Joanie wet on Christie's Bluebird cap, the rivalry between the two sisters increased. When Jean bought Christie her first lipstick, Joanie—still a little toddler person—smashed the tube. Christie brought the lipstick to her mother as tears rolled down her cheeks. That evening, Joanie stood in the entrance hall of the Bayless home, staring out toward the sunset. She said, "Baby Jesus put a ho lot of lick-ups in the sky." Jean and Jim laughed lovingly as the words become blazoned in their hearts. Christie stood, whisked around with a scowl, and stormed out of the room.

That fall, President Dwight D. Eisenhower ran for a second term and was coming to Portland. His ceremonial procession would pass the Board of Trade Building where Jim worked. Jim wrote a note to the principal at Robert Gray Elementary asking that Craig be excused from school to watch the parade. True, Jim had expressed initial displeasure with Eisenhower back in '51, but over the years he had grown to like Ike.

The school principal denied Jim's request.

"Well, to hell with him," Jim said. "He can't tell me no. Who does he think he is? We pay his salary! This is the President of the United States, and he sure as hell doesn't come to Portland every day."

Craig went with his father to view the Presidential parade. He recalls the experience today: "I was thrilled to see the old bald guy sitting in the convertible waving to me while I threw handfuls of confetti on him from a third floor window. That's right! In those days you could open an office window and throw things at the President. Mostly, I was thrilled to be out of school."

Lord James

When Craig told about the confetti for the umpteenth time, Christie said, "Who cares about the dumb President, anyway?"

Craig laughed and grabbed a small ball from the yard. He gave it a little toss into the air and caught it with one hand. "Not me—that's for sure." His sister wouldn't look at him. "What's the matter with you?"

"It's not fair."

Craig laughed again. "So how was school?"

"Oh, shut up." Christie hung her head.

Crouching down to find her face, Craig became serious. He said, "You know, Dad likes you best."

"What?"

He tossed the ball a couple more times before answering. "You're the smartest. You're like him…. You know, when I was at his office, I thought to myself, *I can see Christie behind one of those desks some day.*"

Christie broke into a half smile. Craig ran around in a circle and then shot his ball into an imaginary basket. "I'm just a goof-off. You know that…. I don't know why Dad took me and not you, too."

"Thanks, Craig."

"Wish you'd been there." He pantomimed the making of another basket. "Hey."

"What?"

"Want to wear my *I Like Ike* button?

She chased him out of the yard.

It may be argued that the social culture of the 1950's shaped the lives of the Bayless family and that Jim represented the views of that era. If the times had been different, Christie might have become the business executive and Craig the footloose dreamer. In their hearts, that's where they saw themselves heading.

Christie had a sense that her father valued her abilities, yet she also got the message that he expected those abilities to be applied in a realm designated for women. She learned young that she lived in a world of "pink and blue jobs." Jim's daughters did the dishes and Craig carried out the trash.

The 1960's weren't sure what to do with young girls and women, and neither did Jim. He routed Christie's spirit and opinionated ways down the same path that appeased the restlessness of his wife: public speaking. Christie excelled in writing and speech. It wasn't practical for females to set their sights on a place in the world where there was none.

Yet Craig is quick to offer that his father "had no male chauvinism at all when it came to his daughters." He says, "But remember, we are talking about a time when the women's movement was just starting."

Like many young girls of the era, Christie had a love-hate relationship with the 50's and 60's. She wanted more opportunities, yet she felt a part of a Great Plan valued by society and her father. A strong, nurturing family assured her a sense of safety and contentment. Although a feeling of disquiet rumbled inside her, she thought, Why rock the boat? Why explore issues of independence if it means causing uncomfortable waves?

Christie heard the warning, *Don't analyze life.* Analyzing meant stopping a moment to look at the past and to identify mistakes. Jim never allowed this to occur. "Never look back. Ever forward!" Jim would say. In the early days, Christie would nod and think: I understand. I get it. Okay.

Jean, too, got the message. She perceived Jim on the inside track when it came to understanding the Great Plan. So Jean let him take the lead in decisions about her life. True, it was the war that changed her decision to study speech and drama in college and embark on a career, but Jim felt a working wife would reflect poorly on his capacity to provide for his family. Okay, she said, nodding.

She came to see the wisdom in Jim's philosophy that life goes along best if it follows a schedule. Jim liked to make appointments at 6: 21 and 3:37. "If you're not early, you're late," he'd say. Every morning, 365 days a year, Jim was the first one up. He'd read the newspaper in the same chair in the living room. On school mornings, he'd wake the kids up after he read the paper. There was no variation in the *schedule.*

Like a clock, Jim only moved forward. To his *Never look back. Ever forward!* Jean would add, "Emphasize the good and gloss over the bad," and, "Aptitude plus altitude equals attitude!" She scripted the lives of her family on the calendars. A schedule kept them focused, one foot in front of the other, without time for regrets or what ifs.

But Jim also held the passionate belief that all individuals should exercise their skills led him to encourage Jean's speaking talent. Jean learned how to survive within the system. She had the memory of her childhood friend named Poket who had helped her realize a sense of power over her world. At the side of a man named Jim Bayless, Jean established herself as matriarch in a patriarchal world.

Jean's penchant for fantasy helped compensate for the pragmatic world she helped her husband create around the lives of her children. When she gathered them around her to tell a story, her words chiseled away at the straight lines of the world. For those moments, they believed in truths with round edges.

Chapter Fifteen

Every year around Thanksgiving, Jim continued to make his annual visit to Grants Pass. Jean accompanied him. The children would march into the car as ordered. No one really looked forward to the trip.

Perhaps they took their lead from Jim. He felt determined to show everyone back home how far he had advanced beyond their rural, blue-collar lifestyle. He would phone his Bayless relatives occasionally and make an annual visit, but he would not cross the line he had drawn between his past and his new life. As the children exited the car in Grants Pass, they would gather in formation next to Jim, their toes to a line they couldn't see but knew existed all the same.

Jim preferred keeping company with Jean's side of the family. They lived in the social style to which he aspired. Jean and the children, for overlapping and different reasons, shared Jim's partiality. The children hoped the knack of the Narvers for casual closeness might rub off on their own family, but it never really happened. Today, Christie believes that because her mother had no siblings and her father felt distant from his, Craig and Joanie and she never established a closeness that would keep them forever a part of one another's lives. She says, "Dad thinks it's perfectly reasonable to talk to or connect with your siblings virtually never. I think it's sad."

Craig states that as a young boy, he found his father's relationship with his mother and his siblings "complicated." He didn't mind visiting Grants Pass, but he always felt glad when they headed home.

He says, "We were Presbyterians, they Baptists. It terrified me when we went to their church and the Baptist minister told us where we were going to go because we had sinned." Craig didn't feel he was "evil" and was quite sure that (except for his swimming instructor) he'd never met anyone who was. Certainly not his parents, despite the fact that they drank the "devil's liquor."

On the trip home down the interstate, the children would sit quietly in back and listen to their parents discuss the visit. It seemed to Craig that his father was under a great deal of pressure from his Grants Pass family and especially Nanny Dee Dee to mend his sinful ways. Sometimes harsh words slipped out. The bottom line seemed to be, says Craig, that "other than Dad, we had little in common with the Grants Pass relatives except the Thanksgiving tradition of enjoying a big turkey and lots to eat."

"Are we ever going to go back, Dad?" Christie asked once.

Jim and Jean exchanged glances. Jim immediately regretted his careless words and said, "Of course. They're *family*."

Thanksgiving, 1957, the James Bayless family drove to the ranch of his mother and Dee Blanchard. They saw Martha May, her husband, Roy Fry, and their children Nadine and Bruce. Jim's youngest brother, Don, would show, as well as Roy and Gerry and their three children, Larry, Linda, and Jeanie. Tommy Dee and his wife, Grace, came with their three boys and their daughter, Ann.

The fire in the hearth seemed to draw rather than emit heat. In the eyes of Jim's family, it was Martha May who warmed the room. She was all hair, a thick and curly mound. Smiling, Christie says, "In the 80's when I first saw Eunice, the character Carol Burnett created for her comedy show, I thought, *That's Martha May*." Only her looks, however. Otherwise, Martha May was nothing like the abrasive Eunice. When she spoke, her soft voice and humble demeanor gave a reverent air to the occasion. Everyone liked her.

Her fifteen-year-old daughter, Nadine, reminded Christie a little of Nanny Dee Dee because she spoke often about the Lord. Jean liked Nadine a great deal, but Christie eyed her cousin with curiosity and suspicion as kids do with other children who seem too *good.*

Nadine would one day marry and become a missionary in Honduras. "She's a successful person in life," Jean says today. She proudly compares Nadine to her oldest daughter. "Like Christie, she can bloom anywhere."

The Bayless children slept at the Blanchard farm. Jim and Jean found accommodations at a hotel. Early the next morning, Jim received a phone call. Dee Blanchard had suffered a heart attack and died. "Thanksgiving, 1957," Jim says. He recalls the year distinctly because he had just bought a new Chrysler. The purchase of a new vehicle always served as the perfect calendar to spark Jim's memory. "1959? Another new Chrysler. Craig got braces." Jim bought Chryslers until he retired and then switched to Cadillacs.

Dee's death surprised everyone. Seventy-six years of age, he had appeared physically fit, as usual, that holiday. In his late sixties he had played shortstop on the town softball team and held his own on the court with his son, Tommy Dee, a state tennis champion.

Inez had loved her second husband, yet she never felt the passion for him she had known with Jim's father. She told Dee's daughter-in-law, Grace, that the fire of a second marriage cools quickly when the individuals involved are mature. In fact, such intense emotion is neither needed nor wanted, really. Besides, Grace knew as well as she that Dee was "set in his ways and not easy to live with." Yet Inez deeply admired him. Jim did as well. He says, "I was glad my mother married him. I liked him. He was fine man—tough, yet friendly. He respected me—let me call him Dee. He always thought me very smart."

Jim took his children home to Portland and returned to serve as a pallbearer at Dee's funeral. He says, "I owed him that respect."

Inez traveled to the Portland home of her son annually in the years to come, usually by bus. The Bayless family didn't relish her visits. Craig says, "Dad's sweet, generous, almost humorous side absolutely disappeared in Nanny Dee Dee's presence. He went to the office and did more chores around the house and in the yard than normal. Mostly to show off." Jim tinkered around the house to bring attention to the home his success afforded him. He wanted his mother to be proud of him and of his high status in the business world.

Jean would quietly watch her husband and mother-in-law interact. She'd shake her head at the "two peas in a pod" as they'd bicker, both determined to be *right* about everything. "Inez would quote the Bible right and left," says Jean. "You couldn't debate anything about religion with her because she breathed it."

Inez believed the Truth should be told. She even hurt the feelings of her friends. Martha May tried to tell her, but Inez believed people should know certain things about themselves. That's a good thing, Jean would think, but it hurt sometimes. "She was self-righteous," Jean says today, "but I truly admired her…. She was one gutsy lady." Her feistiness, however, didn't endear her to the children in the Bayless household. Christie describes her grandmother as "haughty, always right, cold, humorless. Built like a square box with dark, gray hair."

Always being right requires a constant effort to keep the mind sharp. One evening after playing a game with the children that required a certain scholarship of knowledge, Inez took the answer cards to her bedroom to study. Jean says, "She probably thought that a teacher like herself should know all the answers." She adds, laughing, "Or maybe Inez simply wanted to study the answers so she could win the game next time she played." The latter possibility made sense. Jim, too, loves games. And he likes to win.

In December of 1957, the children of Hessler Hills gathered, as they did every year, and practiced singing Christmas carols. Then they walked to each home in the neighborhood and sang two carols from their list, followed by "We Wish You A Merry Christmas." After all twenty homes in the community had been serenaded, the families assembled at the home of Ira and Lauretta Keller.

The Kellers served the children tea sandwiches without the crusts, and hot chocolate. The adults enjoyed bar favorites and brandy-spiked eggnog.

Lauretta would tap a spoon to a crystal glass, asking for everyone's attention. Knowing the routine, the carolers gathered around the tree. "It *always* looked the same," says Christie, "cut from the middle of a big tree so the top didn't come to a point. Long branches grabbed at the ceiling."

An honored child, chosen beforehand, read the story of Jesus' birth, occasionally pausing for the children to sing from their resumé of carols. The tradition continued for decades without the Bayless family ever missing a year. Christie's daughter Amy Jean—at eight years of age—would read the story in 1980.

On Christmas Eve, in the privacy of her own family and home, Jean read *'Twas The Night Before Christmas,* by Major Henry Livingston Jr. With the passing of years, she found she had memorized the story. She'd one day perform it at their country club and at the Civic Theatre in Portland.

Every Christmas morning, Mike and Muz Welter arrived at the Bayless home at 5 am and helped create the stage for the day as the children slept. Jim taped the door leading from the children's bedrooms in case they forgot their promise to wait until they were called. "Not that we would EVER consider defying him!" says Christie. "We were very obedient kids."

Once the children were released from the bullpen, they sat patiently as each person opened a present. The ritual suited Jim fine. He disliked mess and chaos. The thought of diving into the gifts also appalled Jean, who says, "I knew friends whose families tore through Christmas in twenty minutes when it had taken them months to get it together." Jean's mother, a "precise little lady," savored the experience of opening her gifts ever so slowly. "Muz, hurry up!" everyone would chorus good-naturedly.

Christie played the piano and everyone sang. Much to her dismay, Joanie would climb on the piano bench and bang the keys. Little did everyone know then that Joanie would be the one to best charm beautiful music from the piano. "The musical member of the family," everyone calls her.

In spring of 1958, Craig turned eleven. "Christie was eighteen months behind in age and eighteen months ahead in maturity," he quips. Joanie, soon to be four, had started talking back to exercise her independence.

Jim called a meeting of the Bayless group. Craig remembered the first time the family gathered in the living room "for an important announcement." Their father made known the coming of a new family member—not a dog as Craig hoped for, but another baby sister.

"So from time to time," Jim was saying, "I'll call a *family conference* when we have matters to discuss that concern the whole family."

Discuss? The word perked Craig's attention. "And do we get to vote?" he asked with a look to Christie, not quite believing their good fortune.

The children were sitting on the couch and Jean sat in a chair. Jim stood before everyone, absorbed in his presentation. Craig and Christie were huddled in excited whispers. Craig raised his brows hopefully to his sister. "There are three of us and two of them. Want to see if we can vote and get a dog?"

A democracy in the Bayless household? The absurdity of it struck both kids simultaneously. They grimaced, realizing they'd been duped into false hope once again.

"Early next year," he said, "your mother and I will make our trip to Palm Springs. We've decided to take you children with us."

Nothing about the Bayless family conferences would ever resemble a democratic proceeding. Jim would continue to use the "conferences" to announce fully laid-out plans that had already been implemented. He simply wanted cries of approbation to match his own enthusiastic estimation of the plan. "I don't remember us ever voting on anything," says Craig.

Wade Hansen, Jim's accountant friend from across the street, introduced Jim to boating that summer. Jim occasionally crewed for Wade with friends, Andy Andersen, his contractor neighbor, and Oren Robertson, head of the Fred Meyer Company. Sometimes they took the 40-foot, Shain motor yacht down the Columbia River and north to Victoria, British Columbia. Wade had named the boat *Gemini*.

Robust and healthy, Wade didn't strike Jim as the frail accountant type. The crew jokingly called their good-natured host Captain Bligh. In turn, he called each Fletcher Christian. He gave Jim a knife engraved with his "name": Fletcher Christian #1. Oren's gift read Fletcher Christian #2 and Andersen's, Fletcher Christian #3.

The boat had a swimboard off the transom. On one occasion, the *Gemini* sat in front of the Empress Hotel where Jean and Jim had enjoyed their honeymoon. Jim, dressed in a dapper blue blazer and white pants for a trip to the city, stepped over the transom to the sloping swimboard. He slipped and with a *swoosh* found himself below water.

Miffed as a wet kitten, he changed his clothes and took them to the local haberdashery, George Straight Clothier, Ltd. "I just purchased these last year and look at the condition they're in!" he announced gruffly. Without a word, an employee took the soggy bundle to the cleaners and later delivered the outfit to the *Gemini*.

Fortunately, says Craig, his own limbs functioned with greater adeptness than his father's. As a boy, Craig displayed athletic prowess, particularly as a runner. He played little league ball, albeit poorly. (Jim did a stint as an umpire but received so much abuse from fans, he quit.) Although slight like his father had been as a youth, Craig gave any sport a try and earned his father's respect. Jim gave him more responsibility for tending the lawn.

"Not a weed to be seen in the Begg's lawn," Jim would say to his son. "Nice pattern in the mowing of the Hansen's lawn, don't you think? I wonder what brand of fertilizer the Andersens use."

Jim didn't have to say it. He wanted the Bayless lawn greener and better mowed than any of the neighbors'. After school and throughout the summer, Crag would mow, dump the grass clippings, and water. Jim, home at six, would ease out of his jacket, loosen his tie, pour a scotch, and occasionally eat a raw tomato covered with salt over the kitchen sink. Then he'd inspect Craig's work.

"Good job, Craig," he'd say. Then directing his index finger away from the glass of scotch, he'd "point out the few errant blades that I had missed and tell me how certain he was that I would correct the condition first thing in the morning. Of course, I always did."

Tending the lawn brought Craig, Christie, and their father together in a common battle against creatures that had no regard for their hard work. The Baylesses owned two chickens named Jack and Susan. "I used to care for fifty," Jim said, sharing a little about his experiences as a farm boy. "The downside about Jack and Susan," says Craig, "is that they pooped across the yard, as well as on the barbeque. Dad always threatened to roast them." Even though Craig hated the task of picking up after the chickens, playful sentimentality led him to later purchase two porcelain chickens named Jack and Susan that he keeps on his mantle.

Another "enemy" came with four legs: dogs. The absence of a leash law in the city gave permission for the neighborhood dogs to visit the Bayless lawn at their whim. "Come here, Rupert," the kids would call to the Begg's "little shorthaired something" when Jim was at work. "Hey, any good smells this morning?" they'd say to the Noall's black lab. Later, as Jim surveyed the lawn with scotch in hand, he'd sight a perfect circle of pale green in the lawn and fume, "Goddamn dogs."

Yet the fiercest enemy of all was the moles—the Townsend mole, in particular: brownish black and about eight inches long with a piggish snout and rat-like tail; apparently earless; eyeless too, it seemed, as only velvety fur covered the places where sockets should have been. Vile creatures! Jim would say, raising a fist at the burrows that scarred his finely-manicured lawn. He was a man used to winning and wasn't about to admit defeat to an army of pin-brained rodents.

"Thus began the ten-year War of the Moles," says Craig. "We rolled out our heavy armaments. We had hoses, sprays, gasses, and traps of every description. We stabbed the varmints, crushed them, drowned them, and poisoned them. But the mole army never gave up. Early in the morning, as the sun rose over Mt. Hood, we would hear Dad exclaim, 'Those goddamn moles are back.'"

Craig and Christie schemed and made a proposition to their father. "Wouldn't a dog help keep the moles away?" The kids looked at one another, nodding in confident agreement. "Especially a breed known for digging and rooting out moles," they reasoned. "A mole biter, Dad. We'll get a mole biter."

"No, the dog would spot the lawn," Jim responded.

They were prepared. "We will clean up after it every second."

"No. Christie is allergic to dogs."

With the help of their mother, they had done their homework. They learned that a shorthaired dog would be less likely to cause allergic reactions. That the hair itself might not be the culprit at all, but instead the saliva or dander, didn't occur to them. Armed with self-serving logic, they responded to their father, "But a shorthaired dog, like a dachshund, doesn't cause allergies."

They waited. Craig smiled. Gotcha, Dad. Christie looked to her brother and liked that he was smiling.

"Okay," said Jim.

"What?" hollered Craig. His arms shot up. "Christie! A dog!"

"Thank you, Daddy," she crooned with polite excitement, and then ran off to tell her mother and Joanie.

Jim called a family conference "to codify the promises made" about their individual responsibilities regarding the new family member. A contract was drawn up. Jim made Craig and Christie sign in blood. They each pricked a finger and dropped a spot of blood on the contract. Craig says, "Mom was somewhat distressed by this barbaric display but silently rejoiced because she had been our secret ally in forming the case for the dog."

The Bayless children became the proud owners of a dachshund named Schnapps. Christie broke out in hives when she petted him. Schnapps yapped incessantly and never caught a mole.

Ever since Jim and Jean first visited Palm Springs in 1955, they had returned annually. In 1959, Jim and Jean decided to take the children along and stay at the Green Gables Apartment Motel. So began the family's long association with "the desert." Craig says, "It was the test ground where Dad could see how fast the new Chrysler would go. As well, we all could play golf without getting our feet wet, a real luxury for people from western Oregon."

As they drove down what would become Country Club Drive, Jim eyed the tarpaper shacks that littered the sand dunes. With his self-assured, "lecture" voice, he said, "Craig, you can get a whole section of this desert just by building one of those shacks and homesteading the land."

"Really, Dad?" said Craig, knowing well the expectation that he offer an engaged response. "What's homesteading?"

Jim eased into the brakes, releasing the cruise control. He liked this dandy new accessory Chrysler had added to their 1958 Imperials. Pulling over to the edge of the baking asphalt, Jim swiveled and said to his son in the back seat. "Craig, all you have to do is agree to spend $800 a year improving one of those desert lots and the government will give it to you."

"That's cool, Dad. Let's buy some. We can build a bunch of shacks like those. No problem," Craig said.

"No," Jim laughed. "Why throw away good money? This land will never be good for anything." He put the car in gear and started again down the road.

128

At that time, it was just blowing sand, says Craig. Rarely did his father make a poor business decision, but in this case, he couldn't have been more wrong.

Everyone played golf this vacation. Even Joanie, almost five, putted a ball around. All the children had received the message that the game was part of their destiny.

Before heading home, the Baylesses loaded the trunk with fresh grapefruits, impossible to get in Oregon during February, and headed home. Jim drove up the coastal highway and veered off to San Simeon where they toured the Hearst Castle. The luxury of the 127-acre estate awed Jim. The kids read placards and fed their father statistics they knew would impress: "Forty-one fireplaces, Dad!" "Thirty-eight bedrooms!" "Dad, this Hearst guy has 155 more rooms than we have."

As the shiny, new Chrysler neared the St. Francis Hotel in San Francisco, Jim said, "Put those comic books away, kids. Sit up and act civilized. Don't embarrass your good name."

An elegantly uniformed doorman opened Jean's door. The kids slipped out of the car slowly and quietly. The doorman motioned for Jim's keys and stepped to the rear of the vehicle. When he opened the trunk, the grapefruits rolled out, escaping into the hilliest city in the United States. The yellow balls gained momentum, careening into curbs and each other. A few bowled into a bicyclist. Others came to a rest when flattened by a streetcar.

Jim stood there chagrined. The kids concealed their giggles. "As my mother would have said," claims Jean, "*We looked like a bunch of Country Jakes.*"

That summer, Jim pursued golf, the first sport he'd ever really played, with a passion. He joined the Portland Golf Club (PGC) and took lessons. According to Craig, "The club pro told my father his stance looked 'like a dog taking a shit.' Undeterred, he continued practicing and playing...Dad attacked a golf ball. He was a natural slicer." Christie jokes, "Dad liked golf mostly because it started at a precise time—9:17 and not *about* 9."

Since a fine country club offered a way to meet new people and entertain clients, PGC became a second home. Christie almost eleven, and Craig, twelve, walked the greens with their parents, learning more about course etiquette than anything. Christie says, "It horrified Dad to think we might play slowly or in any way appear ill-mannered or bothersome to anyone."

Craig sometimes smuggled his BB gun into his golf bag and shot frogs in Fanno Creek while on the course. Christie often played barefoot and climbed apple trees to snag a snack. They both learned to drive a golf cart. Golf became what the Baylesses "do." Jim announced this fact to the world by arranging a family photograph on the first green of the golf club for the Bayless Christmas card.

Although the children won some trophies in junior golf tournaments, Craig says, "Golf talent must be genetic because none of us was ever very good." Christie, who competed on teams for both her high school and the country club, disagrees. "Speak for yourself!"

Golf defined both the family's social and personal life. Christie says, "On the golf course is where we would 'bond' or go to 'be together.' Our family didn't picnic or take walks. In later years, we didn't 'do lunch' or shop. If we had a family crisis or simply wished to spend time together, we played golf."

That Jim had the opportunity to play 36 holes at the Portland Golf Club "Pro-Am" in 1960 had everything to do with money, he admits, and nothing to do with his golf skill. The honor cost him $750. He drew Arnold Palmer as a partner, presenting a situation that both excited and terrified him. Christie says, "Racked with nerves, he couldn't sleep. He knew Arnie's army of fans had no interest in watching a hacker with a handicap of 18 divot the fairways."

The two other amateurs on Jim's team were Bill Triplett and Tom Williams. Jim pulled Craig out of school to watch his duffer Dad play in the big league.

At age fifty-four, Christie confronted her parents about being left out once again. "How come only Craig? Why didn't I get out of school to see Arnold Palmer?"

"Sorry, Christie. It just didn't occur to me," said Jim.

"We owe you one," added Jean.

"And while we're at it, how come I didn't go with Craig to see President Ike?"

"In those days, Christie..." Jim said.

Jean laughed. "We owe you another one, dear."

At the close of the second day of the Pro-Am tournament, Jim's team ranked in third place—thanks to Mr. Palmer. Jim uses his silver bowl trophy as a planter in his office.

Chapter Sixteen

Girls and women grumbled silently in those days about the "pink and blue" privileges of society, yet Jean began on an equal footing with her husband when it came to learning about investing their money. In 1958, Jim joined an investment club, and the women of Hessler Hills created their own. It is telling of the 50's and 60's, however, that the men's meetings, according to Craig, were "liberally fueled with spirits" while the women's group, called "Curves," served tea and cake at their Thursday morning gatherings.

Jim rarely brought up the subject of money at home except when he'd rage on the phone at an associate about the failures within the office of collecting "receivables." He did speak about his clients, however. "Just the mention of U.S. Bank or Fred Meyer would silence all other conversation," says Craig. Keeping his business at the office proved a challenging task for Jim. According to Craig, "There never seemed to be a distinction between a friend, a client, a neighbor, or a business partner." On the other hand, Christie remembers distinctly a "rule" her father repeated: "I never make clients of friends." If it happened naturally, fine, but Jim never intentionally crossed the line of friendship to recruit a client.

During the early summer of 1960, Christie and her friend Sue Thuemmel decided to build a fort. The woods behind the Thuemmel home on Mitchell Lane seemed the perfect location. The eleven-year-olds looked at one another blankly. They hadn't a clue how to begin.

"We'll need some lumber," Sue said.

Christie brightened. "They're building a new house near me. Maybe the construction workers will give us some wood."

"Okay, but how will we get it down the hill?"

"My dad's wheelbarrow should work."

"Are you sure Jim won't mind?" Jim had recently given Sue permission to address him on a first name basis. She used it proudly, realizing she had earned his respect.

Christie shook her head. "He'll like it that we *took initiative*."

Sue laughed. "Oh yes, *initiative*. She'd heard Jim lecture many times on how a person must lean forward and take action in order to succeed in this life. "Okay, let's do it."

Christie, skilled at wrapping her tongue around words, easily persuaded the construction workers to donate their scrap wood. The girls spent the afternoon making trips with the wheelbarrow up and down the steep hill from SW Fairmount Boulevard to Mitchell Lane. After the final load, they each grabbed a hammer, a nail, and a piece of wood. They stood still a moment, thinking.

"How do you make a wall?" Sue asked.

"You're asking me?" Christie said, setting the girls off in a chorus of giggles.

Each girl approached her father when he arrived home from work. Both Grant Thuemmel, president of his advertising and public relations firm, and Jim arrived at the proposed site of the fort still in their business suits. They asked questions and brainstormed to generate a building plan, never letting on that they knew little about carpentry.

The men worked two evenings on the project. "We simply watched," says Sue, "and oohed and ahhed. It was the most beautiful structure we had ever seen."

Christie and Sue spent their early teen summers in the plywood box refuge. They'd lie on their backs, talking about "girl stuff." One day as sunlight came through their one window, they realized it was time for them to start shaving their legs. "We grew up there," says Sue.

Memories about the fort recall a lesson Sue learned that summer from both Jim and her father: "When you get overwhelmed with your workload, remember you can only build your 'house' one nail at a time."

Jim found himself elected that year as a trustee at the First Presbyterian Church of Portland. Craig says, "Dad seemed to hold every lay position in the church at one time or another."

As a trustee, he would encourage the congregation to pledge money for the ongoing maintenance of the church and for various missions such as the "Friendly House." The settlement house, founded by First Presbyterian Church in 1930, offered a helping hand to the affluent and needy alike. "Neighbor helping neighbor" still serves as its mission statement.

The children had difficulty understanding the relationship their parents had with the minister, Paul Wright. Christie says facetiously, "I thought he was Jesus' brother." Craig adds, "When Dr. Wright raised his hands in that robe to give the benediction, I imagined God was speaking. He had a certain presence."

Each Sunday, especially in fine summer weather, the family would have an early morning debate. "Are we going to church?" "Yes? No?" "Let's not!" "We really should!" "Why?"

"Because!" Jim would say, ending the discussion.

Craig says, "Dad carried vestiges of his early religious boot camp and felt guilty if we didn't go. So, more often than not, we went."

Church activities struck the children more an obligation than a reverent act. They attended church camp and sang in the choir; they went to Sunday school as their parents listened to the sermon in the big sanctuary. Church was a predictable part of the Bayless routine.

Today, Christie attends church regularly but says, "Church is an example of how something important to Dad was not necessarily passed on to all of his kids." Craig believes in God and calls himself a Christian, but his family does not attend church. "Our family did all the expected religious things, but somehow I came out without any strong religious convictions." He's "a devout agnostic" when it comes to the miracles of the Bible. He finds it "unreasonable to believe that someone could part a sea or walk on water."

Jim, too, easily finds fault with most of the miraculous accounts in the Bible. Yet he still considers himself a Christian, "a modern one." Although he rarely attends a church service, he believes that "religion stands for everything good in the world." Jim holds Islam as valid as Christianity. The two religions share the same God, he says; only their teachers differ. He also values the tenets of Buddhism, even though Buddhists don't believe in his God. No matter what label a man attaches to his religion, Jim honors his right to practice it

He values how all religions express a compassion for the poor. Jim considers poverty the biggest problem facing the world today. "We need something similar to the Marshall Plan to help the destitute in Africa and Afghanistan," he says. He recalls how Secretary of State George C. Marshall's proposal to Truman restored the economic infrastructure of Europe. The plan later earned Marshall the Nobel Peace Prize.

The governments of the world owe no one a livelihood, Jim believes, but they must offer a leg up to the indigent. "I pay $250,000 a year in taxes and don't mind it a bit if it helps someone get a better start in life."

On June 8, 1961 at 10 am, Craig attended his graduation ceremony from the eighth grade. By early evening, he sat aboard the Union Pacific's "Domeliner City of Portland" en route to Chicago with his parents. From a diner car with dome windows above, alongside Christie, he viewed the Columbia River Gorge. The Bayless family was embarking on what Jean called their "Heritage Tour," back to Jim's birthplace in Browns Valley. They'd also explore the Atlantic Coast. Even Jim had never been that far east.

He hired two schoolteachers to drive his Chrysler to Chicago. He never even considered leasing a vehicle because he wished to tour in the comfort of his own car. The teachers would stay at the YWCA and vacation in "The Windy City" for three weeks while the Bayless family traveled the East Coast. Then the young women would drive the Chrysler back to Portland. Jim and his family would fly home.

Joanie stayed in Portland this trip. As Jim and Jean planned their vacation, they joked that three weeks of Christie and Joanie in close proximity might be more than anyone could bear. It was decided that Jean would propose to her youngest the benefits of staying with her grandparents. She also came with a backup plan.

"...Pleeeease, Mommy, I want to go," Joanie repeated with a typical, six-year-old's persistence.

It was time for Plan B. "It's a very long ride, Joanie."

"But I want to go!"

"Christie's coming, too."

Joanie looked long at her mother, thinking, a forefinger hooked over her lip.

"You'll have to sit in the back seat with her for a long, long time."

Joanie said, "I think I'll stay home with Gramuz and Bobop."

Jim and Jean's seats on the train faced their children. Jim said to them, "I was Christie's age when my family first moved to Oregon." He glanced a moment out the window before continuing. "We drove all the way. Took about two weeks." Craig and Christie shot one another a look. Two weeks? It sounded like forever.

As the Cascade Mountain Range disappeared into the night, Jim played the reel of his memory backwards. "The Bear" story his mother told repeatedly during the trip from Indiana to Oregon came back to him. He said, "*W'y, wunst they wuz a Little Boy...*"

"What?" Jean and Christie said in unison, and then laughed. Christie said, "Say that again, Dad."

"*W'y, wunst they wuz a Little Boy...*" He smiled, pleased that he remembered. In his head, he heard his mother's voice. "*Went out in the woods to...*"

Craig eyed his father curiously. "To what?"

Jim laughed. "*...to shoot a Bear.*"

Jean smiled. "Do you remember any more?"

"*So, he went out...*" Jim hesitated, and then shrugged. He looked at the expectant gaze of his children. "Never mind. A silly story."

Craig sleepily closed his eyes. Over her book, Jean caught Jim's attention and nodded toward Christie.

Jim opened yesterday's *Oregonian.* "Come sit by me, Christie."

"Will you read me the comics, Dad? Please?" Christie asked, quite familiar with her father's preference for reading aloud from the business page.

"You children get enough of comics," Jim said gruffly, and then smiled. "Maybe I can squeeze some practical information into your head. Think there's any room?"

"Oh, Daddy."

Jean traded seats with her daughter. Christie curled up in the seat as Jim opened the business section. He began reading. Christie yawned and fell asleep.

The following morning, the landscape offered a variety of hills, open space, and mountains. The next day, it flattened into the Midwest. The kids pressed their noses in dazed boredom on the smudged glass of the speeding train. Then they swooned—a bit dizzy—back into their seats.

Jim said, "There's a herd of cows…a chicken farm…"

"Stinks like Jack and Susan," said Christie, without looking up from her book.

"Look, Craig," said Jim, pointing. "Your favorite cereal is growing out there."

Craig glanced up. "Wheaties grow in the ground?"

"Put away that game and learn something," Jim said.

Craig obeyed. He followed his father's gaze to the endless miles of soil, dotted with nondescript sprigs of green, until his eyes drooped.

When they arrived in Chicago the following evening, they stayed at the elegant Palmer House Hilton in the heart of the Loop area. The schoolteachers met the Baylesses the next morning and turned over the Chrysler.

"We'll meet you here in a few weeks," said Jean, pleased as everyone else to slip into the familiarity of their own car.

A few days later, the family checked in at Detroit's Statler Hotel for a two-day visit. They toured the Ford Motor Company Museum. Next they drove north to the Canadian side of Niagara Falls, down to New York, and into Boston. Jim loved watching his children explore and learn about the world. Twelve-year-old Christie tried to eat her first cherry stone clam in Boston, Jim remembers, smiling. She demurely spit it into her napkin.

The Baylesses drove on to Washington, DC. The kids hoped to see President Kennedy. Jim was a fan of the Vice-President even though he didn't vote for the Kennedy-Johnson ticket in 1960. He thought Kennedy a rich Catholic floating on his father's money, undeserving of the Presidency. He had cast his vote for Nixon.

Upon arriving in Washington, DC, Jim phoned Johnson's office to learn if the Vice-President would be speaking before the Senate. The

137

Vice-President was out of town, but his office offered tourist tickets for the Bayless family to observe the day's proceedings from the gallery. Jim would need to pick them up.

Craig tried to act on his father's orders to sit in the reception area and keep his hands off the mementoes and pictures. However, a steel canister proved irresistible. Engraved on its shiny surface were the words: *Sent to Outer Space and Back—presented to Lyndon Baines Johnson from his friends at NASA.*

Craig looked around surreptitiously and then carefully unscrewed the lid. Out flew a coiled spring that bounded and then clattered across the room. Craig pounced from his chair to retrieve the evil thing just as Jim emerged from the inner chamber. He grabbed Craig's hand and quickly ushered him to the door. "What did I tell you about keeping your hands off things?"

"Uhh, weh—well…" Craig stammered.

Jim chuckled. The pace of Craig's heart took minutes to slow. He says today, "From that day forward, I never liked LBJ."

In retrospect, Jim thought Kennedy did a good job during his three years in office. He was at work when Oswald assassinated Kennedy in Dallas. Jean called him at his Portland office with the news. Jim remembers thinking, "Like Lincoln, I suppose they'll make a hero of him. A man gets shot and they name streets after him." He thought a moment how he would make a damn good President himself. *Never would get elected, though.* He knew that the American people respected Hollywood types like Kennedy rather than smart businessmen.

When Johnson ran in '64, Jim supported him. He didn't like the Republican candidate, Goldwater, the "hawk" Arizona businessman who had supported Joe McCarthy and disliked Truman. "He was too conservative for me," Jim says.

Following the election, Jim had his first and only taste of politics. He received a nomination from the Oregon election headquarters to serve the new administration in any needed capacity. Johnson's people investigated Jim's background, but no one from the government ever approached him. "I'm glad nothing came of it," Jim says. "I would have made a terrible mistake giving up my position in the insurance business to move to Washington, DC."

Besides, as it turned out, Jim didn't like the way Johnson ran the country or handled the Vietnam War. He applauded the man's decision to step down in 1968.

Generally speaking, politics did not occupy much of Jim's thoughts. He never talked issues with the political figures he played golf with or encountered at social gatherings. Nor were political issues discussed around the dinner table. In fact, Craig cannot recall any conversations about political philosophy or dogma.

His family, however, did discuss the burning issues of the day. In the 50's, they cursed "the vile, commie Russians who were going to cook us at any moment," says Craig. The family "survived Sputnik's assault on America's scientific and technological leadership" by making sure Craig's science exhibit of "nuclear chain reactions, mousetraps, and ping-pong balls" was finished—before the Russians arrived, everyone joked. Craig says, "I remember all the dire warnings and the mandatory school air raid drills, but Mom and Dad never seemed to take it all very seriously." Jim and Jean and were "dead serious," however, about Craig completing the science project before the deadline. "We did it as a family," he says.

When in office, Johnson accomplished at least one good thing, Jim supposes—he signed the Civil Rights Act of 1964. Jim supported the rights of Negroes. Martin Luther King, Jr. was another story, however. Jim thought him a rabble-rouser, unworthy of leading the civil rights movement. "Looking back, he was very good for the country," Jim says, "but naming a national holiday after him was just another excuse for the people in the Federal government to take a day off."

After leaving Washington, DC, the Baylesses drove west across the Virginias to Pennsylvania. Jean fell in love with a lavender hurricane lamp in Philadelphia. As expected, Jim asked, "Where are you going to put it?"

Items introduced to the Bayless household always claimed a permanent place. Jim and Jean created a predictable environment in their home with both the furniture and their attitudes. While the children rebelled some—being cheerleaders for change, as most children are—the truth was, they felt safe.

"We'll put it on the living room game table at the end of the glass wall," said Jean.

"That's fine," said Jim.

They purchased the lamp, and Jim packed it carefully in the huge trunk of the Chrysler. He drove everyone on to Ohio and into Indiana.

After a long while on secondary roads, Jim stopped at a small clapboard house on an acre or two with a tiny pasture in back. Transparent figures formed as Jim stared. He saw the image of his mother exit the front door with a load of wash to hang. He heard his Aunt Murl laugh as she whirled two-year-old Martha May in her arms. Grandpa Bayless and his father were working in the garden.

"Jim?"

"I lived here once," he said to Jean. "Before my father got sick."

Craig and Christie stuck their heads out the car window, studying the house with wonder as Jim drove on, not sure what questions they wanted to ask.

Less than two minutes later, Jim stopped at a poorly tended cemetery. A traditional white church with a steeple stood across the street. The children followed their father out of the car. Jean lagged along behind, taking in all the strangeness that belonged to her husband's past.

Jim pointed to a tombstone. "Roy Washington Bayless." For a moment Jim thought he should tell Craig about his grandfather, about his heritage. He scanned the area with the eyes of a fourteen-year-old, and a sadness, like the sweep of a linen curtain, passed before him. He said nothing.

Craig kneeled and ran his hand across the etchings on the stone. "DIED October 20, 1930," he read, and then did the math. "Thirty-one. No, thirty. He died almost thirty-one years ago."

Jim saw his son's mind calculating more numbers, trying to figure out things a young boy shouldn't have to think about. "You were only nine, Dad," said Craig. He looked at his sister.

Jean had stepped away, uncomfortable in the depressing environs. Jim noticed headstones that sat angled in the earth and resisted the temptation to straighten them. He eyed the marker next to his father's. "Baby Wanda Louise," he said, not for anyone's benefit but his own. It came to him in a flash, the memory of holding her the day she was born, and then it was gone.

They drove south into the town of Browns Valley. Jim jutted his chin toward a house as they drove down Main Street.

"This is where you were born?" Christie asked, her voice a singsong of disbelief.

Craig laughed. "Oh sure, Dad. Where's the hospital?"

Jim didn't answer. Craig sat back, puzzled. His father pointed to small, aging buildings and spoke the names of strangers. Craig felt uneasy.

"I went to school there," said Jim, pointing to a small, two-story structure badly in need of repair and paint. Jim stopped the car so everyone could take a closer look.

Craig's eyes widened as he laughed. "No!" It looked nothing like his Robert Gray Elementary. He ran to a window, his sister at his heels. "Whoa! You've got to see this, Christie."

"Turkeys?" said Christie. "Mom, look at this."

Jean peeked in a window. "Jim, come see. A farmer has his turkeys inside."

He smiled, wryly and pointed. "Over there is the house where I lived when I was about six."

"Where, Dad?" Craig asked.

"Just beyond that pasture. Get in the car. We'll drive over."

A darkness surrounded Jim when he pulled up in front of the house, as if he were suddenly in a movie theatre. A backlight of memories flickered to the ticking sound of a reel-to-reel projector. "It used to have a porch," he said. "My father..." Children's voices from the past and present blended into white noise. "It seems smaller." There seemed to be nothing more to say. He drove away.

They headed north again down Main Street. "There's Uncle John and Aunt Gertrude's place," Jim said. He slowed before a small, one-story home—*more like a cabin*, Jim thought.

"You're kidding," Craig said, sure the day was all a big joke. He pointed and laughed along with his sister.

"Uncle John owned the town garage," he said, stopping before a structure with a lop-sided roof. "I used to call it a *gar-age* because the letters GAR were on this side of the window and the letters AGE over here." The letters were barely visible.

Craig rolled his eyes at his sister, and they grinned.

Meeting Aunt Gertrude, however, took away their smiles. The front door opened as they knocked. No hello or expression of surprise or delight welcomed them. "What's your politics, James William?" Gertrude queried the nephew she hadn't seen in almost thirty years.

The children noticed newspapers sticking out the top of her dress. "To keep out the chill, child," she said, when Christie asked, and shooed everyone through the front door. With her wizened stature, her long nose that widened at the end, and her hair in a bun on the top of her head, Aunt Gertrude looked a bit like the scary, old women from storybooks. Uncle John, age seventy-six, struck them as nothing more than someone very old, but he had more hair than their father. He combed it flat to one side.

"Nola died ten years ago now," said John when Jim asked about his uncle in Crawfordsville. "We didn't really see each other much, you know."

No, Jim didn't know anything about anyone in Browns Valley.

A painting of John and Gertrude's only daughter, Helen, who had died in her early teens the year after Jim was born, hung on the wall. She appeared angelic, with one finger pointing—like Uncle Sam, Jim noticed. He shuddered as he walked from the painting, haunted by the realization that the eyes followed him around the room.

Craig approached an inside door. Gertrude cut him off and grabbed the handle. "That was my Helen's room," she said, and locked the door.

"Can we go now?" Christie whispered to her mother.

But they stayed the night. In the evening, everyone sat on the porch. Christie noticed sparks in the still air. "What's that?" she asked.

"Fireflies," her father said. "Uncle Roy and I used to catch them when we were boys."

Christie and Craig looked with delight at one another. They asked their father, "Can we?"

Aunt Gertrude provided the jars. "Now let Uncle John poke some holes in the lids so the poor creatures can breathe," she said in a manner that sounded like a cackle. The children imagined themselves a bit like Hansel and Gretel.

"Thank you, Aunt Gertrude," they said in unison, and then they darted off, scooping their jars through the air. They giggled as they caught the bits of light flying in the night.

Later, as Christie lay in bed watching her "magic lights," she wondered with adolescent awe that her father had been raised so differently than herself and Craig. That was all the insight her twelve-year-old mind could handle for the time being, and she fell asleep dreaming about her father and Uncle Roy as little boys chasing fireflies in this odd place called Browns Valley. Over the years, Christie often considered this early realization about her father. Understanding that his identity was "founded on a different reality" helped her understand their different perspectives.

In the morning, Craig and Christie awakened with hopes of transporting their fireflies back to Oregon. Jim made the children release them. The "magic lights" would remain in this strange land of their father that could never belong to the Bayless children.

As the family drove out of Browns Valley, Jim tried to explain what he knew about Aunt Gertrude. "After her daughter died, people said she went a little crazy. They called her a hypochondriac."

"What does that mean again?" Christie asked, not really sure she'd ever heard the word but not wanting to admit it.

Craig said, "You know. It's what *you* do when you don't want to go to school—say you're sick when you're not." He smiled mischievously.

Christie puffed with indignation. "I've never!" she said to the surprised look on her mother's face. Thankfully, her father gave no reaction and kept driving.

Craig looked at his mother with feigned seriousness. "I'm just kidding, Mom." He smiled. "Really."

The children—and even Jean—drove away from Browns Valley a little dazed. Craig wondered if little green men from Mars had taken them to some foreign planet. Jim felt a little the same way. He would never see his aunt and uncle again. John died three years later and Gertrude, five years after that.

In Chicago, the Baylesses met up again with the schoolteachers.

"Drive carefully," Jim said, handing over the Chrysler keys. He paused. "Now, don't eat in the car."

"No, sir," they said.

"Good," he said. "See you in the middle of next week then. Don't be late."

The young women nodded nervously. "Yes, sir."

That Thanksgiving, the Baylesses visited Grants Pass and talked of their trip to Browns Valley.

"Can you believe there were turkeys in Dad's schoolhouse, Nanny Dee Dee?" Christie said to her grandmother.

"We also saw a bunch of dead people," added Craig with the typical insensitivity of a fourteen-year-old.

Inez glanced to her son. Jim looked into the distance. He felt her pain and waited for it to pass.

During dinner, the conversation turned to the "family of niggers [who] had recently moved into Grants Pass, but not to worry, the local boys had run them out of town," Craig recalls. Jim and Jean were incensed. "This was not the kind of talk they wanted their children to hear." Jim knew his mother and siblings, and many of the neighbors in Grants Pass didn't understand the concept of equal opportunity, of living in peaceful co-existence with the Negro population. Language such as "second-class citizens" angered him, especially when the Bible was brought in to support their un-Christian views.

During future Thanksgiving visits to Grants Pass, Jim tried to disperse such talk. Craig remembers one conversation about "niggers" during the mid 60's being the reason they "never went back." The Thanksgiving tradition in Grants Pass ended after 1966. Jim and Jean continued an annual trip, usually without the children. Only twice in the decades to come did the children return on Thanksgiving.

Kissing Cousins: Trevor Madden and Taylor Bayless

Clockwise—Roy, Don, Jim, Inez, Martha May

Craig and Christie

Craig, Christie, Jean, and Baby Joanie, 1956

Jean on Jim's arm

Jim and Jean

John, Gertrude, and Jim in Browns Valley, 1961

Muz and Mike

Young Jean on the Telephone

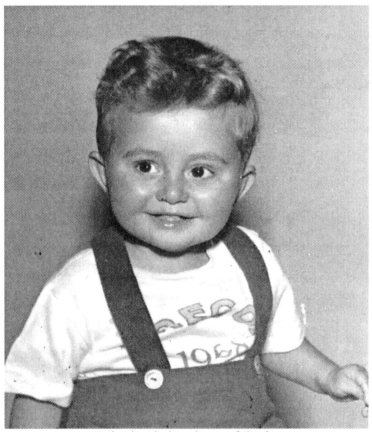

Winning baby photo of Craig

Young Inez

Chapter Seventeen

Jim had entered the world of real estate in 1960. The aunt of Bill Bowes, son of the City Commissioner, worked at Dooly, and his aunt wished to sell a house on NE 21st and Multnomah Street that she had converted into six apartments. Jim paid ten percent down on the $25,000 asking price and borrowed the rest.

"Part of the investment strategy," says Craig, "was to raise rents and ride the rising tide of escalating property values. Keeping expenses low was also important." He jokes, "What better way to reduce expenses than to employ slave labor?" In August of 1961, the same summer as the Heritage Tour back East, Jim instructed Christie and Craig to paint the front porch of the newly-purchased tenement. Christie recalls with shocked indignation how she and Craig walked to the bus and transferred downtown with a gallon of gray paint in tow. Craig says their father felt bound and determined to instill his work ethic in his "soft children." He never let them forget that their future included gainful employment.

The children always had summer jobs. Mowing lawns topped Craig's resumé. With the experience of tending the lawn of the very particular Jim Bayless to recommend him, Craig quickly acquired ten neighbors as clients. He used his father's state of the art equipment and fuel. "I sent out bills and opened my own bank account with the encouragement of my entrepreneurial father."

During the summer of 1961, however, just before starting his first year as a high school freshman, Craig worked as an office boy in the employ of Dooly & Co. He made coffee and deliveries, distributed mail, filed, and ran the mimeograph machine. The office smelled like old paper, tobacco smoke, stale coffee, and printer's ink.

As Jim drove Craig to his first job in the world of business, he eyed his son carefully, misreading the boy's enthusiasm. "No need to feel nervous, Craig," he said. "And there's no reason to expect animosity from the people at the office just because you're the boss' son."

"Yeah, okay, Dad," Craig replied, thinking, *ani-moss* what?

"And don't worry about learning where things are and how they work. The staff will show you around."

"Sure, Dad," Craig said brightly.

When he stepped off the elevator onto the third floor, he looked around. Same ol' place, he thought, recalling all the Saturdays he and Christie had rampaged the floor layout, offices, and desks. "Because of my 'previous training,' my first day was a triumph," Craig says. Only after he arrived home and looked up "animosity" did he have any doubts. Then he shrugged. He hadn't experienced any ill feelings from anyone. Besides, his familiarity with the office said only one thing to him: He belonged there. What else would the son of Jim Bayless think?

In the years to come, Craig would work as an assistant at Dooly, labor in a farm-equipment parts warehouse, and after college, sell real estate. He says, "In each position, I was either directly employed by Dad or he introduced me to the opportunity through his contacts. He always gave me a helping hand when I needed it. He nudged, but he did not shove."

The first summer Craig worked as an office boy with Dooly, eight years had passed since the University Club voted Jim in on the recommendation of Warren Munro.

The formal beginnings of the University Club were on October 8, 1898 with fifty-six charter members, mostly from Eastern colleges: eleven from Yale, six from Amherst, five each from Harvard and the University of Virginia, and four from MIT. It had seemed doubtful that the UC would accept Warren Munro's nomination of Jim, the University of Oregon dropout, as an associate member.

Yet, in 1953, they did just that, and in 1962, the members elected him their president. It was one of the proudest moments of Jim's life.

In keeping with Jim's no-nonsense way of doing business, the meetings under his watch were conducted efficiently. This proved a formidable task sometimes, considering the topics that made it to the final agenda. For example, the minutes of the Board for May 23, 1962 read: "Mr. Hoffman made a motion that a five-dollar charge be assessed to the bills of the members not having dice boxes." The protocol in the club bar required that the men roll dice to determine the payee of the tab for the table. The men without a personal set of dice were assumed cheapskates. Deadbeats. But to keep a light-hearted spirit as the order of business, Mr. Hoffman amended his own motion, stating that members could refuse to pay the five-dollar charge.

Jim hit the gavel with a good-natured grin, bringing an end to the snickering. "Is there a second to this motion?" The motion was seconded and passed.

The Annual Meeting of 1962 lasted only a few minutes. No reports were read. The members quickly adopted or voted down motions. If a subject required discussion, it was waived and added to the basket of the incoming president. Before the members had barely settled into their chairs in the Red Room, Jim adjourned the meeting.

The doors opened into a lounge that displayed "a parade of hors d'oeuvres to stagger the imagination," it says in Jim's final President's Report. There were stacks of Maine lobster, which cost $1.40 a pound, cherry stone clams on the half shell, crab legs and Alaskan king crab, and Olympia oysters in a background of dramatic ice carvings.

Dooly & Co. held their monthly partnership meetings at the University Club immediately following the appointed workday. Jim Hefty, who had joined the firm in 1954 just out of the trenches of the Korean War, became a partner in 1962 and recalls how Jim, pretty much the managing partner around the office, took the lead at the meetings—"Someone needed to." As a result, Jim's pet peeve, the accounts receivable issue, always seemed to headline the agenda. Jim repeatedly threatened to charge interest to the salesmen who didn't collect on their overdue accounts. All the partners knew Jim had every right to throw stones. "He had the biggest production and lowest accounts receivable in the office," says Hefty.

Nevertheless, a couple of the partners would take Jim on, turning the meetings into "knock-down argument sessions that got pretty vocal," according to Hefty. Jack Thomas, although characteristically an introvert, openly disagreed with a number of the firm's policies. Warren Munro and Jim would get into arguments nearly every meeting. It didn't take much to set them off. Perhaps Munro felt eclipsed by Jim. Although Mr. Dooly's son-in-law and a recipient of a percentage of the year-end profits equal to Jim's, Munro had fewer clients and held a less-esteemed position in the firm.

Hefty, although guilty of failing to meet Jim's standards of getting the premiums paid, liked Jim. When he first joined the firm, "Mr. Bayless was my mentor." Over the years, they became friends. "Jim is a very social guy—lots of fun to be around," he says. "The guys at Dooly were always doing something—golf or cards or partying somewhere."

Drinking after work happened frequently. Friends and co-workers would tip a few at the University Club or other "watering holes, and we'd playfully harass each other," says Hefty. One evening after leaving the club, the same cop pulled Jim over twice for speeding. Both Hefty and Jim laugh as they recall the incident. "That's right," says Jim. "The officer stopped me not far from the club and then again on Fairmount Blvd." Shaking his head, he adds, "I don't usually make the same mistake twice."

Work, golf, and fishing on Wade Hansen's boat occupied most of Jim's time during the early 60's. Once, he invited Craig on the *Gemini.* From that moment on, Craig schemed for a way to convince his dad to buy a boat of their own. He says, "The campaign for a dog was mere child's play compared to the all-out assault for a boat." His father seemed disturbingly content to play Hansen's first mate. Craig hunkered down with determination to make Jim understand his destiny as a captain.

Unfortunately, this time Jean would not come to her son's assistance. She'd seen the food preparation expected of Carolyn Hansen every time the *Gemini* headed to sea. A boat of her own? No thanks. Being a "pampered guest" suited her just fine. A boat struck

Jean as unpleasantly similar to a campsite. She viewed boating as "floating camping," says Craig.

Wheedling and joking hints got Craig nowhere with his dad. Jim would simply raise a hand and say, "No more" to Craig's ceaseless appeals.

Craig should have known from experience with the Schnapps campaign that only with a well-reasoned battle plan, designed to anticipate and counter his father's every argument, would he taste victory. Once again, with more determination than confidence, he approached his father.

Tinkering with a sprinkler head in the backyard, Jim half listened to his son's rambling pleas. "I've heard all your arguments before, Craig. I agree that boating is fun." He looked directly at his son. "I've been thinking I'd like to buy some property near your Uncle Ursel and Aunt Merle's at Wauna Lake. Wouldn't you like that?"

"Well, sure. But Dad, a *boat.* It would be so cool."

"Owning a boat consumes all your free time."

Craig looked blankly at his father. So?

"First of all there's golf. I enjoy golf on weekends. And don't forget church on Sunday," he said, walking to the spigot and turning on the water. The sprinkler head spit some water and then began its back and forth gyrations. It held Craig's focus, giving him time to think.

"You could play golf on Thursdays instead," Craig tried. Jim looked at him. Craig hesitated, and then smiled. "As for church...well, isn't boating a religious experience?"

Jim's frown made him look a little like Nanny Dee Dee. He shook his head. "Besides, it's an expensive hobby, Craig."

Oh. How expensive?

"A 28-foot Chris Craft would set us back about $25,000."

Craig's jaw dropped. Wow, that *was* a lot of money. He started calculating how many lawns he'd have to mow. Whoa! He'd be an old man before he could offer even half that amount.

Jim smiled.

Darn! Craig thought, thinking how his father seemed to be sunning in his victory. He stomped his foot like a horse once, and then again.

"I'll tell you what," said Jim, breaking into a laugh. "If General Insurance stock goes up to twenty dollars, we'll get a boat."

"Yeah?" said Craig. He ran into the house for the newspaper. Jean told him to take a glass of iced tea for himself and one for his father. "Yeah, sure, Mom. In a minute," he said, running out the door with the business section of the *Oregonian.* "Dad! Dad, show me how to read this."

Jim smiled. He'd been reading the business section to his children for years. For the first time, one of them was showing some interest.

"General Insurance seemed to move like a glacier," says Craig, "but it did move. I knew because I checked it every morning for months."

Then one day General Insurance stood at 20 and an eighth. Craig *yippeed* around the house and phoned his father at work with the news.

On July 8, 1962, the Bayless family became the proud owner of a 28-foot Chris Craft, which they stored in a boathouse at the Portland Yacht Club. *Aquarius*, they named her, after Jim's zodiac sign. They stole the idea from Wade Hansen, whose May birthday gave rise to the naming of his *Gemini.*

All five Baylesses were on board *Aquarius* nearly every weekend in the warm months. The family would motor out on the Columbia River and anchor in quiet inlets. At the end of each outing, Christie would stand on the bow and slide open the boathouse doors. On the inside of one door hung the sign Jim had asked his daughter to paint: *Lower the aerial, stupid.*

Often the Baylesses met up with other boaters on their excursions. They'd raft the boats together and walk from one to another, visiting.

A friendly, unvoiced competition took place between the women about who could prepare the finest meals. Jean would sigh in good-natured defeat at Carolyn Hansen's "perfect" presentations. Nevertheless, she continued to work hard fashioning her meals.

Food filled three shopping carts and cost fifty dollars for three days on the water. All the necessary provisions filled two cars. Everyone helped unload and transport the supplies in a wheelbarrow to the boat.

When the Baylesses boated alone, usually on their long ventures to the San Juan Islands, Jim took great pride in dining off what they pulled from the sea: clams, crabs, salmon, and oysters. He particularly enjoyed the raw oysters, which he'd open immediately with a knife.

"Here, Craig, try one."

"Sure, Dad," he said the first time. He hesitated as he studied the liver-like, slimy creatures. They're still alive, Dad, he was about to protest and then thought the better of it. If Dad was going to eat the wormy things, then so was he. Craig gagged as he pulled one of the creatures from its shell, and then ate it with prune-faced effort while his father preoccupied himself with the opening of another shell.

Better cook the oysters in their shells on hot barbeque coals, the guys decided. That's the only way Jean and the girls would consider tasting them.

"Disgusting," said Christie.

"Come on, Christie," Craig said, making sure his father was listening. "Try one." He threw one down his throat. "Hmm, they're warm."

During one voyage, Craig and Jim rowed the dinghy ashore to eat oysters fresh off the rocks. They competed, each seeking out a bigger mollusk. "Real seafood for tough guys," says Craig. They'd slurp a live one down without any "wimpy lemon or cocktail sauce."

Then Craig's stomach suddenly lurched. He gazed down at his waistline and imagined the squirmy creatures. Nausea rose to his neck.

Jim noticed his son pale and then flush a green tint. "That's about enough for me. What do you say, Craig?"

On Columbus Day, October 12, 1962, a hurricane referred to as the "Big Blow" traveled the Washington and Oregon coasts. Winds of 120 mph reached the Bayless' hilltop home overlooking Portland.

Jim was at work when the winds hit. Jean had left to pick up Christie from church choir practice. She gave orders to Craig to watch Joanie. Craig, a high school sophomore, had faked an ailment that day in order to avoid a test. When the windows began to shatter from flying debris, Craig gathered Joanie, a week shy of her eighth birthday, and her visiting playmate and racked his brain for a plan.

Just then, the little girl's mother pulled up in the driveway and whisked the dog, Schnapps, and the three children to safety. During the five-hour siege that followed, the hurricane winds lifted the carport roof and dropped it on the house, destroying a third of the structure.

The phenomenal winds prevented Jean from driving up Fairmount, so she and Christie stopped at a neighbor's house. Since the phone lines were dead, Jean had no way to call home. She paced frantically, repeatedly checking the phone receiver for a dial tone. Finally she decided to make her way on foot to the house. Upon learning that two of her children were unaccounted for, she screamed.

Jim had made it home, and with the help of neighbors in hard hats, searched the rubble in and around his home for his two missing children. Finally, during a brief restoration of phone service, a neighbor notified Jim and Jean that their children were safe.

Christie and her parents stayed at the Andersen's that evening. In the morning, Jim went to work, knowing his clients would be desperate to contact their insurance broker. "Mom took the helm of the yacht we called home," says Christie.

Jean directed the movers to take everything to one of two moving vans. One truck would deposit less necessary items at a storage locker. The other van would transport needed furniture and boxes to a temporary home. Christie watched in amazement at the way her mother took charge. She was so used to her father being in command that seeing her mother's obvious skill for organization caught her off guard. Later, when the crisis was over, Christie noticed the wizard mastery of her mother to inconspicuously transfer command back to Jim.

The Baylesses lived two months at Orchard Hills Apartments. The construction workers restored their home back to its original appearance. This time they bolted down the carport roof.

On December 15, Jean's birthday, the Bayless family returned home. The neighborhood of Hessler Hills gave the family a coming home party. Everyone laughed when Jean unwrapped the gift of Margaret Mitchell's *Gone With the Wind.*

Usually of enemy status, the wind, on one occasion, had a role in returning peace to the Bayless household. When it seemed as if Craig would fail science class, Jim looked at his son with perplexed incredulity. He had never pushed his children to achieve all A's, but he certainly didn't imagine they could ever fail a course. No television for Craig, he decided, until this situation could be turned around.

Something Jim always said gave Craig an idea about how he might recover his television privileges. "Dad often proclaimed the hypothesis: *It never rains in Portland when the wind blows from the east.*" Using Jim's state-of-the-art anemometer and wind direction gauge, Craig would test his father's theory. With the plan to enter the science fair, Craig took wind velocity and direction readings twice a day for months. He recorded his results on a graph, and sure enough, his father's hypothesis proved true. More accurately, he later realized, "It never rains at the *Bayless house* when the wind blows from the east."

Nevertheless, Craig passed his science class and won the State Science Fair. Jim beamed. "That's my son," he said.

Chapter Eighteen

The spring of 1963, Jim and Craig attended Power Squadron courses to learn about navigating and handling boats. While practicing what they learned, Craig approached his father with another purchase plan. Jim responded to his son's plea for a water-ski boat and trailer in an expected fashion—he required that one condition be met: If Christie could learn to ski (as Craig had—on a neighbor's boat), Jim would yield and buy them their own ski boat.

"Christie, get up next time or I swear I'm going to drown you!" Craig would scream. He'd ignore the fact that her lips had turned blue in the spring-chilled water of the Lewis River. Eventually, she learned how to ski and the duo got their boat. Jim also bought a dinghy—"for Joanie," he said—and called it the Jolly Joan.

The Walther family boated in the same group as the Baylesses. Quite infatuated with the shy sixteen-year-old Sandra, Craig invited her to join him for a moonlight ride in the ski boat, away from the rafted boats. They motored to a secluded island, and as luck would have it, Sandra returned his affections. They were soon "making out."

In spite of the fact that he had his eyes closed, a blast of light blinded him. His father had decided to show off his shiny, new searchlight to the other "gadget-crazed fathers," as Craig called them. Jim demonstrated the awesome power of the light by first locating the ski boat and then the tender lovers. Humiliated, Craig and Sandra scattered into the shadows. They rode in silence as Craig delivered the lost promise of a new girlfriend back to her boat.

Christie recalls the incorrigible tendency of Jim to "spotlight" her own love interests. He mounted twin beacons to the house fit for monitoring the perimeter of a prison, she says. They always "magically" came on as Christie arrived home from a date.

Jim would smile and shrug at the indignation of his children. He never apologized for his behavior—except once. After Craig married Sandra, he begged the couple's pardon for his indiscretion that evening of their first kiss.

In January of 1964, Jim traded *Aquarius* for another Chris Craft, longer by six feet. He named her *Aquarius II.*

Both Joanie and Craig say they have never seen their father sadder than the day *Aquarius II* sank. The yacht was in the boathouse when an engine-cooling hose broke loose. Craig says, "I will never forget the crestfallen look on Dad's face when he saw the stern of his beautiful boat on the muddy river bottom of our boathouse. Brown water lapped at the wheelhouse windshield."

They resuscitated the boat, but it was never the same. Jim traded it in the following year for *Aquarius III,* a thirty-eight footer that included a stateroom for Jim and Jean. Just as Jim stayed true to one car company, Chrysler, he only bought Chris Crafts. Businessmen who joined Jim and Craig on the yacht often complimented the boy and his father on their teamwork. They glanced at one another with cloaked surprise when Jim consulted Craig on various matters. People rarely saw Jim ask the opinion of anyone.

Wade Hansen fell ill that year. He had mouth cancer. The doctors cut away part of his tongue—then the whole thing. He spoke through a voice box. The odd robotic sound coming from Wade suggested that a part of his being had already gone. The man who had introduced Jim to boating died in May.

Jim kept *Aquarius III* two years before buying the fourth and final boat, a fifty-five footer with two diesel engines. Accommodations to sleep six included two staterooms and a V-berth, three heads, and a contained galley. The yacht towed the sixteen-foot ski boat with ease.

Each generation of *Aquarius* found herself the victim of a number of "nautical fender benders." Jim doesn't take full responsibility, however. He wishes to give due credit to the crew.

"The *women* crew," says Craig, quick to take sides with his father. Then lowering his defense, he suggests in a gentlemanly fashion, "but it wasn't exactly their fault. I don't remember Christie or Mom—and Joanie was too young—ever attending any Power Squadron classes." It was neither expected nor encouraged that they do so. Tongue in cheek, Craig adds, "Perhaps in the early 1960's women were not capable of understanding boat handling."

It was Joanie who was responsible for Jim winning the Portland Yacht Club's not-so-coveted *Boner Trophy*. With snickering unbefitting a classy establishment, the club awarded the trophy each year to one of its hapless members.

Joanie doesn't deny her role in the fiasco. She and her little friend had played with the gears during a visit to Beacon Rock. When it was time to leave, Jim started the engines without noticing that one was in gear. Unwittingly, he stowed items and readied for departure. The boat strained against the mooring lines. The lines held fast. Soon the boat inched away, pulling the dock with it, as well as a dozen other boats. The skippers who were aboard their boats frantically started up their engines. Their crew or passersby whipped free their lines from around the dock cleats, (appearing like the mirror image of cowboys hogtying a calf.) The blur of bodies to the dock and the shouting caught Jim's attention. He jammed the guilty gear into reverse to ease the tension on his lines, and then hit neutral. Although a catastrophe was averted, the skippers voted unanimously to grant Jim Bayless that year's *Boner Trophy*.

Craig wasn't on board that day at Beacon Rock. But neither he nor Jim blames Joanie or the other female crew completely for the nautically-tainted name of Bayless around the Portland Yacht Club. Other "boner" incidents allow them to point a finger at the weather. Boating in Oregon meant boating in rain. Inclement weather only added to problems as Jim discovered that it took more dexterity to park his Chris Crafts than his huge Chryslers.

As well, they give credit to the Columbia River itself that impeded Jim's path with its submerged and floating logs, sandbars and garbage from the cities, refuse from paper mills, and wood from the lumber industry.

Joking aside, Jim would never really blame the river. The problem rested with the negligence of industry. The businesses considered the Columbia a sewer. Jim's fellow cruisers seemed to think the same way. And truthfully, the Baylesses were just as guilty. In the early 1960's, all boaters on the Columbia thoughtlessly dumped their refuse overboard. When the Portland Club yachters "rafted" their boats together, all the toilets pumped directly into the river. Craig says, "We disposed of our cans and bottles as trash, later sinking it in the river. The terms *recyclable* and *biodegradable* were not yet in our vocabulary."

When the Baylesses started motoring to Canada, however, and saw the crystal clear waters, Jim began commenting on the mess in the Columbia. A rule against tossing small items over the side was enforced. Comments such as "Put that pull tab in the trash," were added to the list of Jim's favorite phrases. Referring to a 1964 song by Bob Dylan, Craig says, "The times were a-changin'."

So after blaming the gals and the weather and the river, Craig admits that he and his father weren't exactly top notch boaters in the early days: "In Power Squadron classes we learned the maritime rule governing right of way, the meaning of colored lights and buoys, compass navigation, chart reading, and useful sayings like 'red-right-returning.' We had to do homework and pass tests. It was like school, only fun. Dad and I both graduated, but I doubt that anyone ever failed. In any event, Power Squadron unwittingly cast us upon the waters. They didn't know what a terror they had unleashed."

It was on *Aquarius IV* that Jim committed the boner for which only he can claim responsibility, the one no one—at least Craig and his in-laws—would ever let him forget. Jim might try to make a point about the bad weather, but none of his family members will let him get away with sharing the blame with any *one* or any *thing*.

True, it was foggy that day on the Oregon coast, just south of the jetty at the mouth of the Columbia. *Aquarius IV* had radar and Carl and Arlene Walther's boat, *Carlene,* didn't. Could Jim provide navigation instructions to a safe refuge? Craig says, "To the north were the sharp rocks of the jetty and to the east, a monstrous surf. To the west and south lay limitless open water, but refuge could be found only to the northwest." Jim knew they were on a SSE 160-degree course. Calculating in his head and without conferring with Craig at the helm, Jim told Carl, "Steer 90 degrees," directing *Carlene* east into the gnarly surf.

Really? thought the Walthers. Well, Jim had access to a radar screen, so he must know what he was talking about.

Craig did the math, but it was too late. Carl Walther had changed course and wasn't answering his radio. ("Carl didn't like to leave his radio on. He was saving it for the next owner," jokes Craig.) His boat disappeared into the fog on a course for disaster.

Losing one's way in the south jetty of the Columbia Bar sends shivers up the spine of the best of sailors. The Baylesses stared into the fog to the east, waiting as if they might hear something, or perhaps see the *Carlene* suddenly trajected back at them through the fog. The crew of *Aquarius IV* had no idea if Carl would realize his danger before the surf either swallowed and cast *Carlene* to shore or swept her to the rocks of the jetty.

Fortunately, Carl and crew spotted huge rolling surf off their bow and reversed course in time to make it safely out to sea.

At Carl's funeral in 2002, Craig reminisced with Carl's son, Cardy, about the Bayless-Walther boating adventures. They concluded that Jim's math error, resulting in the Walthers setting a course for perilous danger, topped the list of Jim Bayless' *boners.*

During the summers of 1965 to 1969, the Baylesses cruised to Canada—motoring a hundred miles west on the Columbia River to the ocean, up the coast, through the Straits of Juan de Fuca to Victoria, and north to the San Juans. Jean comments how the accepted protocol of life aboard a boat fitted Jim's personality perfectly. "Hop to it, crew. Let's get this boat shipshape. Stow that gear in its proper place.... On deck now for inspection," he'd say in so many words. Nowhere else but at the helm of his boats, says Jean, was Jim his truest self: "authoritative, opinionated, stubborn, fair, and very worthwhile."

Jim took great pride in the appearance of his yacht. The crew fell within the purview of his concern, and Jean supported him fully. When Wade and Carolyn Hansen recommended Savory Island as a place where they "simply *must* stop for dinner," Jean, imagining a Victorian inn, gave orders that the gentlemen don coats and ties and the ladies wear pretty dresses. "We rowed ashore so that the Canadians could fully appreciate the adorable Bayless clan," says Craig. "Mom's Victorian inn was a fishing camp full of barefoot, hippie vacationers who looked at us as if we had arrived from Mars."

Undeterred, Jim ordered drinks. Jean took a sip of hers, peering around over the rim of her glass. "Canadians," she said, "really should learn how to dress for dinner."

On one occasion when Craig was at college, Grandmother Inez was visiting. Jim and the Bayless women took her on a boat ride. Jim left an aft storage compartment open when he diverted his attention to the barbeque. Upon resuming his conversation, he looked around. "Anyone seen my mother?" he called out. "She was here a second ago."

"My word, Jim," said Jean, "where could she be?"

"The head, maybe?" offered Christie.

Joan reached to close the storage hatch and noticed a gray-haired lady sprawled ten-feet below in the bowels of the boat. "Nanny Dee Dee," she cried out, "what on earth are you doing down there?"

True to her unflappable, Bayless ways, she said, "Just inspecting things."

With Jim and Joanie grabbing at her one arm and Christie and Jean pulling the other, they managed to bring Inez back on deck.

"Not a scratch," said Jean, shaking her head in amazement.

Inez smiled. "God does a good job of looking after me."

Craig calls his father a "fearless boater" because he cruised with his family up the Strait of Georgia, north of Desolation Sound to Toba Inlet, and would have gone to Alaska if business and school schedules hadn't placed limits on their time. Most members of the Portland Yacht Club never ventured farther than twenty miles from port and had no experience with the ocean. "My dad went from a *boner* novice to a world-class captain in just a few years," Craig says proudly.

Those boating years, says Jim, "were the happiest times of my life."

Chapter Nineteen

Christie and her brother and sister would on occasion raise their hands in exasperation at their father, but they adored him. Perhaps their love and loyalty can be attributed to that mysterious devotion nearly all children have for their parents. On the other hand, Sue Thuemmel adored James Bayless, too.

He was like her own father in many ways. Actually, all the fathers in Hessler Hills were. They dressed alike, socialized together, lived by the same schedules, and spoke words that reflected the same morality. It was a "Leave It To Beaver" community. The Bayless adults "were family to me," says Sue. Jean, always the epitome of elegance, frequently invited Sue to dinner. "Please call your parents and tell them we'd like you as our guest for dinner," she'd say, her deep voice breathy and warm.

When Sue grew into her teen years, she encouraged Jim to talk about his work. A passion for business pumped through her veins naturally. At age seven she watched how her father began his own advertising and public relations firm and how her parents made it the largest in Oregon. She took business classes in high school. Jim welcomed her questions. She says, "He taught me that starting at the bottom is fine as long as you point yourself in the right direction."

One day Jim asked sixteen-year-old Sue to a special breakfast. No one else was invited. He prepared the entire meal. Christie, Craig, and Joanie weren't around. Jean went to the bedroom. Sue sat up straight

171

in the turquoise, Naugahyde booth. She smiled, watching as this important man, wearing a tie with his sleeves rolled, waited on her.

It didn't occur to her at the time that Jim might have felt sorry for her. Christie had made the Trojanes Dance Team and she had not. Her feelings of disappointment dissipated as she watched the prominent businessman prepare eggs and bacon and converse as if they were peers. He spoke about the difficulty of achieving goals, how a lot of sliding back to the bottom of a hill happens before a person ever makes it to the top. She couldn't imagine he was sharing anything personal about his own life, but his words had an intimate feel.

"Like Sisyphus, you know," he said, placing a glass of juice and a roll before her.

"Thank you, Jim," she said. There were a number of words he said that she didn't understand, but the message came through all the same.

"You're very welcome, Sue," he said—and not, *young lady,* as he had often called her in the past. He returned to the stove, and then glanced over his shoulder. "Imagine your highest goal and then go after it," he said.

As they sat together eating, he rested his fork and looked at her a moment. "Obstacles will disappear if we are confident enough to confront them."

Sue smiled to cover the flash of painful memory about the Trojanes. Then it was gone.

Following their breakfast, Jim walked her to the door and opened it. He said, "Look at that world out there, Sue. Stare it down. Say, 'Here I come and I've got a lot to offer.'"

Sue stepped to the front walk, smiling and waving, her confidence level a few notches higher. Weeks later, she was elected treasurer of the student body at Wilson High. As an adult, she would start her own foreign language instruction company.

Jim drove Sue, Janet U'Ren, and Craig and Christie to school a few times a week. Hessler Hills looked down one thousand feet on the city of Portland. In winter, the ice and snow made for treacherous driving conditions. Since no sidewalks were ever built and the school bus service didn't extend to the Hessler Hills community, the

Thuemmels and U'Rens shared responsibility with Jim for transporting their children to Wilson High.

One school morning, the four young people awoke almost simultaneously with the same thought as they glanced out the window: A snow day! The trees bowed with inches of weighty white. They jumped from their beds with visions of school-free plans in their heads. Unfortunately, one mile from the Hessler neighborhood, only rain had fallen. Jim would need to transport the teens to school in his large Chrysler down three steep hills—two of them pure ice.

Jim picked up Sue and Janet at the bus shelter he had helped the fathers build in the early 50's. The vehicle, like an elephant on ice skates, made its way down the first hill. Only when Jim started down the second hill—the steepest—did the singsong shrill of overlapping teenage voices still. It was as if someone had pulled the plug on a radio. Then the car turned perpendicular to the road and slid. The mouths of the teens oohed silently. Jim, however, kept the wheels straight and they sidled safely to the bottom of the hill.

They sat there a minute—to the left a muted TV screen of an icy hill that disappeared into white. To the right and below, they could see the bustle of traffic in the valley. Jim righted the car and they drove on. As they made it to the bottom of the final hill, chatter again filled the vehicle. No one said a word about what they had experienced.

They took their cue from Jim, who never was one for reflection. Things happen. You handle them the best you can. Looking over his shoulder never got Jim anywhere. Life had taught him that a man is best served by giving his attention to whatever is coming at him head on.

When Craig left home in the fall of 1965 to attend Willamette University in Salem, an hour away, Jim lost his navigator. The Bayless family's boating adventures began a slow decline as the crew moved away. The bold lines defining Jim's love of boating began to fade.

Craig's flight from the nest saddened Jean, says Christie. Her eldest daughter leaving the following fall would bring on another blow. "I felt a little sad, of course," says Jean. But although she loved her two oldest dearly, their leaving opened new doors in her life.

A part of Jean had always felt a modicum of frustration in her role of wife and mother. She considered her family *a team,* but "I wasn't usually on the team. I was a cheerleader," she says with a rueful smile. "Only sometimes did we put me on the team."

If she had never become a Bayless, if she had been on her own, she might have become an actress—winsome and ravishing. "But not a sex symbol," she laughs, shaking her head. "A comedian. Maybe a Doris Day who can't sing." Instead, she said, "I do" and learned well how to act the silent partner. Instead of becoming a star, she cheered others to stardom.

With the emptying of her nest, Jean saw the opportunity to enter the community stage. She decided to volunteer at Good Samaritan Hospital where she had given birth to her three children. During the next fifteen years, she'd become president of the women's auxiliary.

Her experience as wife to Jim Bayless made her a perfect leader. When bossy ladies would ask other volunteers to accomplish a task and then "pull the rug out by taking charge," Jean would say (as she had said in so many words and so many times to Jim), "Let her do it her way (*Let me do it my way*). She's a volunteer. Let her find her niche. This has to be a team effort."

She became chair of the Red Cross Blood Donor Recruiting and chair of the Safe Neighborhood Program sponsored by United Way. Jean volunteered by reading books into a tape recorder for the blind. Had Jim approved, she would have adopted kids in trouble or become a foster mom. She would have graced the stages of local playhouses. But she understood clearly, says Christie, that "her first obligation was to be available when Dad wasn't at work." Christie pauses. "Yet it was her choice as well. Mom always put his wishes first."

"In those days," says Jim, "the most important role a woman could have is that of wife and mother."

Jean's volunteer work at Good Samaritan Hospital was the one place she stood in charge—alone, without Jim a step in front of her. When Jim first went into business, Christie says, he viewed his future as a leaning ladder he held by its side rails. He stepped to the first rung, determined to use only his own weight to keep the structure balanced. Grasping the hand of his wife, he guided her behind him as he ascended rung after rung. "Climbing the ladder wasn't Mom's idea," says Christie, "but she loved the man and would always support him. Not once did she entertain the thought to let go of his hand."

Although Jean stepped through opening doors as Craig moved on to college, Jim paused with the realization that he would miss his son. Christie witnessed the moment. She wondered, Would it make her father happy to hear that she loved boating? She looked up at him and made a silent plea: *Dad. I'm a willing co-pilot, deck mate, cabin boy, hook baiter, and boat cleaner. Craig is gone. Look at me.* But she knew he would never see her in quite the same way he did a son.

She could never replace Craig, although she wanted to. She tried to—because it was Craig and boys and boating that her father seemed to care most about. But Craig says, "Gasoline and muddy river water didn't hold the same allure for Christie as they did for Dad and me. She preferred boys and clean clothes. On occasion we had to figure out where to pick Christie up after one of her pressing, social engagements that conflicted with the departure time of *Aquarius*."

Choices for women and girls of the 60's, however, were no longer black and white. They had a glimmer into the possibility that they could do it all.

Christie recalls a final summer voyage on *Aquarius IV.* Craig would be a sophomore at Willamette in the fall, and she had started packing for her freshman year at the University of Oregon. One afternoon, in a secluded bay in Canada, she and Craig and Joanie were taking turns riding on an air mattress that was secured to the ski boat with a rope. Jim decided to give it a try. "He'd turn turtle every time," Christie says with a chuckle. "Dad caught our giggles and never did manage to stay atop the mattress."

Seeing the playful side to her father's personality happened rarely. "I so badly wanted a photograph of how I saw him that day," Christie says. As he bounced on the mattress behind the ski boat, laughing, he exuded a warmth she wished she had seen more often during her childhood. She imagined enlarging the photo and hanging it in her father's office. Jim stopped laughing when his daughter mentioned her fantasy, and Christie sighed, knowing that Jim Bayless, the businessman, would never allow the endearing, light-hearted side of himself to become part of the image he displayed to the world.

His every frown devastated her. When she displeased him, she would redouble her efforts to resuscitate his approval. Titles and awards hung on her bedroom wall. She received top grades. During her senior year at Woodrow Wilson High School, she served as Chairman of Student Body Activities on the executive board. In January 1966, she competed against 3100 high school students from throughout Oregon and won the VFW Voice of Democracy speech contest. The Veterans of Foreign Wars awarded her a $150 savings bond and a five-day trip to Washington, DC so that she could compete for the national title and a college scholarship.

Jim and Jean drove her to the airport. Her father smiled and wished her well. She knew he was proud of her by the softness in his eyes. But he doesn't really see *me,* she thought.

Though today, she's not sure what she wanted her father to see. Was it a young woman capable of excelling in the world of business or at any career? Or did she want him to see someone equal to Jean, capable of becoming a good wife and mother? Maybe both.

As she sat on the plane in 1966, memories of the last time she visited the nation's capital, four years earlier, flooded back to her. She had wanted to see President Kennedy. Tears moistened her eyes. She would see him this time—at the Memorial that marked his grave.

Her father didn't understand her sentiments about JFK. "He was just a man who got himself assassinated," he would say, not so much because he had no compassion for the man's tragic end but because Jim resented people whose notoriety bloomed due to the way they died. Perhaps, too, he was a bit jealous seeing the admiration for another man in his daughter's eyes.

Christie saw her father's disregard for Kennedy as yet another example of how he didn't seem to value what she deemed important. He simply didn't understand her at all. Christie says, "During one summer break from college, he insisted I take shorthand so I could 'get a job' after graduation. I tried, but I absolutely could not do that stenographic thing."

Jim didn't know she had dreams of doing something important with her life—although she wasn't sure what. Mostly she wanted the support and encouragement and *time* to discover the career that suited her. But that wasn't her father's way. *Know your goal and go after it,* he told her. But that wasn't *her* way. All her life, he believed *Father*

Knows Best. Christie says, "He would decide how something was going to be, and that was just the way it was. Our family wasn't a democracy."

"And it shouldn't be," says Jim. "Children need direction."

"I wanted to go to Stanford, but Dad brushed that idea off," Christie says.

Jim thought private schools an unnecessary expense for anyone. The University of Oregon was a fine school. Ultimately, Christie would go to the University of Oregon, earn a degree, and then become a good wife and mother without pursuing a career. Early on, she told herself that she was yielding to her father's dictum. But today she says his wishes blended into her own, and she followed the path she wanted.

Jim hated the 60's phenomena of long hair, bizarre dress, and electrified music. To Craig, however, his father seemed to accept the times with astonishing tolerance, even as it enveloped his son. Christie says, "It has always been the case that in my father's eyes Craig can do no wrong."

She saw a different message in Jim's eyes when he looked her way. She knew the country's wave of challenge and confrontation unnerved her father. Jim lost respect for LBJ who forfeited control over the country because of his take on the Vietnam War. When protests about the war spilled into the streets of the 1968 Democratic National Convention in Chicago, Jim marched out and registered as a Republican. He phoned Craig. "I don't know what these Democrats stand for any longer," he lamented.

Although rebelliousness simmered in the youth of the 60's, it never came to a boil in Christie. She melted in the warmth of her father's approval and re-formed to the mold of his conservative attitudes. No matter what he said to her, she always spoke lovingly to her daddy. Today she holds, like individually picked flowers for a bouquet, the times he told her with a word or expression that he valued her.

Two thoughtful gifts from her father stand out clearly in Christie's memories. That the presents came solely from him makes them special. While driving her en route to some activity, Jim asked his daughter to itemize how much money she anticipated needing for her freshman year at college. He'd give her a lump sum for the whole year.

"How about if you just send me money each month?" she said.

Jim took his eyes off the road and gave her a drawn out, "No." Looking ahead, he added, "Part of my investment in your education is that you learn how to budget money."

"Oh." Since she had no paper with her, she pulled *The Highest Dream,* a paperback, from her purse, tore out the title page, and wrote her expense list. When Jim mailed the check to Christie at school, he enclosed the title page to which he added the note: "fulfilled with love, Dad."

In a second instance, Jim bought a green, costume jewelry ring and mailed it to Christie's Tri-Deltas sorority house. He included a note: "To make a nothing day a something day. Love, Dad."

After 1960, Mr. Dooly rarely came into the office. The junior partners of Bayless, Munro, and Rimback had assumed leadership over the company. Jim reigned as the highest producer of sales. He often stopped at the door of Dooly's office and peered in. Jim recalled the times they would visit each day to discuss the business.

Mr. Dooly died in the late 1960's. Jim honored his friend by volunteering to serve as a pallbearer at the funeral. As he listened to the words of the priest at St. Mary's Cathedral, he felt sad, but he had known his old mentor had been ill. Jean says that Mr. Dooly was Jim's closest friend, the person to whom her husband attached the strongest feelings. They had dined at one another's homes. They shared a passion for a company.

At work, the day after the funeral, Jim recalled the office of Maurice Dooly as it had been that November day in 1944 when he entered it to ask for a job. As always when dealing with death, a pragmatic presence filled him. Jim said goodbye in his mind to Mr. Dooly and moved on.

Chapter Twenty

A draft deferment allowed Craig to attend college. In January 1969, he received a notice to report for duty immediately upon his graduation in June. Feeling that boot camp and Vietnam were virtually certain, he joined the Marine Corps Reserve even though he chanced active duty prior to graduation. More importantly, he hoped to avoid an immediate assignment to Vietnam. Whatever the case, finishing college would have to wait.

Craig was able to join his family in March for their yearly trek to Palm Springs. According to custom, they reserved rooms a year ahead at the Desert Braemar. Card games, a family tradition, consumed a substantial amount of everyone's time—that is, when they weren't playing golf. Jim, forever flaunting an air of superiority, was always the one to beat. Loud laughter would accompany jovial rooting for him to lose—although he rarely did.

It was on this vacation that Craig announced his engagement to Sandra Walther. "During a card game in the desert—where else more suiting?" says Craig. The couple had renewed their high school romance when Craig transferred to the University of Oregon for his last two years of school.

"Sandra's mother will handle the wedding plans," Craig said.

"As it should be," said Jean, nodding.

Jim said nothing. He'd had a run-in or two with Arlene Walther over the years. For example, the previous winter, Craig and Sandra left the University of Oregon campus for a ski weekend and failed to make it back for Monday's classes. A phone call to Sandra's sorority house informed Arlene that her daughter was last seen "with the Bayless boy in his yellow Barracuda." Greatly distressed, she called Jim.

"Sandra is somewhere in the mountains with your son. Do you know where they are?"

"No, Arlene, I don't."

"You don't understand! A big snowstorm hit the area. They must be trapped in some motel or bar or something."

Jim said, "Well, good for them. I'm sure they're having a great time."

"Well! I find your attitude a bit cavalier. I'm going to organize a search!"

The snowstorm had trapped the enamored couple an extra night in the mountains. Little did they imagine that anyone would be looking for them. They were, after all, young lovers oblivious to all but one another.

Jim's boating days were coming to a close. His navigator was in the Marines and would soon marry, and Jean seemed to be talking more often than usual about finding a place at the beach. Then someone painted "Jean's beach house" on one of the fenders of *Aquarius IV.*

"Who did that?" Jim growled harmlessly but in his bearish way, without the ability to adjust his tone. Everyone could read that he didn't expect an answer. He had finally taken the hint that Jean wanted to move their love of water closer to the beach. She wanted a beach home.

It was time to look at what new adventures lay in the distance. Without any regrets, Jim decided to sell *Aquarius IV.*

Craig didn't really mind the inevitable end of the boating life, of weeks each summer at the mouth of the Columbia River. It marked the end of an era—of his boyhood. Now a man with a job and fiancée, a different world had his attention. With scoffing denial of its importance, he said goodbye to boating: "Oh, it was fun at first, but after cleaning what seemed like my thousandth salmon, after baiting my umpteenth hook and cleaning up after a seasick guest, after one too many battle with the fog, and the smell of fish and fuel—it all became too much. I don't care if I ever eat another salmon." Truth was, he'd treasure his role as first mate to his father for the rest of his life.

The Oregon coast attributes its charm to foul weather and rugged beauty. Jim bought land in the area of Surf Pines, not far from the mouth of the Columbia River and less than two hours from their Portland home. He built a house that donned a bad toupee of cedar shakes. Big decks and windows directed a view to the wild surf. Lodgepole and ponderosa pines surrounded the area of coarse beach. The family nicknamed their new beach house *Aquarius V.*

Jim and Jean and Joanie spent their weekends at the beach. The collegiates, Craig and Christie, joined them when they could. Jim would stay through Monday mornings and then make the hour plus drive to his Portland office. He loved his beach home. It was perfect. But a beach house is no fun without beach toys.

He bought a Jeep for roaring down the beach, a log splitter, an amphicat, a golf cart, a trailer for hauling driftwood and a chainsaw for cutting it. One day he sunk the Jeep. "I thought the water more shallow," Jim says, smiling. "Everyone laughed at me." If someone else had made the error, it would never have become a family story to pass on during family reunions, but for Jim to make such a mistake destined the tale to live on in the annals of the Bayless family.

A passion rooted in Jim for cutting and collecting driftwood— boom logs, in particular, that had escaped from sawmills. But they were on *his* property now; they were his to haul and arrange about the landscape of the beach house.

The hobby of collecting antique copper and brass also gained momentum following the purchase of a ship's lantern at Guaiacum Bay in British Columbia. Family conversation debated the definition of "antique," but "obviously old" satisfied Jim. The Bayless beach house, abound with an array of shiny pots and pans and curious vessels and tools, took on the appearance of an antique store.

Although Jim has given many pieces to his children, he proudly displays between 250 and 300 copper and brass pots, pans, and nautical items, including ship's lanterns wired to function as electric lamps. Nearly every room has an antique coal bin, filled with nothing these days but bittersweet memories of Jim's early childhood in

Browns Valley. He can still picture Grandpa Bayless returning from the basement with a bin of coal for the stove, his face with a smudge of black like a bruise, his sweat the smell of a cheap cigar.

The beach house gave birth to yet another project for Jim. He became a chef, particularly on the barbeque. Not of the gourmet variety, really, but he took on only the most complex methods of food preparation. He smoked fish on a hickory smoker or sent it to the cannery. He deep fried corn fritters, oysters, and "unidentifiable comestibles," says Craig. Jim cooked salmon in ways that neither he nor anyone else has done since—as fillets or steaks with various marinades; whole on the grill; wrapped in foil with onions, spices, lemons and wine, and steamed in copper vessels or poached in the oven.

Craig completed six months of Marine training and never finished college. "Dad didn't seem to mind," says Craig, "because he never overvalued a college degree. Working was always more important." Jim has since changed that attitude, but he gave his blessing for Craig to simply get on with his marriage and career.

Arlene handled all aspects of Craig and Sandra's wedding that took place December 6, 1969, even though the reception was held at the Portland Golf Club where only the Baylesses were members. Craig says, "Dad just showed up and kept his mouth shut, thank you very much!"

Craig and Sandra rented an apartment at the Royal Firs, the large complex Jim had purchased that year. Not long after, since Craig was doing quite well as a real estate broker for Norris, Beggs, & Simpson, they built a home on Fairmount Boulevard, across the street from Jim and Jean.

For years, a strain existed between Sandra and her in-laws. Being neighbors certainly didn't help matters. Craig states that his parents saw Sandra, who is "painfully shy," as cold or aloof. Sandra viewed Jim and Jean's "aggressive friendliness" as "demanding or threatening." Craig knew his parents hoped he'd marry "a perky, cute little party girl. Instead I married a dark, brooding, quiet, smart girl." A polite discomfort stilted the conversation when the parents got together with Craig and Sandra.

"A drink anyone?" Craig would ask. "Dad?" He'd pour a scotch for his father and for himself as well. He had acquired his father's preference for the drink. Long ago, due to "some imprinting process," Craig learned that "there are very few things better than a good scotch on the rocks." Perhaps the "imprinting" took place, says Craig, during the time he finally convinced his father the family should own a dog, or when he learned his father might buy the family a boat; both fond memories gather around a glass of pale yellow liquid on ice Jim had held as they talked. Or perhaps it happened as he watched his father read the newspaper each evening, a scotch on the end table next to his chair. For Craig, when sipping a Glenlivet, the warmth of all the old memories blurred as one.

On April 4, 1970, Jim and Jean arranged an engagement party for Christie and Marc Kelley, her boyfriend since high school. The supervisor of student teaching at the University of Oregon frowned at Christie's request to leave early that Friday, but Christie couldn't imagine displeasing her parents by being late.

Craig didn't approve of Christie's fiancé. He had roomed with Marc one term at UO only to throw him out. In a take-off on the nuts & candy company, "we called him *Ralph Rotten,*" says Craig. "Dad accepted Marc because he's what Christie wanted."

"I wish Dad had voiced his concerns more clearly," says Christie.

At the time she thought her father's objections stemmed from the fact that Marc didn't have any money. Jim had given Christie a speech that said basically, "How much harder can it be to fall in love with a rich instead of a poor guy?" She snapped back: "It's a good thing Mom didn't take that advice."

More accurately, Jim objected on the grounds that Marc's priority seemed something other than Christie. Intuition and a good judgment of character told Jim that young Kelley would one day hurt his daughter, and he didn't like that at all.

Christie says, "I was young and didn't understand Dad's message. And he didn't state it passionately enough, early enough, clearly enough."

She married Marc David Kelley at first Presbyterian Church. Her parents planned both the wedding and reception. Dr. Paul S. Wright performed the ceremony. Joanie was the maid of honor and Craig, an usher.

Jim told Christie she should have her reception at the University Club. "It's beautifully decorated at Christmas," he said.

Typical, thought Christie. I'll get a classy wedding—but on a budget. We'll use the club's décor—dead Christmas trees—and not have to pay for decorating.

"January 3rd is an ideal date," said Jim. "Since the club is closed on Sundays, we'll have the facility to ourselves."

On the up side, thought Christie, somewhat peevishly, the women can enter through the front door. Women were permitted access to the front entrance on Sundays and for specific events.

Yet when standing dressed all in white on her father's arm, Christie's emotional flurry of internal dialogue disappeared. She says wistfully, "There is a story that Dad cried twice in his life. First, when I was born. Second, that day in January of 1971 I married."

Christie started out her married life living at her father's Royal Firs Apartments. Marc and Christie gave Jim and Jean the joy of their first grandchild on December 2, 1972. But the Kelley marriage was not doing well.

The couple bought a house just a few miles from Christie's parents—"to be close to Mom, partly because my marriage was a disaster and also because she was willing to help me raise Amy Jean," says Christie. "We were really co-moms"—of AJ and then baby Lisa, who was born on June 4, 1975. They called their grandmother *Jeana.* Amy Jean had added the "ah" for emphasis on one occasion when no one was paying attention to her. The name stuck. The girls called Jim *Papa.*

AJ often saw Mary Begg, who lived next door to the Baylesses. "She gave you your 'banky' when you were born," Christie told her daughter. AJ slept every night with that blanket—and still has it today. When she slept over at Papa and Jeana's, AJ would crawl into their bed early each morning, her 'banky' in hand. She'd raise the sleep shade masking Papa's eyes in order to waken him.

He'd feign sleep a few moments longer.

"Papa, Papa," AJ would say, jumping on his stomach.

Then Jim would pop open his eyes and swipe her 'banky'. Giggling, AJ would try to wrestle it back from Papa.

Jim soon changed the direction of the game. He would use his index and baby finger to simulate a telephone. "Hello? Is this Mrs. Begg?" He'd raise the blanket for a closer look. "I've found a blanket. Perhaps you know who it belongs to?…You don't?"

"It's mine, Mrs. Begg! AJ's!" she would cry out, giggling all the while.

On the playful conversation would go until Jim said, "Yes, you are quite right, Mrs. Begg. It's time for me to get ready for work…. AJ, will you take care of this blanket until we find the owner?"

She'd follow her Papa around as he shaved, repeating his words and adopting his mannerisms. When Schwartz appeared, Craig's pet schnauzer from college he had willed to his mother, AJ would refer to it the same way her Papa did: "Damn, dumb dog." For the longest time, says AJ, "I thought that was the dog's name. I couldn't understand why people would either laugh or hush me."

When AJ and Lisa reached school age and spent a night with Papa and Jeana, Jim drove them to school the next morning on his way to work. Fifteen minutes before it was time to go, he'd stand at the door telling the girls to hurry. AJ says, "To this day, every time I get ready to go out, I hear him calling: *You're gonna be late, you're going to be late*—and I never am!"

Jim liked to help AJ study for her spelling tests. "Let me see this week's words, Amy Jean," he'd say, and then drill her throughout the week. AJ says, "He made me spell *giraffe* repeatedly until I got it right." The word was on the list for bonus credit. "Papa would say, 'Life doesn't come with a safety net very often, AJ. Always take it when it's offered.'"

AJ and Lisa believe their Papa mellowed over time. "I never knew Papa as the often gruff man my mom remembers," AJ says, even though her grandfather enforced strict rules. No eating ice cream in the car or in the house. No eating at all in the dining room—only the kitchen—because they might spill and mess the nice table. No entering the living room alone. But it never occurred to her that life could or should be otherwise until her cousins Trevor, Taylor, and McGregor came along. AJ was eleven when Trevor was born.

"Suddenly the rules weren't there anymore," she says. "Papa softened with the years, and dramatically so when he retired."

Christie would drop Lisa and AJ at her parents' house when she had Junior League projects to do. Jean routed them to school and back again and delivered the youngest girl to her doctor appointments. Lisa had inherited the "lazy eye" problem, strabismus, from her grandmother. The girls saw more of Papa than they did their own father, a political lobbyist who traveled often.

Jean says, "Jim didn't like Marc. My father didn't like Marc. The boy was good-looking, arrogant, and not helpful to Christie. My father thought that if Christie was up on the roof doing something, Marc should be there, but he was all front and no back, always ducking responsibility around the home because he had to go out and be political. His lobbyist views irritated the hell out of Jim."

Jim thought Marc a braggart, "too interested in his muscular self." The young man always had an excuse to be somewhere else than with his family. Lisa once said, "You can always depend on Papa to be home when he says." If he said six o'clock, he'd be there "on the dot." Jim says, "Christie never knew when Marc might arrive home. Sometimes he stayed out all night."

As her father had taught her, Christie admitted her mistake. "Daddy," she said, "You were right."

"I was very glad when she got divorced," says Jim.

Christie, however, says sadly, that when she told her parents she planned to divorce Marc, "Dad treated me a bit like I had a plague. The message was 'you should try harder, be more of a wife—less opinionated—bad things don't happen to good people.' Dad was sure he knew the formula for the good life: Good people who tell the truth and keep their desk neat don't get fired. Get up early, take care of details, be organized, be on time and your life will work out perfectly—just like mine."

Christie felt she had disappointed her father, and that was something she could hardly bear.

Just months after Christie married Marc, Joanie traveled to Europe in her senior year with the high school choir. She was the first in the family to see Europe. Then she headed off to college at the University

186

of Oregon in 1972 for two years and moved back home to finish her education at Lewis and Clark College.

She married Mike Madden December 7, 1975 in a format that was a carbon copy of Christie's wedding and reception. Strong-willed like her father, Joanie opposed a number of the suggestions made for the program of the event, but she eventually yielded. As Jim watched his daughter at the altar, he recalled her at the piano, playing his favorite music—Beethoven's sonata "Clair de Lune." She's the only one, the family stories go, born with any musical talent.

Chapter Twenty- One

Although the shenanigans of the youth and the political leaders in the late 60's convinced Jim the country had lost all reason, he possessed a certain satisfaction about his own life. His yearly income suggested a successful businessman. He held the largest partnership interest in Dooly & Co. and had expanded his real estate investments.

After purchasing the apartments at NE 21st and Multnomah (the tenement that grew a mite prettier after the grumbling Christie, almost twelve, and Craig, thirteen, gave its porch two coats of gray paint back in 1960), Jim bought the building next door. He had hoped to destroy the two structures and build a small apartment complex, but he couldn't get a building permit. Instead, Jim traded his properties toward the purchase of an apartment house in Beaverton called The Belaire. He continued to buy and trade.

Jim walked with his head a little higher. His well-groomed and proud presence drew attention; he knew it and he liked it. He would pause his step in a room and listen for the sound of opportunity. He kept an ear on John Boyd, whose company of Wheeler, Boyd & Ballin had merged with Fred S. James (FSJ) in 1969. In the fall of that year, Jim considered merging Dooly & Co. with the James firm.

He flew to Chicago to meet with Art Jens, head of FSJ. It was Election Day. "I remember that," says Jim, "because if I could have had a drink, I might have had enough nerve to say, 'To hell with you, Art.'" Negotiations were a little rough, but Jim came back to Dooly advising the partners to merge with FSJ.

"It's about to go on the New York Stock Exchange," he told them. "A merger makes plain good business sense." Besides the fact that Jim owned the largest partnership interest, he also held stock. When Dooly merged with James, the stockholders could exchange their stock on a tax-free basis.

The naysayers didn't want to become little fish in big pond. They'd have to take a pay cut to cover corporate overhead. Jim knew they had a point, but then again, he had plans to be part of the "corporate overhead."

Jack Thomas grumbled. "I'm about to retire. I can't afford a decrease in wages right now."

The pay cuts would be significant. Jim's own take-home would drop from $125,000 to $45,000. Nevertheless, he said with a frown, "Look to the future, Jack. We'll more than recoup our losses when the value of our stock hits the national marketplace."

"How can you be sure?"

Jim steeled his gaze, looking first at Jack and then across the faces of the other partners. "I'm sure."

The partners didn't really have much choice. Dooly & Co. merged with FSJ. Jack Thomas chose to retire. Optimistic about the future, Jim added to his budding real estate empire by buying a new, eighty-six unit apartment complex called the Royal Firs. "We're now a million dollars in debt, and we can afford it, Jean," he said with a grin. "We must be doing something right."

The combined firm remained in the Board of Trade Building the first year, doing business as Dooly & Co. The second year, the business called itself Fred S. James / Dooly, until they became Fred S. James. John Boyd from FSJ managed the office. When he became the regional director, Jim took over as manager. FSJ moved to consecutively larger quarters until in 1974, Jim signed a lease in the Columbia Square Building, which spanned a full city block. FSJ sprawled across one full floor, spilling over onto a second, covering 55,000 square feet in total.

Eventually the insurance company became known simply as *James*. Was it coincidence or fate that Jim's personalized license plate, *James,* referred to himself as well as the company in which he was a rising executive?

Two life-altering events transpired in 1975. Jim, at the age of fifty-four, experienced a persistent itching on his back. A dermatologist diagnosed diabetes. An internist agreed and instructed Jim to take a three-day course at Good Samaritan Hospital. "Or," he said, "I can tell you the same information in ten minutes."

"I'll take the ten-minute version," said Jim.

He controls his diabetes with four shots of insulin a day. "Jean does a marvelous job of preparing meals that are sugar free. I give myself the shots." When they go out, Jean carries the needles in her purse. "Don't forget to shoot yourself," she'll say.

While Jim was figuring out how to live with diabetes, Transamerica Corporation bought Fred S. James. He received a check for all his stock and handed it to Jean. She counted the zeros, and then threw her hands into the air as if signaling a touchdown.

"One million..." he said as Jean embraced him. "One million, five hundred thousand, to be exact." He couldn't stop smiling. "I told you one day I'd be a millionaire, Jean."

"Yes, Jimmy, you did. And I'm the one who believed in you."

He bought the fifty-six unit Stone Creek Apartments, located across the street from the Royal Firs, and he named the complex Royal Firs West. He now owned 142 units.

When John Boyd retired in December of 1979, Jim slipped into his position as regional director for the Northwest. The job required constant travel to the offices in Salt Lake City, Medford, Portland, Yakima, Seattle, Spokane, Anchorage, and Boise. In time, Jim was asked if he would like a position at the home office in Chicago. But Jim loved his life in Oregon. He declined.

In spite of Harry Grannatt's formula and later because of it, Jim had done well in the insurance business. On September 20, 1976, Jim attended Harry's funeral. He'd spent his career listening to Harry's odd ideas and quirky sense of humor. *So smart, he's dumb,* Jim thought that day, recalling how the words had played liked an obsessing jingle in his head for thirty-odd years.

That night Jim leafed through Harry's book, *The Pied Typer.* On page eighteen, he read:

> *When I was in school*
> > *And learned how to spell*
> *They taught me a rule*
> > *I remember quite well:*
> *Put "i" before "e,"*
> > *So I learned when a brat,*
> *Except after "c,"*
> > *It's as simple as that!*

> *...But while I'm proficeint*
> > *At spelling, I've feared*
> *Though the rule is efficeint*
> > *The words do look wierd!*

Jim smiled in spite of himself. "See you later, Harry."

The Baylesses had visited Palm Springs nearly every year since 1955. They decided to sell their Astoria beach house in January of 1977 and buy a condominium at Thunderbird Country Club. The seller, a Russian countess named Irina Tolstoy, had furnished the villa like a Russian museum.

A home in Palm Springs. "Jean thought she had died and gone to heaven," says Jim.

They now owned a residence in the community of Rancho Mirage, "the playground" of Presidents and celebrities, eleven miles from Palm Springs. But Jim says the names of celebrities didn't affect him much at all—didn't then and never would. He had always thought the way the media highlighted accomplished people should include businessmen. Then he'd be impressed. Phil Harris, Alice Faye, Frank Sinatra, Desi Arnez and Lucille Ball, Bing Crosby, Bob Hope, and Gerald Ford were no different than James Bayless. They all came to Rancho Mirage to play golf and live in the sunshine.

The Baylesses belonged to three country clubs: Astoria for when they went to the beach, Thunderbird in Rancho Mirage, and Waverly in Portland. Jim no longer held a membership at the Portland Golf Club. He had quit one day in anger. When guests from New York were visiting that Jim wished to impress, he telephoned the club to request a particular day and starting time. The slot was unavailable.

"Fine! Who needs your club?" he yelled, hanging up the phone. The next day he joined Waverly Country Club and remains a member to this day.

Ten days before Christmas, 1978, Jean's father died at the age of seventy-eight. The bright eyes of the handsome white-haired man had dimmed over the past few years, and the taut lines of his oval mouth had weakened. His high cheekbones, which seemed perfectly matched to his friendly, outgoing personality, couldn't conceal his faltering spirit. Perhaps the heavy smoking caused the cancer. Just as likely, the asbestos in refrigerators and soda fountains that he worked on in his used appliance store killed him.

Many of Mike's friends, as well as Jim and Jean's, attended the memorial at St. Andrew's Presbyterian and the gravesite service. Craig gave the eulogy. He says, "Bobop was the most universally-loved man I have ever met."

Jim said little about the passing of Mike Welter, but it didn't go unnoticed that he had passed long periods at his father-in-law's bedside. He sat, turning the pages of memory, recalling how Mike had worked around the Fairmount house with the love and care a man typically devotes only to his own home. All the Sunday dinners came back to him that they shared in front of a television set, an informal honor reserved only for "family." Christie says, "I think Bobop was the father figure Dad never had."

Jim accepted Mike Welter blindly and completely. "He never seemed to expect Gramuz and Bobop to live at the standard he held other people," says Christie. "They were the only people in Mom and Dad's circle who weren't climbing the ladder of success."

The close relationship between the two men centered around their projects. Mike often dressed in the overalls and baseball hat he wore at work. After a morning of toil, the men would pause and enjoy a beer. Their enthusiasm and conviviality around the ritual impressed Craig. He'd watch the foam make its way to the top of a mug and then miraculously stop at the rim.

"Please, Bobop. How about a sip?" Craig begged the first time, keeping tabs on his father's response from the corner of his eye.

Holding the mug with two hands, Craig dove into the foam. Mike grinned as the boy's upper lip and nose disappeared. When he came up for air, Craig said, "Nothing! It tastes like something, but mostly nothing."

His father and Bobop looked at each other and laughed. Craig joined in. In the years to come, memories of the friendship between his father and Bobop always surfaced when he downed the head of a cold one.

It surprised everyone that the energy of Mike Welter evaporated before that of his wife, the thin and frail Elsie who had never seemed capable of making it on her own. A smoker and conservative who said little and balked at change, Elsie always wore a housedress and sensible shoes. For church, a small hat with a short veil sat upon her head. She'd wrap herself about her handbag. Her hair had turned white prematurely, making her appear far older than her husband during their middle years. If approached, she was kind. When she had "a few snorts" in her (as she called a drink), she could be funny and sweet as she played the few piano tunes she knew. Her grandchildren adored her. Christie chose Gramuz to guard the secret of her plans to re-marry.

When Mt. St. Helens erupted five months after Mike's death, no one was home at the Bayless household, which would have been the perfect place to view the wonder. Sunday, the eighteenth of May 1980, Jean and her mother were spending the weekend at the home of a friend who lived at the beach.

It appeared dark as Muz and Jean drove the slippery roads home the following morning. They couldn't imagine what had happened in the world. Grey ash covered everything. The lush green maples and Douglas firs around the Bayless property that had stood summer-ready but a day ago, now appeared cloaked in dirty snow.

At 8:32 am, the clocked time of the eruption, Jim was flying with business associates to Colorado Springs on a chartered plane. He missed viewing it from the sky by fifteen minutes.

As regional director, Jim realized he was at the peak of his career, but there were times he gave a thought or two to an early retirement. Not that he was sure what he would do with his free time. Play more golf, perhaps. Or travel. He'd seen a little of the world, but there certainly were places out there he hadn't.

For one, Yugoslavia, as it was called then. Before joining Jim's firm, Don Stathos and Ron Ashbracher of Don Stathos Insurance Agency had won a trip to the Balkan state from United Pacific Insurance. Since Jim held the position of Regional Director, the men invited the Baylesses to join them and their wives on their trip in early October.

Jim had never before stepped on Communist soil. The body of Marshal Tito had barely turned cold when the Bayless entourage arrived. *Communist.* Others called Tito *Socialist.* The words stuck in Jim's throat, but he couldn't help thinking about the man, this peasant born Josip Broz who had adopted the pseudonym "Tito" when working in the communist underground. Broz had risen from a common farmer to the President of Yugoslavia.

The politics that directed the minds of men like Tito and Stalin and Khrushchev rarely entered Jim's mind. Farmers he understood— his father and Grandfather Bayless working the soil in Browns Valley. As well, Jim understood the desire to pursue a position of leadership. But his life revolved around simple terms of truth and honesty and honor. He repeated platitudes of proper conduct to keep the world straight in his mind, and he possessed neither the time nor patience to unravel the complexities of the political world that seemed to keep company with cruelty and deceit.

Barely unpacked from the trip to Yugoslavia, Jim and Jean enthusiastically took on the wedding plans for Christie's second marriage.

Christie had met Rick Gorsline in a nightclub the 1st of December 1979, the year of her divorce from Marc. A friend from work told Christie that she and Rick were "naturals" for one another. They weren't, however—he, an athlete, "a racquetball player who had no desire to have kiddies," while she was looking for an "honest, fulltime parent for my girls," He earned a living as a car dealership sales manager—not exactly what Jim would have chosen for his eldest daughter.

But Jim could see how Rick loved both his daughter and the little girls. The relationship seemed inevitable. Jim picked the wedding date. "And let's have the reception at the University Club," he said.

"Okay, Dad," she said, sure Rick wouldn't mind. "But a small wedding at St. Andrew's Presbyterian, I think."

"Before my birthday party," he instructed.

Christie looked at her father, wondering why the hurry.

"It would make things simpler."

More *proper*, you mean, Christie thought. Much better for his daughter—the mother of two children—to introduce her escort as "my husband, Rick," rather than some ungainly, socially unacceptable title. Rick and Christie married, January 13, a week before Jim's 60th birthday.

Rick admired Jim right from the beginning, and his opinion hasn't changed over the years. "He's not an easy guy to know," says Rick, "but he has character. I've seen it. I have a tremendous amount of admiration for Jim, and I'm not the only one. He has the respect of some really high-end folks. Few young men can blazon a goal in their hearts and follow it to the end. Jim made his life turn out exactly the way he wanted."

Rick put in many work hours when the kids were young at jobs he didn't really enjoy. He did it for his family, and Jim approved. Rick wonders if his father-in-law knows how much he wanted to fit in the Bayless family. He fantasized about hanging out with Craig and Mike and playing golf, smoking cigars, and "talking about chicks—crazy stuff. Doing things that real brothers do." And he tossed around the possibility that Jim might become "like a father" to him. It hasn't happened, but "what the heck—I keep hoping," Rick adds.

"In general, my parents tell me they are proud of me," Christie says, "but I know they wish I were more conventional, married to a career CEO of a company they've heard of and a member of the country club.... But I raised two healthy and college-educated daughters. Amy Jean, who produces the news on a cable station, is the 'successful child' they've always wanted."

With time, distance, and effort, the strained relations among the Walthers, Jim and Jean, and Craig and Sandra soon eased. In 1980 the young couple moved to Houston where Craig worked as a branch manager for Cushman & Wakefield, one of the largest real estate firms in the world. Sandra and Jean became warm companions. They joke about writing a book that will be part cookbook and part mystery, Jean says, laughing. "We never quite get started, but we love talking about it."

Today, Craig and Sandra make Jim and Jean pop their buttons. Cushman & Wakefield transferred Craig to their Chicago offices in 1986, and he went on to become executive vice-president and partner at Milepost Industries. "Craig is smooth," says Rick. "He's a business guy who dresses fine, smells good, and is married to a woman who is smart and looks good. He owns a fancy house, travels on business, and is the vice-president of his company. They make lots of money. Craig and Sandra are every parent's dream come true. Craig is Jim and Jean's dream of the perfect son."

Joanie and Mike Madden chose a private life. They set up permanent residence within shouting distance of where they grew up in the prestigious west hills of Portland. Joanie worked during the early years of her marriage selling radio advertising. When her husband became a self-employed homebuilder, she got her real estate license for the purpose of listing Mike's spec homes. Mike keeps to himself—isn't much of a talker, especially about business. Jim's relationship with him is reserved but respectful, similar to his relationship with Rick.

February 15, 1983, Joanie gave birth to a boy, Trevor. Jim couldn't have been any prouder than the day he first became a parent himself. The following year, Sandra and Craig would deliver to Jim and Jean a fourth grandchild, Taylor. Trevor's brother, McGregor, came along in May of 1985. The family of Jim and Jean Bayless totaled thirteen.

Chapter Twenty-Two

Jim celebrated his sixtieth birthday at the University Club. Christie's daughters, AJ and Lisa, seven and four in age, respectively, sang "Happy Birthday to Papa." Craig, Christie, and Joanie each said a little something about their father with reverent humor. For the most part, however, Jean held the microphone.

Jim's mother attended the celebration. She later mentioned to Jean that she would have liked to speak. Jean thought, I thought of that, and I didn't ask you. She says today, "Inez' comments on Jim's past would not have been fitting for the occasion. We were all facing forward that day. Jim had no inclination to look behind."

Jean believes she held Jim's best interest at heart. She knew how her husband disliked talking about his years before the war. In fact, he avoided talking about any past—even theirs. He also became irritable if topics previously discussed came up in conversation.

Christie has seen all her life how Jean, quick to sacrifice her own needs, lovingly and with a smile, has catered to her husband's wishes. Christie says, "As a kid, Dad's refusal to discuss the past didn't really matter to me, but as an wife and mother, I think often how that characteristic of his affected Mom. Women want and need to rehash party conversations, to discuss disappointments and happy events, and Dad wouldn't do that. Not being able to just talk to her partner must have made Mom's life quite lonely at times."

Jim's reticent ways set the tone for the family's social dynamics. Christie feels that they seldom talk about "real things." Their

197

conversations have always been a series of "sound bytes." She says, "When we get together, we play cards or golf. We are like the characters in that play *The Cocktail Hour* where the man always goes to the office, the woman wears the pretty pearls, the daughter has some ghosts in her closet, and the son tries to tell the family he carries a deep, dark secret. During the cocktail hour, everybody hides behind their smiles as they fail to talk about all the issues. To a great extent, there you have the Bayless family. We only speak to relate who said what to whom and what is good and what's for dinner and what is pretty and perhaps you'd like another drink."

It's likely that Jim is responsible. Like so many of his generation who grew up in the Depression, he wanted his adult life to focus on "what is pretty" because his childhood left a hole in his heart he can't heal. Or maybe his mother is responsible. Jim and Jean believe that when Jim ran from his past to where he felt good about himself, Inez pulled him back, chiding that he had not yet lived up to his potential.

On one occasion, during one of Jim and Jean's biannual visits to Grants Pass in the mid-80's, they were driving Inez to church. It was a silent morning except for the autumn leaves crackling below the wheels. Suddenly, Inez' voice boomed from the back seat of the large, luxurious Chrysler, "Jim, you hitched your wagon to the wrong star."

Both Jim and Jean flashed her a startled look. With a swift turn of the steering wheel, Jim pulled to a stop at the railroad tracks. He swiveled around, bracing his arm across the top of the front seat. A controlled anger both pushed and contained his words. "You've always wanted me to be only one thing—your brother Randy, a preacher." His face pulsed and reddened. "So you say I hitched my wagon to the wrong star. Well, let me tell you—" He faced her straight on. "I hitched to exactly the right star, and you're benefiting from it. You're riding to church in a nice car. I have a very successful family, Mother, and you have three wonderful grandchildren. You've certainly got some nerve to criticize me."

He turned away, took deep breaths, and then looked over his shoulder. "I've got a good notion to not even take you to church." He sighed. "But let's forget you said that."

In 1971 his mother won the nomination to represent Josephine County in Oregon's *Mother of the Year* competition—"based on her outstanding qualifications as an ideal mother," the newspaper article said. "Good for her," Jim had said. The thought, *Did anyone ask him?* reared for only a moment.

Inez said nothing, even though a silent response to such a berating was quite unlike her. But perhaps she saw it surface in her son for the first time: a deep pain for all the deaths, all the loss, all the wanting he had known as a child. How could she not understand those feelings?

As they continued on to church, she stared at the back of Jim's head. How different he was from her other sons. Then she smiled with the thought:…different even in the way he was losing his hair while Roy and Donald had kept their thick, full manes.

She wondered if Jim knew she loved him—had always had his interest first in her heart. Did he think her a good mother? She sighed, wondering if it had always been that her tongue and arms felt drugged, unable to comfort him. She sat statue still for the duration of the ride, her hands knitted tightly together in her lap.

In future years, en route to church, she would remember that day in the car again and again and feel an ever-so-slight weight press at her chest. After October 29, 1988, it disappeared as she stepped towards the church and passed a marble table. A plaque caught by the sun would gleam. Inez always stopped, read it, feeling both uneasy and proud, and render a tight smile. "Presented by James Bayless to Inez Blanchard," it read, "recognizing 50 years of service to the community of Grants Pass for her teaching and church service." It is there today, although Inez has passed on to be with her Lord in heaven—and with her beloved brother, Randy, who followed her two years later.

Elsie "Muz" Welter died at Thanksgiving in 1982 after complications from osteoporosis and a broken hip. She was eighty-one-years-old.

Jim and Jean heard of her death on their way out the door for a couple weeks in Palm Springs. Jim chose to not cancel the trip. "Put her in cold storage until we get back," he claims he told the nursing home.

That he said those exact words is probably unlikely. Jean constantly rebuffs her husband for his callous comments about his memories. Her recollections reflect a man with a softer edge.

Nevertheless, Jim and Jean went to Palm Springs and held a funeral service for Elsie a few weeks later.

One might think that a "gadget man," as Craig referred to his father, would embrace the computer age. But the leap to technology that required an understanding of virtual memory and microprocessors and cyberspace was a twilight zone Jim refused to enter. It was ledger sheets he understood. Craig says, "Dad's desire for the latest gadget stopped with the VCR and the microwave." In 1983, Jim's firm, gone international since its merger with The Sedgwick Group, made plans to switch to computerization, Jim said, "I don't want any part of it." He had been in the insurance brokerage business forty years. He was about to turn sixty-three, an age to think about retiring and not about playing the game with a whole new set of rules.

He could afford to retire. Smart investing and luck had given him financial security—in spite of one major mistake: In 1978, he invested with Lloyd's, the prestigious London-based insurance market.

When Jim would travel to the home office of Sedgwick, located in London, he did business with Lloyd's. As he walked along the Thames River near his leased flat, he'd bandy about thoughts of investing with them. Acceptance by the organization would mean the recognition of James Bayless—beyond U.S. borders—as a man who had achieved financial success.

The thought of becoming a "name" had an alluring quality for Jim. It was as if he could smell the addictive aroma of freshly-ground, Columbian beans coming from Edward Lloyd's business that got its start as a coffee shop on Tower Street back in 1689. More than an insurance company, Lloyd's is a brokered market of competing and co-operating underwriting syndicates that take big risks with the hope of big returns.

Everyone but Jean's mother encouraged Jim in the Lloyd's venture. He joined twelve of the underwriting syndicates and proceeded to lose half a million dollars as a proliferation of asbestos claims hit the insurer along with malpractice suits. Then the Exxon-Valdez spill occurred in March 1989. Six months later, Hurricane Hugo hit, leaving $7 billion in damages in its wake for the 'names' of Lloyds to cover.

Fred S. James executive Bill Burch relates a story about when he and some other business associates learned about Jim's financial loss. "Certainly bad luck for Jim," he says, "but I have to tell you..." He starts laughing. "I could have made myself a few bucks. Jokingly, I bet some guys at work I could predict how Jim would respond to the Lloyds fiasco. *At least I have my real estate,* he'll say. And that's exactly what he did say." Still laughing, Bill wipes his eyes. "I could have won fifty bucks," he says. "The man has no sense of humor about money. It's the moon and the stars to him.... *What's so funny, Bill?* Jim would ask me. *Can't explain it, Jim,* I'd say, patting him on the back. *There are some things you just can't explain.*"

So, yes, the Lloyd's investments were a mistake. "You were right, Elsie," Jim would chuckle years later, even though he knew full well that her advice was based on characteristic timidity and not market knowledge.

Then there was the door to a potentially smart investment he didn't open.

"I wish he had listened to Dan and me," says Mary Ellen Callahan, a Rancho Mirage neighbor of the Baylesses.

During the early 80's, Mary Ellen and her first husband, Dan Monen, met Jim and Jean on the links at Thunderbird Country Club. The couples became frequent names on one another's social calendar. Although the Baylesses introduced their friends from the cornfields of Omaha to various wonders of the Northwest, they never visited Omaha.

"It's a shame," says Mary Ellen." Dan was the attorney of Warren Buffet, the largest stockholder of Berkshire-Hathaway, a Fortune 500 corporation. My husband made millions and millions of dollars because of Warren's good investment advice. I urged Jim and Jean again and again to visit us. I wanted to introduce Jim to Warren, but it never happened."

"That's the long and short of it," says Jim, "*it never happened.*" He hesitates. His eyes reveal nothing. Then he adds with a pedantic air, "It never serves to wonder what might have been. What's the point?"

He thinks a minute. "Besides. Using my own investment advice, I have made millions in real estate."

Jim retired January 31, 1984. He turned over his job of regional director to Don Moreford, the manager of the Spokane office. Jim had an eye for good businessmen. Eventually, Don became head of Sedgwick's Board of Directors.

The firm threw Jim a farewell party in March at Portland's Red Lion Inn. Bill Lilly, a partner and personal friend, served as Master of Ceremonies. When watching Bill, Jim recalled his early days at Dooly with Bill's father, Claude, the elderly partner who, to Jim's amazement, seemed content to handle only small accounts and receive only the very smallest percentage of the profits.

Ethel Pugh and Michael Wyckoff attended the party. Only four years earlier, the fun-loving women had thrown a "Thanks For the Memories" party when Jim became regional director.

Speaker after speaker said a few words and presented him with humorous gifts, including a ledger sheet from 1952 indicating that Jim was paid $225 twice a month. "I was in the hole that year," Jim interjected with a laugh.

He received an authentic-looking (but "fake") Western Union telegram that poked fun at his undying devotion to the Chrysler Corporation. It read:

DEAR MR. BAYLESS:

I WANT TO PERSONALLY CONGRATULATE YOU STOP ON YOUR CONTINUED SUPPORT OF OUR CHRYSLER CORDOBA STOP AND I AM SURE THE MARKET WILL CHANGE SO THAT SOMEBODY STOP WILL BUY YOUR USED CARS AT HIGHER THAN SCRAP PRICES.

BEST REGARDS:

LEE IACOCCA, CHAIRMAN, CHRYSLER CORP.

With the kids grown and Jim retired, living in Portland lost most of its appeal. A place at the beach sounded better. Two homes, like bookends around their lives, had always served the Baylesses well.

They had their place in the desert. It was time to replace their Portland residence with a home by the sea.

Jim and Jean made plans to build their new beach house in Warrenton, a town of less than five thousand people, situated across Youngs Bay from Astoria, the "Little San Francisco of the Pacific Northwest." Forest, three rivers, and the Pacific Ocean surround the area. Jim and Jean sold their Portland home to live the winters in the desert and spend the summers and winter holidays on Warrenton's Strawberry Hill. From their new home on Malarkey Drive, they could view the Columbia River flowing into the ocean and south. One visitor said, "I can see to San Francisco in the south and all the way north to Seattle."

The Baylesses now owned an Oregon beach house and a villa in Palm Springs. Jean thought a moment about how her life had played out differently from the way she had imagined. When Craig and Christie were young, she told them stories about how they'd one day have a dog or two, lots of sisters and brothers, and a musty old house on the beach. Christie says today, "I suppose she just loved Dad more than she did her own desires."

Jim had little intention of spending all his retirement at either one of his homes. In May, two months after his farewell party, he and Jean boarded the transatlantic liner, the QE2, in the company of their old Portland neighbors, Larry and Margaret Noall. The 963-foot Queen Elizabeth 2 transported them in six days, at 32.5 knots, to Southampton for their visit to London.

People commonly associate ocean liners with romance. Ships such as the Titanic come to mind and the love story that steals the focus from the downing of the great ship. Jim, however, didn't take the cruise for romantic reasons.

A flair for the romantic isn't Jim's way. Save romantic love for the pages of fiction, he figures. So far as he knew, it didn't flow in the Bayless blood. His father died when Jim was too young to consider how his daddy loved Inez. Did he ever look at his wife with tenderness? Did he reveal any inkling of a romantic nature?

Not even Jean, his number one cheerleader, can lay honest claim that the Lord remembered to create Jim with even one romantic bone. "He has never been poetic," she says with a sigh. Then again, in Long Beach, just last month, they were having dinner on the Queen Mary, a ship a hundred plus feet longer and double the tonnage of its sister the Titanic. That night, Jean wrote in her date book with schoolgirl exclamation, "Jim proposed marriage again to me!"

One can only guess, however, how that evening played out. Neither Jean nor Jim recalls the occasion. It seems no Cyrano whispered in the ear of the feckless lover that evening.

Nevertheless, if Jean's notes record the truth, the incident happened. Perhaps the moment was sparked by the fact that retirement allowed Jim to spend more time with his wife. Although he knew better than anyone that he lacked what it took to sweep women off their feet, he conjured up a certain romantic charm. Perhaps as a retired fellow, with middle age in his rearview mirror, Jim found a second wind; he saw again a bit of the young man that could drum up the nerve to ask a pretty girl at Jantzen Beach to dance.

Martha May and Roy Fry had been married thirty-six years when Roy died. In 1983, her husband six years in the grave, Martha May fell in love again. She rarely visited her brother, but when Inez announced a July visit to Portland, Martha May decided to accompany her mother.

Jim looked askance at his sister. "What does he do for a living?" he asked at dinner.

Martha May straightened, realizing Jean must have told him about Chuck. She smiled. "He's a machinist in the plywood industry."

Jim paused, remembering his father-in-law, Mike, so skilled with his hands on any machine and a good man—the best, really. "Okay."

Okay? Martha May looked at her brother, irritated that he thought she wanted his approval. He went back to eating. She watched him. Well, perhaps she did—want him to give a nod to her happiness. It would be nice, she supposed. She picked at her food, and although a large-boned woman and taller than average, she felt herself shrink smaller than the petite and slender Jean, seated across the table. At fifty years of age, Martha May still saw herself as James William's little sister.

"We met at church," she tried. "I sang in choir with his wife before she died. And Chuck knew Roy."

Jim cut his turkey, turning the fork continental style to stab the white slice, and chewed slowly. He dabbed his napkin at his lips and said, "Chuck."

"Yes. Chuck Davis. He's a wonderful man who loves the Lord." She glanced around the table and settled on Jean. "And I love him."

Jean paused in her chewing and smiled back.

"He plays golf," Martha May added.

Jim glanced at his sister over his water glass. Jean said, "Martha May, may I offer you more salad?"

As the family sat around after dinner with coffee and cake, Jim brought out a golf putter. "Picked it up in St. Andrews, Scotland," he said, handing it to Martha May.

She ran her hand across the smooth head of the club: alternating, laminated layers of two exotic woods, one the gold of fall leaves, the other red as berry juice. She fingered the small inlay of ivory. "Beautiful," she said.

"It's a present."

Martha May raised her eyebrows.

"For that new man of yours," Jim said, with a grin that made Martha May think he had just told a joke and was wondering if she got it.

"Oh!" A tingling of surprise shot from her stomach. She nearly dropped the club.

Jim sat down and took a sip of his scotch, setting it down next to his untouched coffee. "With one stipulation," he said.

She waited.

"If this *love* doesn't go anywhere, I want the putter back."

For an active man who loved to play golf, it seemed a bit unfair when Jim's body started betraying him. True, he had been dealing with diabetes for a decade now. The bouts of iritis, an acute inflammation of the eye, had plagued him most of his adult life. But he considered himself a basically healthy man. Injections of insulin and the frequent popping of aspirin had become integrated into the routine of his life.

Then in 1984, the same year Jim retired, he experienced his first Mallory-Weiss tear, a rupture of the esophagus where it connects to the stomach, brought on by the prolonged use of aspirin. Next, he went blind with glaucoma in his bad eye. Then a cornea ulcer appeared.

Jim closed his bad eye. Fluid leaked down his cheek from irritation. "What are my options, doctor?"

Used to Jim's no-nonsense approach to matters, the doctor said, "Well, we can replace the cornea or just remove the whole eye and be done with it."

"What would you do, sir?"

"I'd take it out."

"Well, let's do it, then," said Jim.

Now a one-eyed Titan, he still knew how to forge thunderbolts—nothing could slow him. He continued to drive—just as he had over the years when the iritis blurred his vision in that eye, just as he had when the glaucoma took its sight. He continued to play golf.

As a retired gentleman, Jim could play all the golf he wanted. He still belonged to Astoria Country Club for the summer months. During his visits to Portland, he played at Waverly Golf Club. He'd been a member of the Thunderbird Club since 1977. Fellow golfers, Jim Tonkin and Warren Bean who Jim met when playing at Thunderbird, invited him as their guest to a private men's club called the Committee of 25.

"We need members, Jim," said Warren Bean.

Jim eyed the two men with little interest.

"Special men, of course—those of integrity who can help us build the status of the club again," Tonkin added.

Warren grinned. "We have a good time, Jim. We're a bunch of gung-ho retirees who don't want to sit on our thumbs."

The Committee was a pitiful club in those days, certainly nothing compared to Portland's University Club. Its membership had slumped from the twenty-five who started the Committee some forty years prior. Meetings were held in a caddy shack at the O'Donnell Golf Club in downtown Palm Springs, snug against the base of the San Jacinto Mountains.

Jim joined. He enjoyed the "gung-ho" retirees. Then, he figured he might as well join the O'Donnell Golf Club, too, so he could catch some golf on Tuesday mornings before the weekly luncheon of the Committee. The course held the distinction as the oldest in the

Coachella Valley with only nine holes. It had changed little since its conception in the 1930's.

The Committee began in the 1950's. The founders accomplished good works. The residents of Palm Springs can thank the original Committee members for their first street lights. But the mission statement of the Committee has changed. "Now we don't do anything except what benefits our members," says Jim. "It's a purely social organization."

Like Jim, the members are Republicans. Jim served as treasurer from 1989 for five years. In 1995, the members elected him president. Under his watch, the club expanded to one hundred members—with a waiting list—and built a dining facility. It opened its doors to the wives—on Thursday evenings only—allowing them to hear a speaker and have dinner with their husbands. The Committee hosted entertainers such as Merv Griffin, Tommy Smothers, and Bayless neighbor Carol Channing. Political types spoke such as Oliver North and Jack Kemp, Presidential hopeful Lamar Alexander, the mayor of Palm Springs Sonny Bono, and his wife who succeeded him, Mary. Jean nodded in agreement when a woman friend made the comment about Mr. Bono: "He was a hippie. I wouldn't think of going to hear him speak, but he removed his earring and looks respectable now in a suit."

Jean shared the podium with Jim many times at the Committee, telling tales about the trips they have taken. Although her husband declares that the Committee has lost its philanthropic bent, Jean has done her part to instill interest about issues of consequence. The members invited her in April, 1984, that first year Jim joined, to talk about her involvement in Childhelp USA, an organization dedicated to meeting the needs of abused and neglected children through treatment, prevention, and research. Jean had always cared deeply about children everywhere. She felt determined Jim's retirement wouldn't end that.

Maybe now Jim would join her in her pursuits to help others less fortunate. Yes, they would still travel. Yes, they would continue to enjoy all the leisurely activities their wealth afforded them. But in addition, she hoped that, as a team, they would find a way to give back to a world that had been so kind to them.

Aquarius IV

We wish you a Merry Christmas
Jim, Jean, Craig, Christi and Joanie Bayless

Bayless family Christmas card

Christie, Joanie, Craig, Jean and Jim onboard Aquarius

Jim and friends on the links with Arnold Palmer

Craig, Sandra, and Taylor

Jim and Inez, 1980's

Punch Green, Clark Bullock and Jim

Chapter Twenty-Three

In 1985, Jean and Jim took a cruise to China, and then traveled inland to Beijing. Jim wanted to see the Great Wall, one of the great wonders of the world. Over 4500 miles long, he learned. The first three thousand miles cost three million lives. *One thousand lives per mile,* he calculated, his reserve toward death a finely-honed art after sixty-odd years of practice. The wall extended in a blur into the Gobi Desert. Then a guide said, "By today's standards, this first section would have cost 260 billion American dollars." Jim looked quickly at the guide, unsure he had heard right. He glanced at the wall with a better understanding of its reputation as a "wonder."

Upon returning home, he began immediate plans for their next cruise. No one under Jim Bayless' roof ever wondered where he or she would vacation the following year. "I like seeing the future right in front of me," says Jim. In April of 1986, he and Jean would cruise from Barcelona to southern France, and then to Venice. When Libyan terrorists bombed Berlin's La Belle discothèque and President Reagan, in a declaration against international terrorism, sent American bombers to wage war against Quaddafi, Jim only shrugged at suggestions that traveling the Mediterranean might be too dangerous.

He would deny it if asked, of course, because such a contention would suggest unsound thinking, but Jim's mostly unscratched life made him feel a bit invincible.

Jean loved speaking to groups about their travels. "Mom never held a microphone she didn't like," says Craig. The congregation at Pioneer Presbyterian, the oldest Presbyterian Church west of the Rocky Mountains and the one Jean and Jim attended at the beach, delighted in Jean's ability to link her experiences with spiritual messages.

Jim would watch his wife at the podium as she spoke in emphatic, practiced phrases, her face always smiling, telling him and the world that their life was perfect. He felt proud to be her husband.

After her father died in 1978, Jean had escorted her mother on a cruise on the Mississippi Queen, the largest and most luxurious paddle wheeler ever to travel the river. She enjoyed the trip immensely. In 1987, she convinced Jim to take the cruise with her.

They boarded the steamboat at New Orleans and disembarked at Memphis with the music of the calliope's steam whistles still playing in their ears. Jim had never been much interested in the "King" of rock n' roll, but he yielded to Jean's urgings that they take the tour of Elvis' *Graceland.*

At first he studied the wall of Alabama fieldstone that surrounded the estate. He nodded in agreement to the graffiti: "Here under protest" and "Let me get this straight—Paul is dead, but Elvis is alive?"

Then he noticed Elvis' private airplane, inscribed on the tail with the letters TCB. The same letters appeared on the King's diamond cufflinks. He wondered aloud, "What do you think, Jean? What would TCB stand for?"

"It was his motto," an employee told them.

Jim's look asked the question again.

"TCB—Take Care of Business," the employee said, smiling.

Jim nodded his thanks. So Elvis had respect for something beyond his celebrity status. He put business first. Lord James left *Graceland* with a new appreciation of the King.

Jim and Jean rented a car in Memphis and drove to Bowling Green, Kentucky. Jim wished to see his Uncle Randy. The men hadn't seen one another since Jim's boyhood days in Indiana. He'd seek out Randy for his mother—because she'd asked him to—and a little, yes, out of curiosity. He wanted to see what the man had to say for himself after seventy-four years on this earth. Would he stand as tall as the image his mother always drew of him?

Jim didn't quite know what to think when he saw his uncle—a somewhat arrogant man of the cloth for no righteous reason Jim could discern. Randy Orville Yeager, with a Ph.D. in American history, taught at a small college. He had spent his life working on an encyclopedic treatise on the New Testament that he had carried in the trunk of his car until its publication in 1985.

Jim stared at his uncle and wondered at a legacy of nothing more than eighteen volumes of study about the Bible. *Here is the man my mother hoped I would become.* He stared hard at the alien figure, his mind trying to superimpose his own face on the man before him. It could never have happened, he thought, drawing a deep breath, then letting the feathers settle smooth across his chest.

Jim and Jean traveled on to visit Craig and Sandra and their daughter, Taylor, who lived in the Chicago area. During their visit, the five of them would take a road trip to Browns Valley, two hundred miles away. As they passed endless miles of corn and soybean fields, Craig tugged to recall his memories of the last time he visited the "little burg" with his mother, father, and Christie twenty-five years earlier. A blur of tombstones and turkeys and the face of Aunt Gertrude passed like a Hessler Hills wind through his memory.

A family lived in the farmhouse where Jim had been born more than sixty-six years earlier. Someone lived in the bank. The train station and most of the town's structures Jim remembered were gone, the sites overgrown with grass and weeds.

"Pull over here," said Jim. Something stood on a spot he wished to recall.

A local farmer approached the car. "Can I help you folks?"

Craig assumed that strangers in this area were indeed an anomaly. Kids playing in the ruins of abandoned buildings paused and approached the car. "What kind of car ya got here?" a boy asked, his one eye closed in a squint.

"A BMW," Craig replied.

"I ain't never heard of no such car," the boy said.

Craig studied the dirty boy a moment. He pointed to the emblem on the hood of his car that clearly stated BMW.

"Still ain't never heard of it," said the boy.

Craig shrugged "at the Hoosier urchin." No sense debating the issue. He thought to himself, "Thank God Inez had the sense to leave this place. If Dad had stayed, he might have married a cousin and I would be an idiot."

Jim laughs to hear his son talk so because Craig's winsome ways disallow any other response from the father who has created the perfect son. Handsome and athletic, a prosperous businessman with a loving wife and family, Craig is the man Jim always wanted to see when he looked in the mirror Yet when Craig jokes about Browns Valley, a wisp of sentiment passes through Jim, a simple wish that some things about his childhood might have been different. If his father hadn't died, maybe. As he stood next to Craig before the gravestone of Roy Washington Bayless, he wished for a moment that the grandfather and grandson might have known one another. But, of course, if Jim's father had lived, Inez would never have transported her children to Oregon, Jim wouldn't have met Jean, and Craig never would have been. So Jim shrugged, everyone piled into Craig's BMW, and they drove off.

Yet Jim pauses thoughtfully when Craig says, "I have since whizzed by the exit to Browns Valley on Interstate 65 many times—nothing beckons me to turn off." His thoughts wander to the small ghost town of Roseberry, Idaho, not far from where his oldest daughter, Christie, and her husband, Rick, live in McCall. A small, bright white church sits alone in a pasture of grass. A half dozen rows of tombstones rise up across a narrow, dirt road in an area not much bigger than a large backyard. The area resembles the Freedom Baptist Church and adjoining cemetery of his childhood.

When visiting Christie in McCall, Jim enjoys the experience of Roseberry as if he's back in Browns Valley. When they pass what appears to be a graveyard of old farm machinery, Jim tells his daughter the name of each one and what its purpose was, long ago. "Looking back isn't something my father does very often," says Christie. She attentively basks in these rare moments of sentimentality.

In 1988, Grants Pass High School celebrated its centennial anniversary. "We wish to honor you," said the letter from the school's principal, Greg Ross. Jim and ninety-nine other alumni had been chosen as representatives of "the many people that have helped make [GPHS] a truly outstanding school...by leaving a legacy of excellence."

They took Jim's picture and placed it in a pamphlet titled *Hall of Fame.* Someone composed a paragraph about Jim's accomplishments. His information appeared under the "B" section along with Thomas Blanchard Jr., Class of 1966, the grandson of "Dee" Blanchard and the son of Tommy Dee—so a step-nephew of sorts to Jim. Tom had played football for the New York Giants, among other teams, and just last year had signed on to coach at GPHS.

On June 6, 1988, in the Heater Newman Memorial Gym of GPHS, Jim glanced at his nephew across the room. I've always liked your father, he thought, recalling how when working in a sawmill at age sixteen, Tommy Dee had loaned Jim fifty dollars to attend Medford Business School.

Later, Jim shook the young man's hand warmly. *I owe it all to your father,* flitted through his mind. *Your father and a man named Mr. Calvert—an insurance man from Grants Pass.*

Forty-four years ago, they gave Jim the ball, but he ran with it to the end zone on his own.

Weeks later Jim attended a fundraiser for George H. W. Bush at the Annenburg Estate in Palm Desert. "Punch" Green, National Committee Chairman of Oregon at the time, had encouraged Jim to buy the $2000-per-couple tickets in support of the Vice-President's campaign for the Presidency.

Jim admired Walter Annenberg: his estate with seven small lakes and a golf course, his business success as an entrepreneur and generosity as a philanthropist, his prestigious appointment by Nixon as ambassador to England, and his philanthropic gifts in the name of education.

As Jim stood sipping good scotch at the elegant estate, dressed in formal attire next to his beautiful, blond wife, he experienced a flash of fantasy. How fun it would be to forecast the future in the ear of a small boy in Browns Valley still sitting, according to Jim's memory, in an outhouse, turning the pages of a Montgomery Ward catalog.

Jean moved through the reception line on Jim's arm. As everyone in turn shook the hand of Vice-President and Mrs. Bush, a photographer snapped a picture for publicity purposes.

"Where can we get our copy?" Jim joked later with Punch.

"Doesn't work that way, pal," Punch said, smiling. "Well, gotta go take care of things."

As Punch stepped away, Jim called out, "What's the matter? Forget to put film in the camera?"

Chapter Twenty-Four

Jim Bayless doesn't consider himself an Annenberg, even on a small scale. The tag *philanthropic* doesn't really fit him. The word compassionate feels a bit long in the sleeves as well. "Domineering, confident, ambitious, religious..." he labels himself. But philanthropic? "No, not really." He shifts in his chair, and then adds, "People who have as much as we do would probably give more." He sits taller, assuming a defiant bearing he's more accustomed to. "I don't think of myself as generous. I certainly wouldn't give anything if I couldn't afford it. Besides," he says slowly, "what I give is tax deductible."

His beginnings as a *benefactor* "all began on the Astoria golf course," Jim says. "I was playing with a Chinese friend, a photographer, who said that with all my money, I should be helping young people who can't afford to send themselves to college. Jean and I talked about it. We decided he was quite right."

Jim had never been persuaded by all the hoopla around getting a college education. He hadn't needed one to stake his place in the world. His own "education" spanned a lifetime. He learned as he went, forging a prosperous career that would eventually allow him to travel and touch first hand the pulse of the world. Jim came to admit, however, that a few solid years of study early on about business and the world might have done him some good. College could have provided a jumpstart to his successes.

A number of factors prompted Jim and Jean to choose Warrenton, Oregon, for their first stab at philanthropy. They had a connection to the town since they worshiped on Sunday at Warrenton's Pioneer Presbyterian Church during the months they lived at the beach. Offering a scholarship award to the high school would allow them to give back to a community of the coastal area they had enjoyed for over three decades.

The high school served children of blue-collar workers that, more likely than not, couldn't afford a university education. "Nearly all the students in the graduating classes, which average about forty students, need financial help," says Jean. "We could throw a dart." Jim knew only too well how a lack of money might forever leave a young person with his nose pressed against the glass to his dreams. Beyond that, he and Jean would take particular pride in the fact that the meager awards given to the small high school promised that the Bayless donation of a full college scholarship would receive special recognition. In 1989, they offered their first award.

"The Bayless Scholarship is the buzz word around school," says Jean. "I get goose-bumps during the awards ceremony."

Warrenton holds the event during the school day. The whole student body attends. Jean prefers this format rather than holding a special ceremony for just the winners and their parents: "I want the younger students to know that the scholarship lies in their future if they choose to stand up and go after it. I heard a freshman boy tell a friend, *That lady says I can do it.* And three years later, he did."

The ceremony takes place in the school gym with most of the student body in the bleachers. The seniors sit in chairs on the gym floor. On markings indicating center court stands a podium flanked by chairs for the representatives of community groups, individuals, and foundations who present awards that vary from twenty-five dollars to a couple hundred, to the Bayless scholarship of eight thousand. All stand to recite the Pledge of Allegiance. Most of the kids are white, "many in baggy clothes with an attitude to match," says Christie, who has worked as a substitute teacher at Warrenton. Only those in competition for the awards sit upright and attentive.

Her speech is Jean's favorite part of the whole process, even though she thoroughly enjoys how she and Jim pick their yearly winner. They take turns with the applications, ranking them according

219

to the criteria of financial need, grade-point average, involvement in their school and town activities, and their likelihood to graduate. Then Jim and Jean compare notes, delighting in the fact that they often wave in the air the name of the same applicant as the most deserving.

But presenting the speech—dressed as if she came directly from a *Vogue* photo shoot, her husband a glossy image from *GQ*—is the highlight of the yearly event for Jean. "It's the part Mom likes best," says Christie. "She composes her speech with the full intention of encouraging the students—and particularly the girls—to look at her and see that the confidence, poise, and success they see before them can be theirs."

Jean says, "One year, I noticed a girl with a guy who had his arms all around her. She might have been a sophomore. She managed to get herself untangled and watched me ever so carefully. I know she was thinking, *She seems so important. I could be like that.*"

Jim stands next to his wife during the speech, silent but pleased how she draws the spotlight to the both of them. He announces the recipient of their award, which pays to any Oregon state college two thousand dollars per year over a maximum four-year period.

The restrictions Jim places on the scholarship are quite specific. "Why pay the extra costs for a private school?" he often says, not really asking. "Our public institutions are quite satisfactory." And Jim won't pay for more than four years. "Students should get through in four." The eyes of his family members will drift. They've heard this speech a dozen times throughout the years.

A harangue by Andy Rooney on *60 Minutes* in January of 2002 led to fresh material for Jim's speech. "Finishing college in a reasonable time period would be a simple matter if the kids didn't get so much time off. Joanie's son Trevor, for example, came home from Carroll College a week before Christmas and doesn't go back until the middle of January! I agreed with Andy Rooney's every word."

In 1998, when Jim was ill and he and Jean could not attend the Warrenton awards ceremony, their daughter Christie offered to present the Bayless Scholarship. She had been substituting at Warrenton High for a few weeks and many of the teachers and students knew her. In a conversation with another teacher about her plans to present at the upcoming ceremony, Christie said, "Isn't it obvious I'm Jean Bayless' daughter? I look just like her." The teacher replied sheepishly, "I never would have guessed—your shoes are so *quiet.*" Christie laughed, knowing the teacher was referring to Jean's trademark gay, colorful shoes.

Christie had spent many an occasion laughing at her mother—and father, too, poking fun at them with flippant humor. As daughters often do, she had exerted years of effort to not become her mother. And yet there she stood at the podium, representing Jean Bayless and feeling proud. The words—her mother's, her own—related a belief that a college education is vital to success and maturity. It struck Christie then, the import of her parents' goals for the students at Warrenton. They wanted for them just what they've always wanted for their own daughter, that they succeed in life.

Jim and Jean receive notes and letters from the students they have sponsored over the last decade, thanking them not only for the money but also for the opportunity. Due to the power of some phenomenon that defies statistics, all their award recipients have graduated from college in four years. Cathy Gach, the principal at Warrenton, wonders if college acceptance boards might glean some insight from Jim and Jean Bayless. Christie wonders: Perhaps the power of Jean's award speech actually stays with them all four years. *Dare they disappoint Mom and Dad? Dare they fail to meet the expectations of this couple that possess so much hope for their success?*

One recipient had a difficult journey, requiring time in a community college before finally making it at a university. She persevered, with the Bayless couple cheering on the sidelines, and then she graduated. *Of course,* thought Jim and Jean, nodding and smiling as they in turn shook her hand at the podium. In 2001, they attended her wedding.

College and then marriage—the perfect sequence of events for a young woman, Jim thought as he dressed for the wedding. Jean was helping him with his tie. He couldn't help how he thought about women. His daughters had chided him on occasion about being sexist. But such an attitude had paid off in his own life. What would he have done without Jean? Would he and so many people around him have benefited if she hadn't chosen *wife* as her profession of priority?

"I don't like the Pentecostal Church," said Jean, glancing at the wedding invitation before they headed to the ceremony.

"The *love, honor, and obey* part has its merits," said Jim, as he checked his tie in the mirror.

Jean saw clearly behind the "joke" that reflected her husband's sense of truth. A slight frown appeared on her smooth brow, reminding anyone who knew her well that she had spent a lifetime biting her tongue to focus on Jim's view of the world. But she also had her moments. She could tell anyone who asked—and even those who didn't—that she had made her own choices and felt no regrets.

The groom came down the aisle first with the bride trailing behind. The minister said *obey* a number of times. Jean closed her eyes briefly each time to ask God for patience. With the final blessing of the minister, the couple left the church as they came, the bride trailing the requisite number of steps behind the groom. Later, Jean watched as Jim put his arm around the bride's waist and said, "Forget that *obey* business." A smile burst across Jean's face. After fifty-seven years of marriage, the man could still surprise her.

Jim stepped away to sit down, and Jean brought him a scotch. "Thank you, Jean," he said, his glance and tone honoring and respectful. Then he turned away, raised his glass with a sophisticated air, and resumed speaking to group at his table. He was relating his favorite tale about how fruit manufacturers manage to leave a maraschino cherry unmarred after removing its pit—he knew for a fact because Bun Stadelman, one of largest cherry processors in North America, had told him.

Jean approached the groom and whispered, "Forget that *obey* business." He looked blankly at her just as the bride had to Jim. Neither, it seems, had been listening to the minister. Jean smiled. How typical for two people in love, she thought. She sought out Jim again and caught his smile, always perfect, always the same. If she asked, what would he say he remembered about their own wedding?

She sighed. She wouldn't ask. Long ago she'd learned what he felt in his heart and what made it to his lips were two different things. He'd say the church and the ceremony were beautiful. He'd say he wasn't nervous because he's never been nervous in his life. He'd say he didn't have to look at her directly because he knew she was there at his side—and always would be.

Jean watched the groom kiss his bride tenderly. A wedding ceremony, she mused, should only be about love and a lifetime commitment to that love. Nothing else. Learning to obey will never get a marriage through money and family problems. It won't nurture trust or devotion.

Her radar for Jim's baritone voice reached her easily across the crowd. "…and not a blemish on the cherry!"

She smiled. And learning to obey won't make you want to laugh at the same old story you've heard a thousand times. Only love will do that.

$\mathcal{C}hapter\ \mathcal{T}wenty\text{-}\mathcal{F}ive$

Jim was five years into his retirement when the Committee of 25 elected him treasurer in 1989. Tuesday afternoons and Thursday evenings he devoted to the Committee. He played golf three or four days a week. During the summer, he and Jean would move back to the beach. They traveled.

In March of 1990, they visited Israel to "walk in the footsteps of Jesus." They saw everything from the Basilica of the Nativity where Jesus was born to the Golan Heights where He spent his last days of peace before the final journey to Jerusalem. Bits and pieces from the Beatitudes recited in Jim's memory as they stood where Jesus gave the Sermon on the Mount. He could hear the words on the lips of a parade of preachers, beginning with Pastor Lamkin at the Oregon Christian Center. At the Jordan River, Jim tried to imagine the humbled John the Baptist baptizing Jesus, but he could only picture his own dunking in Sugar Creek.

Jim and Jean recall the 1992 trip to Africa as one of their favorites. The cruise ship started in Sydney, Australia, sailed south to Tasmania and on to Durban, South Africa. A chartered DC3 plane waited at Johannesburg and flew a group from the ship to Botswana for a week. Four couples and a guide filled a safari car that drove slowly down trails in the early morning and again at twilight. The guide had looked at Jean when he advised the group to wear quiet colors.

Jim says, "We saw tigers, lions, zebras, and herds of elephants. Hell of a different experience seeing an animal in the zoo and in the wild. We even saw a python."

They took a side trip to Zimbabwe, to the Zambezi River and Victoria Falls, which span a mile and drop four hundred feet, the farthest drop of any falling water in the world. After reaching the gorge below, the spray rebounds a thousand feet back to the sky.

"It was quite the adventure," says Jim, with childlike glee. "We got wet. Soaked to the skin. Even ruined the camera." He smiles, remembering. "But it was thoroughly worth it."

They stayed at the Victoria Falls Hotel, built in 1904, an ostentatious structure of Edwardian style, reputed for its "romantic" ambiance (although Jim would never use those words) as the evening buffet is served under the stars and the falls provide a muted roar behind the music.

After returning to the ship, Jim and Jean headed to India and took a side trip to the Taj Mahal. The poet Rabindranath Tagore described the marble mausoleum as "whispers in the ear of eternity." A 19th century surveyor suggested authorities preserve the "pearl of moonlight" under a glass case. Discussion Jim heard about devising such a "glass case" intrigued him. It seems that an oil refinery in the surrounding city of Agra had blackened the sky and produced cracks in the Taj's white marble.

Another aspect of his visit to the mausoleum, however, disturbed him. He was appalled at the gruesome stories that Shah Jahan, the emperor who ordered the temple built, had the hands of the craftsmen severed and the eyes of the chief architect gouged so that they would never again create anything to compete with the beauty of the Taj Mahal.

Grief due to a deep devotion to his wife, Mumtaz Mahal, motivated Shah Jahan to build the mausoleum. She had been his inseparable companion, his comrade during battle, and his counselor who encouraged his benevolent acts for the needy. She died giving birth to his fourteenth child. When asked how he felt about the reason for the building the Taj, Jim replied without a moment's hesitation, "It was a waste of money!"

His voice boomed with emotion. "The outer grounds are teeming with dirt and grime and peasants selling things. I imagine the people are as poor now as they were in the early 1600's." His voice softened. "It's a shame. So much poverty just beyond walls inlaid with turquoise, jade, and sapphires."

In August of 1993, Jim and Jean traveled to London. Jim made his way to Lloyd's in his continuing battle to disengage himself from the company. Jean said she'd like to visit Buckingham Palace. "But, I wasn't excited about taking another museum tour," she said, recalling their visit to Russia. "The guide at the Summer Palace of Peter the Great went on forever about all the art of those ancient people with bulging eyes," she says. "Then I got chastised because, feeling tired, I sat on a royal trunk or something. When I tried to go ahead of the tour, I was told to come back."

Neither Jim nor Jean tolerated well the common procedure for viewing museums. Tour guides expounding too long on whatever topic and the tedious momentum of shuffling along behind mesmerized tourists tried their patience. To save Jean a repeat of the St. Petersburg experience, Jim made arrangements through Lloyd's for a private car to deliver Jean to Buckingham with a pre-purchased ticket.

People in the long line stared as the limousine passed and dropped Jean near the entrance. A suited, British gentleman with a chin he jutted repeatedly, just slightly, offered his arm to Jean, and they walked in. Then he left her on her own. "I'm sure everyone was impressed," she says. Then someone came along and attached herself to Jean with conversation. Jean sped up her pace and lost the woman. She headed up "a magnificent stairway" and down again, relishing in the joy of doing it alone, free of anyone who might impede her singular flow.

Jim and Jean had taken the whole family with them on exotic trips: to Hawaii in 1965 and 1986 and to the Cotswolds of England in 1977—less Christie's family that time because Christie would travel to Europe later that year with her two daughters and Jean. In December of 1988, all thirteen of the Jim and Jean Bayless bloodline flew to Puerto Vallarta. The oldest grandchildren, Amy Jean and Lisa, sixteen and thirteen, respectively, accompanied Christie and Rick. Craig and Sandra's daughter, Taylor, and Joanie and Mike's boys, McGregor and Trevor, were all preschoolers.

Jim rented a house to stay at Mismaloya Beach, where filmmakers shot Tennessee Williams' "Night of the Iguana." Rick says, "We stayed at a magnificent, hillside mansion with a waterfall, swimming pool, and parrots flying around. A paradise." When the thirteen gathered in the living room, Jim smiled with deep pride at his lineage.

"There's a humorous family story about that trip," says Rick. "A young, Mexican woman did our cooking. Her husband helped out making the beds and such and working in the garden. Neither one spoke any English. Amy Jean had studied Spanish for two years in school, but because she's so shy, even if she were on fire, she wouldn't make a sound. So communicating with the help was difficult. One evening, after a number of Mexican beers, margaritas, and a fantastic meal, we were stuffed. The cook cleared the table and immediately brought in a key lime pie. 'Oh no,' said Jean, 'not yet.' She threw her arms up in her typical, theatrical way. Jean could have been saying *alligator* for all the woman knew, but she did get the message to take the pies away. Well, after a half hour or so, we were ready for dessert and Jean went into the kitchen. 'Oh no!' she exclaimed for the second time that night. We all rushed to the kitchen." Rick starts laughing. "You should have seen the horrified look on Jean's face! It seems the cook had thrown the key lime pies into the garbage…. The family is still laughing about that one."

To mark their 50th wedding anniversary, Jim and Jean announced that they would like everyone in the family to join them in France for two weeks during August of 1994. As usual, they would foot all expenses.

Amy Jean had a conflict of interests. Working at Boston University on dual undergraduate degrees—one in Broadcast Journalism and the other, International Relations—she had hoped to practice her Mandarin and teach English in Shanghai that summer. Rick and Christie wouldn't hear of it.

"You know how it works, Amy Jean," Rick told her. "The whole family goes or Jim and Jeana cancel the whole deal."

"But—" AJ said softly, then nodded. She'd never been one to put up a fight.

"Go next year," Christie said, her mind always scheming with ideas—and then a better one. "Isn't that a possibility? Maybe you'll want to stay even longer than the summer." When AJ opened her mouth to respond, Christie added, "Sorry, no discussion. France is a family requirement."

Truthfully, though, Christie thought the France trip a wonderful opportunity for her girls. Rick agreed. They'd always appreciated the rich cultural experiences Jim and Jean's vacations offered. Over the years, however, Christie often found herself wishing her parents would just find a simple vacation spot—on Laguna Beach, for example. Why not someplace comfortable and relaxed where they might sit around, focusing on one other rather than the surroundings? No, it had to be castles and chalets on foreign soil or, if domestic, someplace like Martha's Vineyard.

Amy Jean sighed.

Her mother smiled, and then cocked her head with an empathetic twist of the mouth as if to say, *You know the drill by now, daughter dear.* Rick gave her one of his hugs that embraced the tiny AJ like a bear trying to get his arms around the spindle-shank of an aspen.

The Bayless brood stayed two weeks near Nice in a renovated castle built in the 1400's. Jim rented three vans, one for each family. An English-speaking cook and maid service added to the ambiance of luxury. The bedrooms all had private baths. Besides the castle itself, only tennis courts and a pool interrupted the 1500 acres of garden and greenery. Jim taught his favorite card game, Pitch, to Craig's daughter, Taylor, age ten, and to Joanie's boys: Trevor, eleven, and McGregor, nine. Then he spent delightful hours each day, poolside, trying to hold his own against their determined effort to beat him.

One evening, Jim directed the entire family to the terrace. Jean, in hot pink long slacks and an "artist's" smock spattered with gold, purple, and pink splashes of color, walked at his side. Dressed for dinner in classy tan pants and a pale silk shirt, open at the neck, Jim announced with a formal air his formation of the Bayless Family Partnership. To avoid the gift tax law, which takes its share of anything over $10,000, Jim would make his children and grandchildren limited partners in his real estate business.

"Craig, you and your sisters now own six percent," Jim said. His smile extended to Joanie and Christie. "Taylor, Trevor and McGregor each have 1¼ percent." The boys, dressed in tennis shoes, baggy shorts to the knees, and black t-shirts with cartoon figures, gave a thumbs up. Jim sought out the dark-haired AJ, his eldest grandchild, so petite and easily lost in a crowd. "The same for Amy Jean and Lisa."

Lisa, fair-haired and an alert, round, bright presence, stood close by. "Thank you, Papa," said the young woman of nineteen. She hugged Jim in the sincere, loving way she always had.

A paper identifying Jim and Jean as the general partners followed by a list of the eight limited partners made its way around the room. Trevor called out to Rick. He and McGregor, thinking their uncle "cool," honored him with the affectionate name of "Uncle Skippy." Trevor asked, "Uncle Skippy, what are all these names here for?"

McGregor interrupted by teasing, "Those are all the people you have to kill off so you can get all the money."

Everyone roared. Jim and Jean smiled and waited for everyone to focus once again with appropriate decorum on the import of Jim's announcement.

"Jean and I will retain 75% ownership," he continued. "I'm proud that I made that money and can pass it on to my family."

Jean mailed off a check for $38,000 to each of their three children last year. "Christie sort of depends on it, while it's a little extra for Craig and Joanie," Jim says. "We don't give Christmas gifts any longer. Everyone opens a check as our present." He adds, "Every few years Jean and I increase the percentage of the 'partners.' Last year grandchildren each received around $8,000. They're fine kids. I'm damned proud of very one of them. That's saying a lot when so many kids these days are bad apples."

Family Vacation in France, 1994. Lisa, Jean, Amy Jean, Jim, McGregor, Trevor, and Taylor

Christie and Rick Gorsline

Jean and Jim

Joanie and Mike Madden

Amy Jean Kelley Goodwin

Joanie, Mike, Christie, Muz, and Craig

Taylor Bayless

McGregor and Trevor Madden

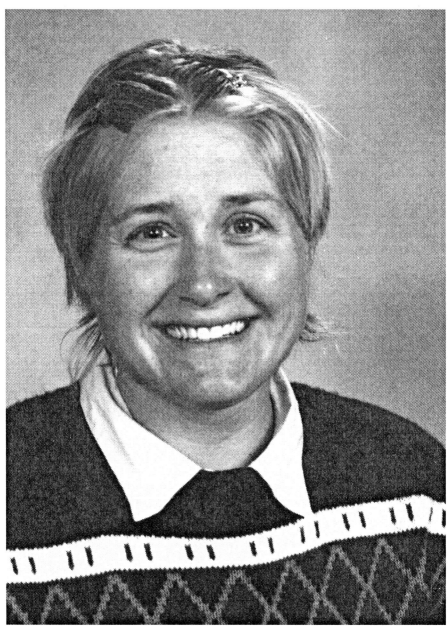

Lisa Kelly Parmentier

Chapter Twenty-Six

Jim and Jean understood the respective lifestyles of Craig and Joanie. Their conversation and social calendars suggested they were of the same ilk as their parents. On occasion, however, the focus of Christie and Rick confused them. But when Christie broke the news to her parents in 1991 that she and Rick planned to buy a Crealock 37 sailboat, Jim and Jean looked at one another with bright smiles and said, "How wonderful."

Secretly, however, Christie and Rick had a dream that flaunted opposition to everything her parents believed in. The couple held no reverence for the work ethic that bound them to fulltime jobs and the investment of their money for retirement. Rick, a manager of car dealerships, was no Jim Bayless and never would be. His and Christie's breaths went shallow at the thought of working until they were "too old to enjoy our lives." *Let's sail off and see the world,* they schemed. *Let's do it while we're young.*

In the spring of 1993, Christie drove her father back to her Redlands home from one of Lisa's track meets. "Dad," she said, drawing out the vowel with cooing warmth.

"Christie," he replied, smiling.

Christie took a deep breath and oozed excitedly, "Rick and I plan to sell our home and move onto our boat, *Nanook*."

Jim watched his daughter, listening carefully.

"We paid off the boat. We have money in the bank. We'll both work until we have enough money to sail off." She smiled. "Like you and Mom, we want to see the world." She inhaled. Her foot slipped off the accelerator. *One sentence too many, Christie.* Now her father would say they hadn't yet paid their dues. He'd say, "Your mother and I can travel now because we have worked hard all our lives for the right to enjoy our money."

But instead, Jim smiled and said, "That sounds absolutely wonderful."

Christie breathed. In October of 1995, she and Rick sailed out of Long Beach, their hearts on a course for a sail around the world.

A year later, almost to the day, Jim and Jean realized a dream of their own. After selling their beach house, they moved into a luxury home at Thunderbird Heights in Rancho Mirage, California. Traditionally the owners of two homes simultaneously, a single residence would now do, but one that was twofold in spacious elegance from anything they had owned before.

If standing just inside the front door, the 6700-square-foot house appears as simply a living room with a cathedral ceiling and gray slate flooring. The eye is drawn immediately to the light pouring in at the glass back wall, which slides open to the pool. A sparse but perfect number of chairs, sofas, and glass tabletops dot the room, dwarfed by the vast space above them. Doorways off this main area lead to bedrooms, a family room, an office, a dining room, and the kitchen that flank one side or the other of the one-story house.

Jim and Jean had spent less than four days in their new home when it happened. Jean phoned her three children with the news: "Your father has had a stroke. A serious one."

It was early Halloween morning. Jim was reading the newspaper in his favorite chair. When he stood and tossed the paper, it fell short of the ottoman. At breakfast, his spoon missed the bowl. Jim mentioned these incidents to Jean. "I'm taking you to the hospital," she said.

Jim got into the passenger side of the car just fine. Five minutes later, however, outside the emergency entrance to Eisenhower Hospital, he couldn't get out. Getting help so quickly, the doctors said, probably saved his life.

From the ER, the medical staff transferred him to ICU. "The next day," says, Bill Burch, retired president and CEO of Fred S. James and one of Jim's first visitors, "he announced he was ready to begin physical therapy." The nurse smiled and said, "I'll tell your doctor."

Jean told the children not to catch a flight right away. Their father's life wasn't in danger and a Thanksgiving visit would be soon enough. He would begin therapy immediately and continue at home.

Six days later, the hospital released Jim. Sam, a fulltime physical therapist, originally from the Philippines, arrived with the necessary equipment that same day. Jim had dismissed the option to receive inpatient therapy for a few months at Loma Linda's University Medical Center, two hours away. A rehabilitation facility at his home struck Jim as more ideal.

"Nicer for Dad, but harder on Mom, I think," says Christie. Jean could have stayed in a hotel while others attended to Jim's rehabilitation needs. She could have found time for an occasional break and spent time alone at the new house. But something about recuperating at his own hearth made it easier for Jim to believe he could get past this more recent medical annoyance. From the moment the doctor announced his diagnosis, Jim clenched his jaw in determination that the condition wouldn't interfere with his life for very long.

Sam, "a good Christian," he proudly confessed, attended Jim from seven in the morning until seven at night. Jean liked it that he wore a white uniform and said, "Good morning, ma'am. Good morning, sir." Neither she nor Jim, however, appreciated his overzealous, evangelical tendencies as he worked. "Let's stick to business," Jim admonished.

Sam's constant presence began to grate on Jean's nerves almost from the very beginning. Then two female physical therapists started working with Jim an extra couple of hours twice a week. Jean felt an outsider in her own home. Stewing with resentment, she tried to find her place. She'd scoot Sam away from business beyond the scope of his job description—such as the wash. "He'd love to put Jim's swim trunks in the washer and then a hot dryer," Jean says. "One day he got hold of a good pair of Jim's slacks and a cashmere sweater. He ruined the both of them."

Jim's attitude toward the therapists was *Come in. Stay as long as you need to. I'll do whatever you say.* But Jean didn't like it that strangers had a place in her home before she'd found her own. She hated it when one of the women therapists sat on the bed in the master bedroom when trying to maneuver Jim. The therapist soiled the bedspread with the soles of her shoes as she braced herself against the bed frame. And the woman called her husband *Jim.* "Miiissster Bayless," Jean would correct.

Jim forbade any negative comments about the therapists. They were his lifesavers. *Just let it all be over soon,* Jean would pray.

The women therapists talked Jim into having a ramp built on the left side of the house so he could make it from the pool area to the garage. Jean could then help Jim into the car and place his wheelchair in the trunk. "I didn't go for the idea," Jean says. "Construction workers would bring more chaos. Unfortunately, I sounded like a witch concerned more about the house than Jim." Agitated all over again, she adds, "The truth was, they didn't know him. He wasn't going to stay in that wheelchair. So why go to all the wasteful effort?"

But they did. A couple of thousand dollars later, a ramp with green, indoor-outdoor carpeting bordered the back of the house and around the garage. No wheelchair, however, ever crossed it. The man who planned to play golf again put all his energy into exercises that would get him to walk rather than ride a ramp.

"Mom and Dad were committed to avoiding, both publicly and privately, the label *invalid,*" says Christie. "There would be no hospital-looking environment at the house. No walker or wheelchair in the living room. They were determined that Dad would soon walk everywhere on his own."

Craig's family arrived for Thanksgiving. Christie flew in the day after. She saw her father before he noticed her. He was in a wheelchair, his whole right side sloping, his face "droopy" as he tried to write with his left hand. She reached out weakly for the arm of a chair as she sat. "I was absolutely horrified, freaked out, devastated," she says. "Where was my tower of strength? My dad's not a big man, and certainly not muscular because he has never really worked out. But," she adds, "he had always presented such a strong image. Oh! To see him there, unable to get up...to see him slacked off on one side...."

Years and years before, I visited him in the hospital and was horrified then, too, for no other reason than he was in a prone position. He'd had minor surgery to his knee, I think. But it occurred to me that I had never seen my father lying down."

Jim looked up, then, and said, "Hello, Christie."

"The way he says my name 99% of the time," says Christie, "feels as though he is slipping a velvet blanket over me. So adoring."

She felt it instantly then, the certainty that flows in the veins of every Bayless, that this negative state of affairs would not linger in their lives for long. Her father would soon be out of that chair. She felt the will of her father saying, "I'm still me inside of this body and before long, you'll see it too."

Jean took a trip to Oregon for a needed break. "Dad didn't understand," says Christie, "that he wasn't the only one who had the stroke. Mom suffered every excruciating minute, struggling to recover right along with him."

Jim returned immediately to handling his real estate. "Taking care of business is his reality, his anchor," says Christie. It played as an important role as any therapist in helping him walk again.

Since Jim couldn't write, Christie wrote checks for him and balanced figures according to his precise instructions. With a laugh, she says, "I acquired insight into how some of his employees must have suffered." Jim didn't say, "Now, this is what I'd like you to do. I'll be back in an hour." Instead, he micromanaged over his daughter's shoulder every minute. "Key in this number. Good, now hit *add*."

"Dad," Christie said with a tender lilt in her voice, "who's going to take care of the books for you?"

"Jean will."

"Dad?"

He looked at her, his middle child who had a tendency on occasion to call him on his proclamations for the family.

"Mom would take on the world if you passed it to her, but I don't think you married her to become your secretary."

He immediately hired Kim, a staff person at the Committee of 25. When she quit due to a family concern, Jim hired George, the controller for Thunderbird Country Club.

Jim was on his way back. He had resumed control of the real estate business, even if he could accomplish the task only by "micromanaging" someone else's hands. He worked hard at home with his therapists—obsessively hard. At six weeks, he could stand.

He ached for contact with the outside world. Responsibilities beckoned him. Four more months of his term of president for the Committee of 25 awaited him. On December 12th, Jim asked Ward Lewis, the vice-president, to drive him to a meeting. Jim stood when the Committee members applauded his return, and he fell. Fortunately, someone caught him. When Jim attempted to stand at the microphone a week later, he fell again.

Jim offered to resign as president. Vice-president Ward Lewis and Tom Moore, retired president of ABC Network and Jim's eventual successor as president of the Committee, responded, "That is not acceptable."

Then Jim's diabetes started acting up. Emergency medics came frequently to the house. Jim's stroke and the ensuing complications took a toll on Jean. After noting in her date book each backward step, she would raise her chin and think, *Unsinkable us!* She spoke the words like a mantra to recoup her spirit and to restate the commitment to Jim she first made more than fifty years ago.

Another important woman in Jim's life had drawn strength in a similar fashion: his mother. When Inez experienced hard times, she would repeat the verse from II Corinthians 4: 8.9—*We are troubled on every side, yet not distressed; we are perplexed, but not in despair...persecuted, but not forsaken; cast down, but not destroyed.* Inez said, "That verse helped me so many times [over the years]."

In rallying support for their president, the Committee of 25 re-elected Jim in March 1997. The following month, they hosted a tribute to him titled, "This is Your Life." Craig, Christie, and Joanie sent thoughts and memories to be shared at the ceremony.

Craig said, ".... It is not well known that James Bayless was and continues to be a Renaissance man. He has at various times been a landscaper, barbeque chef, begonia farmer, angler, poultry farmer, umpire, vacation planner, lumberjack, antique dealer, real estate developer, entrepreneur, church elder, driving instructor, explorer, scotch taster, judge, jury, executioner, father of the bride, father of the groom, in-law, outlaw, bartender, grandfather, and a yachtsman who won the coveted "Boner's Trophy" from the Portland Yacht Club…*Golfer* is not on the list. Most of you have probably endured a round or two with Jim. I'll leave it to your discretion to decide whether or not Jim is a golfer…. We all know that about six months ago, Jim suffered a stroke. This has temporarily challenged his mobility. Not to worry. The determination that drove him to strive for and win the coveted Boner's Trophy will see him through this crisis. He will emerge like the butterfly—okay, the moth—more beautiful than before. Love you, Dad!"

Christie said, "…To my dad, more than anything, *character counts.* He's impressed by the values a person demonstrates. Today we hear about business and political leaders with a variety of versions of the truth. But Dad raised us heralding the motto: *Tell the truth and you'll never need to remember what you said….* Dad is honest. Just ask the IRS. They audit him often and can't find a single extra dollar to charge…"

Joanie wrote: "…Jim always knew where he was headed, years in advance. His idea of spontaneity was making vacation plans five years in advance instead of the usual ten. Jim's favorite saying was, 'I may be wrong, but I'm never in doubt.' That brings light to all his personality traits. Here are some of his phrases heard during his children's formative years: Who's feeding the damn dog? *What are your plans for next summer, Craig?—it's already October.* Schoolteachers get too much damn time off. *Joanie, be good or I'll let Christie out.* Put down the goddamn comic books and look at the Grand Tetons. *Kids, you can go to any college, as long as it's in Eugene.* Girls, marry for money—you'll learn to love him."

Bill Burch, Jim's former boss, came in person. He said, "Well, James. We share many things including the same birthday, we worked for the same company, and retired on the same day…. Unfortunately our company—now called Sedgwick—belongs to the Brits, but that's another story…."

Bill pulled out a hand-written letter. "Jim, can you guess who wrote this?" He read:

> *Jim greatly influenced my career at Sedgwick. In fact, he hired me. I remember when we first met Bun Stadelman,*

whose family owns one of largest fruit companies in North America. That's when I got my first insight into Jim's abilities. Normally when making a call, you expect to exchange some pleasantries. Not with Jim Bayless. We shook hands, business was handled, and out the door we went. On the way home I asked him, "How do you take it upon yourself not to do any chit-chatting?" His response was, "I do business when I'm doing business. I do pleasure when I'm doing pleasure. I socialize when I socialize." Later on, I met some of Jim's clients and asked them about Jim's style. The response was unanimous: "He values my time. I wish more conducted business as he does.... I have great confidence in his ability to handle my affairs...."

Everyone smiled knowingly at Jim. Bill continued reading the letter.

When Jim first hired me, he said I could have a company car similar to whatever vehicle I was driving. At that time I was driving a Porsche. A Porsche? Jim said, obviously surprised. He couldn't quite understand why someone would pay $25,000 for a car. I told him the type of person who would spend that kind of money on a car is the same kind of person who would buy a 55-foot pleasure boat."

The room chuckled.

I was the manager of the Portland office, Bill read on, *when Jim told me he was thinking about retiring. After a year passed, I approached him and asked if he could be more specific about his plans. He said, "I'm leaving tomorrow." I said, "Jim you can't leave tomorrow. You have to give two weeks notice." He said, "You've got my two-week notice. I'll use my carry-over vacation for the two weeks time." I shook my head and said, "Jim, you know that's against our policy to carry over your vacation days. In fact, you're the one who made that rule." His reply was, "Well, if I made the rule, I can break it." Jim left the next day.*

Chuckles cascaded through the room. Bill folded the letter. "Have you guessed who wrote this, Jim?"

"Of course," Jim piped. "That's Ron Kutella. Now he's president of the whole company."

Bill placed the letter in the inner pocket of his jacket. "I used to call Jim *Mr. Gray*. When he asked me the reason, I told him to remember that the world isn't just black and white. *Look for the gray, Mr. Gray,* I said."

Familiar with Jim's dogmatic style, the crowd laughed and applauded.

"Jim," said Bill, "you are held in our community as one of the founding fathers of the brokerage industry. Your legacy is the Portland office. According to Ron, you were responsible for it becoming the second largest office in Sedgwick's North American system with net revenues of over thirty million dollars. And that represents a premium sum of over three billion dollars."

The room stood, clapping and nodding to Jim in appreciation.

Chapter Twenty-Seven

At the close of March, on a Tuesday, Sam failed to show for work. Jim and Jean never saw him again. Apparently he had returned to the Philippines. So Jim pretty much took over his own therapy. He says today, "I could write the book on the subject." He attended the gym at Eisenhower Hospital every other day and otherwise worked out at home and in the pool. Jim was determined to walk without a wheelchair in tow at Lisa's college graduation. By May, he could walk fine with a cane. The wheelchair became obsolete as far as Jim and Jean were concerned.

In a burst of energy, he'd take off walking like a toddler who had just discovered the new trick his body could do. Jim worked out with a vengeance in spite of the fact that he hated the assisted exercise program at Eisenhower. But nothing would keep him from going. Nor would he ever miss his walking exercises in the pool. "There goes the Energizer bunny," Jean would say. When awaiting Amy Jean's arrival for Lisa's graduation, Jim exited the car to stroll the airport. No sense sitting when he could be exercising his legs.

Jean cheered him on. Both of them spoke with disdain about anyone who suffered a stroke and decided to stay in a wheelchair only to wither and die: "They just didn't try hard enough.... Three men in Thunderbird had strokes about the same time. One got well and is playing golf, and the other guy died.... He gave up.... Never tried to get out of his wheelchair."

Christie says, "Dad's singular purpose in life has always been – like a horse with blinders—to go THERE. Never has this been more evident than since his stroke. He said, *I'm going to walk. I'm going to play golf.*"

A few weeks after the stroke, she saw him looking from his wheelchair at the golf trophy he won in 1992. It sits on a wicker table in the family room. Jim and his partner, Ted Lilley, took first place at a Phil Harris Golf Tournament. Each won a lady's purse designed by Judith Lieber. "It's the only time I took first place in anything," says Jim.

Christie's voice lowers softly. "Our biggest disappointment is that he couldn't get well enough to play golf again."

Jean says, "We worked so hard at therapy even though his chances at recovery were not good. His one arm and leg didn't get the wake-up call and that's that."

"But just because I can't play golf doesn't mean I can't get out on the course," Jim says.

When the word got out that Jim would never play golf again, people offered their condolences. The muscles in Jim's face would grow defiantly taut. "I've never regretted a thing in my life, and I'm not going to start now," he'd say.

He went out and purchased a new golf cart. If he couldn't play the game, he'd caddy for his family.

Despite a few minor accidents with the golf cart, life assumed a semblance of normalcy. Then Jim and Jean took a trip to Waikiki, and he fell and broke his arm.

"It was that damn sand," Jim explodes. He felt betrayed by his body at the setback.

Jean took on the brunt of her husband's disappointment. In her date book, she wrote, "Difficult time for us both." But in language that reflected the oneness she felt with Jim, she added, "We are mending. We are unsinkable!"

Those words didn't surprise Christie. "My mother has struggled to 'mend' her marriage fifty of her nearly sixty years with Dad," she says. "I believe my parents deeply love one another, but their personalities have always been out of sync. More accurately than *mend,* they place patches over their differences and never look at them again."

Years after his stroke, Jim religiously continues his exercise regime. He spends an hour daily in the pool. Someone always needs to watch him. He likes that. Usually, that someone is Jean. He used to set his watch on the table and repeatedly ask, "What time is it?"

Jean recently purchased a large clock for the pool area, and she looks forward to visits by family members. "You'll stay with Jim at the pool, won't you?" she asks.

Jim goes to the gym between 3:00 and 5:00 every other day. He'll say, "It's 3:10. I'm going to the gym"—which means, "Let's go now. I'm ready."

"You best not be in the middle of something. And you'd better not have too many errands," says Christie. "If you're late picking him up, you're in trouble." To avoid that problem, she once said, "Dad, why don't you bring along that Robert Schuller book you've been reading—in case I'm a few minutes late?"

Jim's frown told her she had asked the wrong question. He wanted to get home. Where he's comfortable. Where everyone respects the fact that he's Lord James. He believes: *I've earned that right.*

Everyone in Jim's family (except Jean) wishes at times he'd use a wheelchair. During occasional weary moments, a wishful sigh escapes Jim's lips as well. It would be nice to have a wheelchair at home so he might get to the phone before the message kicks in. Nice to have one to get around at the mall so he wouldn't have to worry that a hurrying elbow might knock him down. Someone told him that quality wheelchairs are very light, easy to fold and place in the trunk of a car. But there was no need to pursue the conversation. Jean quickly said, "We don't need a wheelchair," looking at Jim with admiration. He smiled. Of course we don't.

With the coming of September, Jim said to Jean, "Should we do that hundred-day cruise I booked last year?"

Jean's face glowed. "Yes! Why not? We can manage!"

The ship departed out of Athens, south through the Suez Canal and into the Red Sea. The Arab countries had always treated Jim well. Before the stroke, Jim and Jean walked into the desert in Jordan in the company of Bedouins. This time they toured in a private car. A placard with the words "Welcome to Jordan, Mr. Bayless" sat in the windshield. The sign now hangs in Jim's office at home.

In the United Arab Emirate of Dubai, Jim and Jean shopped for Amy Jean's wedding present. She planned in December to marry Chris Goodwin, a fellow International Relations major she had met at Boston University.

They found Dubai quite modern in comparison to other regions of the Arab world. "Oh look, Jim," Jean said. The wind had blown open the robe—called an abbayah—of a young woman, exposing a miniskirt. Another woman was using a cell phone.

Amy Jean and Chris picked a bed & breakfast on a rocky promontory overlooking Zihuatanejo Bay as the site of their wedding on December 2, 1997. The location accommodated her mother and Rick who were sailing on Mexico's Pacific Coast.

Reaching the site required a hundred-step climb. Rick and members of Chris' family made plans to carry Jim on a chair.

"No, definitely not," said Jim. "I'll walk."

Jeana, as Amy Jean continues to call her grandmother, read the benediction. She knew it was important to both Papa and Jeana that the wedding include a religious aspect even though AJ and Chris considered themselves "very non-religious."

"Oh look, Chris," Amy Jean said, smiling, as she gazed down into the box of the wedding present her grandparents had purchased in Dubai. She held up a St. Christopher's medal on a gold chain.

Jean looked to Chris and back to AJ. "Chris. St. Christopher. You see?"

Amy Jean and Chris smiled at one another. "Yes," said AJ, "we see. Thank you."

AJ was living in Chicago when her Papa had his stroke. Although not one for tears, she cried for a solid day. The next time she saw Papa was at Lisa's graduation, nearly eight months after his stroke. She says, "Jeana and my mom both say Papa was doing much better by then—and I'm sure he was! But his slowness of speech, difficultly walking, and overall frailty startled me. I think the thing that got to me the most was his frailty. He'd always been so strong and so much younger than other kids' grandparents—this was the Papa I used to wrestle with over my blanket! How could he have become so old?"

During her wedding reception, Amy Jean glanced thoughtfully at her Papa. She considered how good he looked compared to when she saw him last. It occurred to her that she had always imagined Papa the way he was when she was seven: "strong in mind and body, quick tempered but full of love and fun to play with."

Chris was standing at the table where Papa and Jeana sat. Appearing more like a teenager than a man of twenty-three, Chris listened with boyish politeness as Papa talked about the cars he'd owned. The word *Chrysler* made it to her across the din of conversation. Chris was saying something. Papa took a long look at his new grandson-in-law. Amy Jean smiled. Chris probably told him he'd never owned a car. Didn't know how to drive. "A New Yorker born and raised, sir."

Amy Jean looked down at her wedding dress and then out to the bay. When she looked at Papa again, she was with him on one of their "long adventures of exploration" from the first beach house. She saw herself as a little girl at his side, riding in the Jeep to the beach after a big storm to "hunt" driftwood and haul it back to the house. Then she saw herself and Papa off the road, picking blackberries. He was telling her about all the chores he did as a boy. He was telling her how blackberries grew everywhere in Grants Pass, how they could choke acres of land, and how he would eat them until his belly felt sure to explode. Papa was smiling and she started laughing for no other reason than it was fun to laugh with Papa.

The day following the wedding, Jim and Jean hired a driver to take them to a coffee plantation, not far from the neighboring city of Ixtapa, that produces organic beans. Jim had never seen one and "I'm curious," he told his granddaughter. Amy Jean smiled. "That's my Papa," she said, for a second expecting him to add, "I'll get the Jeep."

Chapter Twenty-Eight

Jim and Jean never said exactly. Various conversations over the years, however, led Christie to believe that a number of their cruising scenarios played out something like this: They would be on deck admiring a sunset when a nearby couple would say, "Oh there's a pretty sailboat. Isn't that beautiful?" And Jim or Jean would respond, "Oh, our daughter and son-in-law plan to sail the world. They'll probably be in that very spot next year."

Christie says, laughing, "Our plan received a good response from their peers, from total strangers who look and smell good. Thank you, whoever you are."

By the time of AJ's wedding, however, the sailors were still in Mexico, and the bloom was off. Christie and Rick visited Rancho Mirage the following summer. Her parents' friends would say, "So what do you do?" Christie and Rick would respond, "For the most part, we don't work. We just live on our boat." They'd look at one another, and then add in unison, "In Mexico." Then they'd laugh. Her parents did not. Later, Jim and Jean would shoo Christie and Rick with a flip of their hands. "Go now and finish your plan. Be off!"

Instead, the Gorslines sold their boat and toured the United States in an RV and Europe on a motorcycle. They embraced and proselytized a new philosophy of life called *cruising,* defined not only in terms of boating. Christie says, "The cruising lifestyle gave us permission to live *serendipitously,* whatever the means of transportation."

Jim sighed and said to his daughter, "I thought you were going to sail two years and then Rick would get a real job and you'd buy a house."

We never said that. We never wanted that, thought Christie.

That's not the way to do things, thought Jim. Look at Rick here. A man should have a job until he retires. Earning a living builds and sustains character. You're a fine wife and mother, Christie—certainly a successful woman in my eyes. A successful family, however, depends on both adults playing out their roles.

Today, a conversation with her father will play out in Christie's imagination: "Dad, why do you insist that there's only one way to live this life? Don't you know I have always subscribed to most of your theories? I mean, Rick and I always use placemats and cloth napkins—on the boat, in the camper. Even when we toured Europe on the motorcycle!"

Jim smiles as if he can read her mind, and Christie beams back. She believes: "Dad's iron will, his correctness and apparent self-assuredness are often hard to live up to, and equally difficult to live with. But I've inherited a part of him. While Dad sometimes doesn't like what I'm doing, that smile at the corners of his lips tells me he appreciates how I'm really an awful lot like him—I'm part of his legacy."

The fact that Jim has the opportunity to pass on a financial legacy assures him that his philosophy about the working life is accurate. If he hadn't participated in the workforce from age fourteen to his retirement, if he hadn't followed the continuous path from milk boy at Heard's Dairy to regional director at Fred S. James and real estate owner, he would never have the means to leave the legacy he wanted.

By the close of the 1990's, Jim had established two scholarships and made business partners of his children and grandchildren. In 1989, he had started the Bayless Scholarship at Warrenton High School. Second, when AJ was about to enter college in 1993, he established the Bayless Grandchildren Scholarship to cover the four-year tuition at a local state college for each of his five grandchildren. During the 1994 family vacation in France, Jim announced the formation of the Bayless Family Limited Partnership. "We've been a marvelous financial help to our children," says Jim, "and they appreciate it. I know because they say so."

Next, Jim wished to give to the Church. He imagined Inez watching him from Heaven's window, smiling slightly but her feelings of disappointment betrayed by her eyes. A mother's hope never dies, he thought. *But I'm eighty-two, Mother. Accept that if I haven't become a preacher by now, it isn't going to happen.* He said aloud, "I've given to the Church—and will continue to do so—my own way."

First, he gave money to the church he and Jean attended when living at the beach. "Of service since 1846, Pioneer is the oldest Presbyterian parish on the West Coast," says Douglas D. Rich, the church's pastor. "A tiny place," says Jim. "Can't hold any more than sixty people. I always say that if the Lord showed up on any given Sunday, there wouldn't be room for Him."

Jim presented the church with Costco stock worth $50,000 and two stipulations: one, that the money be used only to improve the church structure, and two, that the monthly bulletin always mention the Bayless Endowment Fund. In added recognition, the congregation presented Jim with a photograph of the church taken one Easter. A cross of yellow and white daffodils, nearly the width of the church itself, aprons the grounds. Jim proudly hangs the framed photo behind the desk in his office.

Jim also donated $50,000 to the First Presbyterian Church in Portland. Although no longer a member, he wanted to give something back to the place where his family began—with his own marriage—and continued to grow—with the weddings of Christie and Joanie.

Jim suffered his second Mallory-Weiss Tear episode April 27, 1998. He grumbled in despair at how his body continued to betray him. Over the last year and a half, he had survived a stroke and one bout after another of insulin reactions. Now this.

He roared like a lion with a thorn in his paw, clearly announcing his anguish, but letting no one near. When he would snap at the hospital staff, Jean would draw his temper toward herself until the worker could finish whatever task and be off.

The ordeal of Jim's recovery took its toll on Jean. She had survived his stroke, and she had been at his side through every battle with his diabetes, but she couldn't present a strong front by herself. They were a team, she and her Jimmy. If he indeed was faltering, Jean needed reinforcements. After ten days at his side in ICU, she decided to phone her three children. "Meet me at the house," she said. "I need you."

They would all come, of course. Their mother had never before made such an insistent, yet desperate, plea.

Craig, Christie, and Joanie met at California's Ontario airport, not far from Palm Springs. They rented a car together and drove to the home of their parents. For two days they comforted their mother and placated their father.

Jim recovered. Everyone survived. It's what a Bayless does best.

Jim raised his chin and continued to do what he'd always done: look forward. Retirement had become synonymous with travel, and Jim planned to do a lot more.

In June of 1999, Jim and Jean took the whole family to Molokai, Hawaii's poorest island. In Craig's words, Molokai is "mostly red lava dust and howling wind." Until 1969, the lepers of Hawaii were banished to Molokai's northern shore, Kalaupapa Peninsula. The author Jack London once called the area the "pit of hell, the most cursed place on earth."

Craig's daughter, Taylor, wrote a school essay in the style of Charles Dickens, relating the historical hardships of the island. She introduces the character of Halawa, the personification of Halawa Valley, the island's first settlement thirteen centuries earlier. She wrote:

> *A solitary figure addressed them in a hushed, reverent tone...Around his throat hung a boar's tooth, and his feet, tough as any shoe, were bare yet comfortable on the cold, moist, sharp stones....*

Had Taylor asked her Papa, he would have told her he understood more than she might imagine about the barefoot Halawa, the man and his feet, "tough as any shoe." Jim understood hardship and about being poor and vulnerable. But most of all he understood Halawa's pride—and his love for the island's raw beauty.

A brilliant, blue liquid sea rushed into the valley's mouth, preceded by its own snow-white breakers that swirled and foamed around and over dark pieces of long-fallen cliffs, to expend their furious violence until exhausted, the waves gently lapping a curving sand beach....

Jim found the coastline beautiful. Nature reminded Jim—a one-eyed diabetic, seventy-eight years of age and the victim of a stroke—of a man's inner strength. He loved the manmade luxuries that his money afforded him, but the farm boy in him also appreciated the god-given beauty of nature, free for farmers and businessmen alike to enjoy.

For Taylor and his two other grandchildren, Jim exudes nothing but pride. Photographs of all five cover a glass table in the living room and hang in the hall opposite the kitchen of their desert home. "Our grandchildren are all different and all great," Jim says proudly.

He enjoys looking at the picture of Lisa, as a little girl, and himself riding in a golf cart at the beach house in the Gearhart, Oregon. They are dressed like the American flag for the 4th of July parade. "Christie's Lisa is a sweet girl," he says. "She graduated from Northern Arizona University and now teaches special education in Molalla, Oregon. Her sister—our oldest grandchild, AJ—works as a producer for MSNBC in New York."

He picks up a family picture and points to Joanie's boys. "All hair and taller than me—the both of them." He smiles. "Trevor's a sophomore at Montana's Carroll College. He loves to fish." Jim and Jean have kept a flyer Trevor created to promote his lawn-mowing business when he was in high school. "He's a comedian like his mother, Joanie," Jim says. The flyer reads:

Dear Potential Customer,

I, Trevor Madden, am happy to announce that spring is here, and you know what that means—it's time for you to hire me to mow you lawn and do odd jobs. Imagine this: swift, friendly service delivered to you by none other than myself. I will set up a weekly mowing date, and I will perform at rock-

bottom prices. Of course you are thinking—"But this sounds too good to be true!"...I know the only thing you want now is my number. Well, here it is. Operators are standing by...Remember, if you are unsatisfied with your lawn, someone else probably mows it.

Grandmother Jeana created his business card. It read: *Trevor Madden, since 1983* (the year he was born).

Jim points to a photograph of six-foot-four McGregor, Trevor's younger brother. "He plays the drums." He also competes on the Lincoln High School tennis team and volunteers as a coach for the Kids Basketball Association at Portland Parks & Rec. "He'll head off to the University of Portland in the fall."

Craig's daughter, Taylor, towers over her mother in the photograph. Broad shouldered with a champion swimmer's body, she offers a pretty smile. Taylor attends the Tish School for the Arts, a respected film school at New York University. "Her parents sent her to an out-of-state school," says Jim. "That's okay—Joanie did the same with Trevor. Both know what I believe: A local state college is good enough for anyone. If they choose to make up the cost difference for the tuition, that's their business."

Jim has the feeling all his grandchildren will become successful adults. He knows people think his definition of success centers around the dollar. "Perhaps I attach too much importance to money, but *my* definition isn't the *real* definition." He speaks slowly, as if he has been rehearsing the lines his whole life. "A successful person is one who has achieved admiration and respect from his peers: the people who struggled in life to attain the same goals. Success isn't just money. Take Einstein, for example. He was a schoolteacher like Lisa. Success is about what you achieve and if you're happy."

257

Chapter Twenty-Nine

On January 9, 2001, Jim and Jean left for a trip around the world. They traveled on the Seabourn Line: "the Porsche 911 of the cruise industry," Jim quotes from a brochure—" its ships small, sleek, luxuriously decorated and extremely expensive." He says, "Our style of cruising is costly. About a thousand dollars a day. But we enjoy it and I can afford it. The three-month-plus, round-the-world cruise cost a total of $125,000."

Six days into the cruise, the very moment the ship crossed the equator, Jim and Jean were visiting with Mary Hayes, who used to work at Dooly & Co. "She went on a date with Jim once!" Jean exclaims, smiling. "That was before me, of course."

They talked with Lucille Conrad Outhwaite over lunch. The former ballerina had performed in Germany for the pleasure of Adolf Hitler. She was very young at the time and knew nothing of the man or what he'd become. "He kissed this hand," she said, raising a limp right wrist.

Jean didn't know what to think. She'd always taken great effort to avoid the dark side of life. And she'd never been one to encourage anyone's confession of feelings about an experience. She wasn't about to start now. Such a horrid topic was better left alone.

"I don't know how the dancer felt about her encounter with Hitler," says Jim. "I suspect she wanted us to read all about it in her book. She handed us a copy—*Birds of Flight: The Diary of a Dancer.*" He straightens and speaks with marked indignation. "She charged us for it, if you can believe that. I never read it. I'm quite sure Jean didn't either."

By the end of February, the ship reached Vietnam. The public bathrooms offered "as my father was known to say," says Jean, "lots of room for development." Jim entered a stall in his wheelchair and looked first into an empty toilet bowl and then at a barrel of water with a bucket. Well, doesn't that beat everything, he thought. Later he read that six million rural families in Vietnam have no toilets at all. They use the rice patties.

Nevertheless, both Jim and Jean declared Vietnam the country they most enjoyed that cruise. They found the people friendly.

Typically, tourists don't tout Da Nang as one of their favorite places. It offers little to see, and beggars fill the street. But because of the inexpensive prices for quality items, Jim and Jean pronounced Da Nang "the best place in the world to shop." Jim had a silk shirt made for a mere twelve dollars—while he waited. "Fits perfectly," he announced. And they bought small pieces of marble. Realizing he'd need an extra suitcase to tote their treasures home, Jim purchased one of leather for only $25.

A private car and driver drove them around, as was the case in every port. Jim also enjoyed riding in a rickshaw. Jean loved the lotus blossoms that floated in the rice patties.

In Singapore they found a lovely world globe with a lapis lazuli base. When visiting Agra for the second time, home of the Taj Mahal, Jim picked up a silk oriental rug for his office.

The Al Bustan Palace Hotel just outside Muscat, the capital of Oman, was a structure far grander than the Taj Mahal. In fact, Jim had never seen such a luxurious place. While he had grown accustomed to the idea that, in monarchies, the poor seemed far poorer and the rich far richer than within the borders of America, the grandiose majesty of this palace made him pause.

Later, in Oman, Jim heard a story about the Muscat sultan, Said bin Taimur, father of the present ruler. Sultan Said opposed education and any freedom of movement in and out of the country. In short, he believed in no change for his people. *No change.* Jim shook his head in disbelief. The story recalled an incident in Turkey. He was sitting on a bench outside a castle, waiting for Jean. Three native, young men in their twenties approached him. "Excuse us, sir. May we ask you something?"

Jim waited.

"You're an American," one said. "What's your advice to us?"

Without movement or expression, Jim responded, "Accept change. Don't fight it. In fact, encourage it."

"Thank you, sir," the spokesman said, and he walked away with his friends.

Jim wondered if the young men understood what he meant. They might. He did at their age. Jim had already learned that death happens—you accept it and move on. He had already experienced how rigid, religious views can smother a boy—you accept that God takes different forms in the eyes of different people, and that, more often than not, God by any other name is your God, too. And he had already learned that change is inevitable, and if you're looking forward, change is good.

On Monday, March 26, Jim received a fax from Craig that Punch Green had died the previous Friday at his home in Palm Springs at the age of seventy-five.

Jim, who had just turned eighty, had thought his friend would outlive him. A weight filled him until he pushed it away. If he'd ever had a friend, it was Punch. Good ol' Punch. They shared the same politics—conservative with a liberal view.

Jim thought a moment about his own day last Friday, generally an unpleasant one on the Sinai Peninsula. His throat had been sore from a viral plague passing through the ship. Their driver spoke no English. The endless Arab marketplaces, called souks, and the bartering had made him and Jean weary. "Take us back to the ship," Jim said in English with increasing loudness. Eventually the driver got the idea.

Looking out to the sea from the veranda, Jim lowered his gaze. He fought a moment the realization that Punch was the only man he had ever envied: in 1981 when President Reagan nominated Punch to serve as a Federal Maritime Commissioner and in 1989 when President Bush appointed him as Ambassador to Romania.

Jim flashed to an image of his friend waving an American flag. Any fan of Punch knew the flag story. The pending execution of dictator Nicolae Ceauçescu had shaken the country with violent chaos. Punch stood at the window of the American Embassy in Bucharest, grinning as he swayed to and fro with his flag. A crowd of Rumanians cheered below. It was later written that the ambassador "made life-and-death decisions daily under intense and unrelenting pressure. There is not a single member of the Embassy staff who would not run through a brick wall for Punch Green."

Jim straightened and looked out across the sea. He pictured Punch laughing, probably at one of his own jokes.

Over the next month, the ship continued on to Italy, Barcelona, Cadiz, the Canary Islands, Barbados, Puerto Rico, and eventually Florida. Two and a half weeks later, Christie and Rick visited in Palm Desert and fixed grilled knockwurst for dinner. Jim vomited, causing another rupture to his esophagus—his third Mallory-Weiss Tear. Medics rushed him to the hospital.

At midnight, a couple of gray-faced doctors suggested everyone go home. "It's too dangerous to operate. Prepare yourselves. He may not make it. We have to wait and see," one said.

Jean paled. "He should never have eaten that knockwurst."

"Probably wasn't the food," one doctor assured. "No one is to blame. He has a history of these types of ruptures. Could have happened anytime." He smiled kindly. "Go home and get some sleep, Mrs. Bayless."

Two hours later, a groggy Jean answered the phone. "I suggest you get here right away" was all she heard.

At 2 am, a doctor approached Jean, shaking his head incredulously. "A tough old bird," he said. "Looks like your husband is going to make it."

The next day, Jim's doctor said, "You knocked on the pearly gates, Mr. Bayless. But St. Peter didn't want you yet."

"The hospital kept him a week," says Jean. "The second they released him from intensive care, Jim wanted his cane. He imagined he could sprint across the room. His first day home, I saw him talking on the phone to the manager who handles our apartments in Portland. You'd never know he had gone through hell and back again."

Jean knew her Jimmy was truly back when the next day she found him heading to the pool to exercise. He would be well enough to speak before the Committee of 25. The president, Jim Curtis, had sent out a flyer to its members promoting Jim and Jean Bayless as the upcoming guest speakers. *Our esteemed former president,* it read, *has agreed to relate the experiences of his 36,000-mile-around-the-world cruise. He will share the microphone with his lovely wife in recounting the highlights of the trip. Will this work? Not ever in our records has one of our former presidents agreed to share center stage with his wife.*

The morning of September 11, 2001, Jim sat in his office. The television blared with the news of the terrorist attack on Washington and New York. He glanced up at the framed sign hanging on the wall: "Welcome to Jordan, Mr. Bayless."

He thought about the riches he had seen from the Red Sea to the Persian Gulf. Mostly he thought about the poverty. He understood the anger of the people at having so little when everyone in the United States has so much.

"My experience is that most Muslims are good people," says Jim. "Some zealots got out of control, is all. They forgot the concepts of their religion to be good."

Craig says, "Dad was raised under the cloud of religious intolerance. The hatred that resulted on September 11th was brewed in the same type of cloud. Dad hates religious zealots in any form. People need to understand that times change, all things change. Accept it. His message is *Be tolerant.*"

Jim has always tried to live by the tenets of basic goodness found in religion—without going to extremes. "My views hurt my mother and estranged me from my sister and brothers, but it was never really in me to adopt their fundamentalist ways. It's terrible what happened on September 11th. Overly conservative people are responsible."

People call Jim Bayless conservative. He knows that. "Well, I *am* conservative. About working hard and investing your money wisely. About being a good Christian. But I'm not extreme."

Jim identifies with Robert H. Schuller, commonly known as "the evangelist without a gospel." If ever Jim had yielded to his mother's wish that he become an evangelist, he likes to think he would have become a preacher like Dr. Schuller. Jim admired Schuller in 1999 when it occurred to the preacher that the evangelist way of pushing Muslims to become Christians was "utterly ridiculous." Such preaching would no longer be his message. Jim admired how Schuller could change with the times.

"The purpose of religion," said Schuller in a *Chicago Tribune* interview, "is not to say, *I have all the answers, and my job is to convert you.* That road leads to the Twin Towers. That attitude is an invitation to extremists." After Sept. 11, he said that the emphasis should move from proselytizing "to just trying to help everybody who had hurts and hopes."

Jim met Dr. Schuller in December of 2001. Jim respects the preacher not only for his approach to religion but because he's a businessman. "A frustrated architect, really," says Jim. "He delights in building magnificent structures like he has in Garden Grove."

Jim and Jean took a bus with The Committee of 25 to Schuller's Crystal Cathedral, home to the Crystal Cathedral Ministries and a congregation of over 10,000 members, to see the Christmas play, "Glory of Christmas," a world-renowned production of the events surrounding the birth of Jesus. More than the musical backdrop of the amazing pipe organ and prerecorded eloquence by the London Symphony Orchestra, Jim enjoyed the majesty of the live animals, the camels, donkeys, and goats that paraded across the stage and down the aisles.

Jim has an autographed copy of Schuller's autobiography, *My Journey: From an Iowa Farm to a Cathedral of Dreams.* He considered naming his own biography *My Journey.* "But no," he decided, "I have had my own journey. I want a different title."

During the aftermath of 9/11, Jim asked everyone which news station they were watching for coverage of the war in Afghanistan. "Tune in to MSNBC," he'd say, proudly. "My granddaughter AJ is producing the news."

In January, AJ produced two weeks of one-hour shows from various cities in Indonesia and the Philippines about the worldwide al-Qaeda terrorism network. AJ's film crew happened to be the only one on Basilian Island when troops arrived to rescue American tourists from the militant Islamic group, Abu Sayyaf. As a result she produced a package for NBC Nightly News. "Quite a coup for a producer from a cable network," she says with pride.

June 13th, 2002, AJ's sister, Lisa, married Steve Parmentier, a tax consultant from Canby, a suburb of Portland. The wedding and reception took place at the home of Jim and Jean.

Lisa says, "Since I have never had an emotional relationship with my biological father, Papa's dependability and love have been even more special. I spent lots of time with Jeana and Papa as a child. Papa has been there for me since the day I was born."

Jim walked Lisa out the sliding doors of the house, down a narrow path between the pool and seated guests to where Steve and the minister stood. They stepped slowly as Jim walked the precarious route with Lisa on his right arm. His cane balanced his left side. Tears of pride streamed down his cheeks. Rings of narcissi and gladiola floated in the pool.

"Since the stroke," says Christie, "my father allows others to see that he can be vulnerable. He's become more introspective and more accepting of people who are different from him. He wasn't that way when I was a girl."

Christie remembers visiting Grants Pass as a child. "Why didn't we just have fun with the fact that they were so different? We kids got the impression that if we stayed too long, we'd get grease under our nails and start using poor grammar.... Insecurity," she offers as the answer to her own question. "I think my father has always been afraid that too much focus on his birth family would cause him to lose hold on that ladder he was climbing." She thinks a moment. "All his life, my father needed to be something different from Inez, Martha May, and his brothers. He believed that money would make it happen."

A daughter can't always see the whole truth, however. "I've always felt connected to my mother and siblings," says Jim. "They are the James William part of me—there to remind me where I came from and that I dreamed of understanding more than Baptist fundamentalism and small town living."

Given the right time and place, and if Jim could find the right words, he'd tell Christie that he has finally discovered how to become the person he's always known lay deep inside. Sometimes it takes eighty-odd years for things to come together.

Christie says, "I see the ways my father has changed. He has grown."

"Of course I've changed," says Jim. "Things change. People change. I regret nothing in my life because that would mean I didn't accept that the world is always changing. A man has to look change in the eye and say, 'Okay,' and then move on."

"Take, for instance, what happened after Lisa's wedding," says Christie. "I mentioned to Dad that the sprinklers had not been turned on again. He got out of chair as fast as he could and headed to the office to use the phone. "Those Mexicans," he ranted. "They never do what they're supposed to do."

Christie followed him and then did something she'd never done with her father. She raced to stand in front of him and spoke right in his face. "Dad, you hired a gardening service. If you don't like their work, fire them, but don't blame an entire culture because a few don't do their job."

Jim stopped and smiled at his daughter. "Thank you," he said, wondering if she knew how many times in his path forward he has slipped back a few steps.

"I see now," says Christie, "that he likes to be challenged, likes to be intellectually stimulated by hearing opposing discussion." She smiles. "He may be a man of eighty-two who has had a stroke and walks with a cane, but I can say with more conviction than I've ever said it: My father is a man of many strengths."

To make sure he doesn't miss out on any adventure, Jim occasionally yields to requests that he use a wheelchair. A few months after her wedding, Lisa took Jim on a picnic from Portland to Mt. St. Helens. He wanted to see what it looked like with the top blown off. Jean didn't care to go. She preferred to remember it a snow-dipped cone, a beautiful whole in the frame of her living room window.

Joanie, who often borrows a wheelchair to take her father on a "speed fast" walk, took Jim to see Howard Hughes' airplane, the Spruce Goose, a less-than-aeronautical "flying boat," designed during WWII to deliver supplies to U.S. soldiers around the world. Joan borrows wheelchairs often when her father visits. Jim toured the plane in a wheelchair.

Jim continues to plan his vacations with great forethought. He and Jean have taken so many cruises—eighteen—that one liner offered them a free one. In July of 2002, Jim and Jean cruised to Alaska. "Beautiful," said Jim. "Maybe the best yet."

It was the raw, rugged beauty of wilderness that he enjoyed, nature as wild rivers, defiant mountains, and steely glaciers. He likened it to the human spirit, to *human character,* what he values above all else. As he stood at the railing of the cruise ship, he drew a deep breath in the crisp air and felt at home. He smiled. Jean smiled too. "What is it, Jim?" she asked.

"We've had a good life, Jean," he said, realizing that the best in himself had everything to do with Jean. Becoming a successful man requires a working partnership with a successful wife and mother.

As she always has, Jean notes Jim's plans in a date book. A new clubhouse is scheduled to open in November of 2003 at the Thunderbird Country Club, and Jim has booked the first reservation. Lord James announced his request a year in advance that each member of his family make an appearance. Everyone, of course, will attend.

In May of 2004, he and Jean will aboard the new Queen Mary 2, the biggest and most expensive passenger ship in history, and take their quarters in a penthouse. They will travel the Atlantic once again, from New York to Southampton. Water perhaps best symbolizes how James William Bayless saw his life—something to conquer, something that often threatened to pull him under. But he, Lord James, with hard work and good fortune, found a way to sail across it.

About the Author

Sarah Zale writes freelance and poetry, and teaches writing in San Diego. California. Her interest in writing biography began in Mexico when she wrote the stories of Canadian and American women sailors.

Printed in the United States
1366800003B/112-162